Julia Phillips   Energy Exchange

Julia Phillips   Energy Exchange

TABLE OF CONTENTS

Energy Exchange: An Introduction

Energy Exchange, as a book and a concept, describes an interactive dynamic that is central to my work. As in my studio, this volume—my first monograph—began with the title, which describes a conceptual framework. Taking its cues from my sculptural practice, the title conveys a relation between two entities. There are power hierarchies at play in the imagined interactions that my sculptures portray: a social and interpersonal dynamic, an exchange of energy. In recent years, my research interests in psychology and behavior have expanded to an additional subject of personhood, namely our spiritual disposition. The book's title implies something transactional, referring simultaneously to physical, mechanical, psychic, and spiritual exchange. It is a concept that embodies much of this book's content and my artistic practice at large.

Three of the five texts are conversations, representing exchanges with dialogue partners—Janet Dees, Jamieson Webster, and Fia Backström—who share specific interests with me. Additionally included are two essays, by Daniella Rose King and Magdalyn Asimakis, with whom I have been in close conversation over the last several years.

The artworks featured in this publication were created over the last decade, after I moved from Germany to the United States. As a dual citizen, and as a bilingual and bi-ethnic person, I am in a particular position to think about how language constitutes culture and vice versa, and how a vocabulary can reflect the mentality of a place. Discourses are often specific to a language and a location, and those I have experienced in the United States have profoundly influenced my practice and provided a lexicon of expression that I never encountered in German. This has fed my interests in postcolonial studies, social belonging, diaspora, psychoanalytic theory, gender studies, and Black feminist thought, which weave through both this book and my work.

As a result of the cultural shift I am describing, and my conversations and research being conducted in English, I have come to articulate most of my artistic ideas and titles in English as well. The decision to have all texts translated into my first language, German, was led by my wish to contribute to an exchange of discourse and of culture between the English- and German-speaking regions in which my work is exhibited. Yet it is important to acknowledge that some words/thoughts/concepts do not translate and aren't fully graspable in another language, and so I have chosen to leave my titles untranslated. The creative process cannot simply be removed from its original terrain and transplanted into a new one without a larger effort of contextualization, which I hope this book provides.

Julia Phillips, 2023

Energy Exchange: Eine Einleitung

Energy Exchange bezeichnet eine interaktive Dynamik, die für mein Schaffen von zentraler Bedeutung ist. Wie bei der Arbeit im Atelier stand am Anfang dieses Buches – meiner ersten Monografie – der Titel, der einen begrifflichen Rahmen absteckt. In Anlehnung an meine bildhauerische Praxis beschreibt er eine Beziehung zwischen zwei Entitäten. Bei den imaginären Interaktionen, die meine Skulpturen zeigen, spielen Machthierarchien eine Rolle: soziale und zwischenmenschliche Dynamiken, der Austausch von Energie. In den letzten Jahren hat sich mein Forschungsinteresse in den Bereichen Psychologie und Verhaltensforschung auf ein weiteres Gebiet erweitert, nämlich unsere spirituelle Beschaffenheit. Die im Titel dieses Buches bezeichnete Transaktion besteht in einem gleichermaßen physischen, mechanischen, psychischen und spirituellen Austausch – ein Konzept, das einen Großteil dieses Buches und meine künstlerische Praxis insgesamt bestimmt.

Drei der fünf Texte sind Gespräche mit Janet Dees, Jamieson Webster und Fia Backström, mit denen ich jeweils bestimmte Interessen teile. Daneben enthält der Band zwei Beiträge von Daniella Rose King und Magdalyn Asimakis, mit denen ich in den vergangenen Jahren in engem Austausch stand.

Die in dieser Publikation gezeigten Arbeiten sind in den letzten zehn Jahren nach meiner Umsiedlung von Deutschland in die USA entstanden. Als Bürgerin zweier Staaten und als bilinguale und biethnische Person kann ich auf meine eigenen Erfahrungen zurückgreifen, wenn es um die Frage geht, wie Sprache Kultur und Kultur Sprache konstituiert und wie ein Vokabular die an einem Ort vorherrschende Mentalität widerspiegelt. Diskurse sind häufig sprach- und ortsspezifisch, und die Diskurse, denen ich in den USA begegnet bin, haben meine künstlerische Praxis tiefgreifend beeinflusst und mir Ausdrucksmöglichkeiten eröffnet, die ich im Deutschen so nicht finden konnte. Sie haben mein Interesse am Postkolonialismus, an Fragen der sozialen Zugehörigkeit, an Diaspora, psychoanalytischer Theorie, Gender Studies und Schwarzem feministischem Denken geweckt, die sich durch dieses Buch und mein Werk ziehen.

Aufgrund des beschriebenen Kulturwechsels und der Tatsache, dass ich Gespräche über meine Arbeit auf Englisch führe und auch in dieser Sprache recherchiere, habe ich die meisten meiner künstlerischen Ideen und Titel von Arbeiten auch auf Englisch formuliert. Die Entscheidung, alle Texte in meine Erstsprache Deutsch übersetzen zu lassen, war von dem Wunsch getragen, zu einem Diskurs- und Kulturaustausch zwischen dem englisch- und dem deutschsprachigen Raum beizutragen, in denen meine Arbeiten ausgestellt werden. Dabei war allerdings zu berücksichtigen, dass sich manche Wörter/Gedanken/Konzepte nicht vollständig und ohne Abweichung in eine andere Sprache übersetzen lassen; daher habe ich mich entschlossen, die Titel nicht zu übersetzten. Der kreative Prozess kann nicht aus seinem ursprünglichen Umfeld herausgelöst und in ein neues versetzt werden, ohne eine größere Kontextualisierung vorzunehmen – von der ich hoffe, dass dieses Buch sie bietet.

Übersetzt von Sylvia Zirden

Julia Phillips, 2023

We relate so much through the gaze.
—Julia Phillips, 2022

The eye cannot take unless at the same time it gives.
—Georg Simmel, 1921

Historically, research has overlooked the dual function of the eyes—how the gaze simultaneously perceives and transmits information to others.[1] The act of seeing and being seen is the result of multisensory learned experience, a push and pull, a relation between light, the eye, the brain, and of course the cultures of the viewer and the viewed. The gaze can produce intense and unpredictable physiological responses and involves the exchange of subtle and overt signals, including the gaze itself, facial expressions, speech, and gestures. And beyond sight, looking and being regarded by others takes place in language and in sensory registers. It is olfactory, spatial, and informed by memory and perception. It is the product of a deeply complicated interplay of factors.

Julia Phillips' sculptures, installations, videos, and works on paper engage with complex modalities that consider how we look, how we see, and how we are seen. The means of looking—the eyes—come into serious focus as a device for seeing and for recognition. Other phenotypes are suggested through size, proportion, texture, and color, as well as literal casts of the artist's body, to indicate one's observable traits—height, complexion, gender—from one's anatomy to how one moves and how one's body behaves. These markers dictate how we exist in the world and how we are apprehended.

Seen: The Eyes, the Gaze, and Julia Phillips' Sculptural Politics of Looking

Daniella Rose King

In 2015 I wrote an essay titled "Dirty Looks" for the Whitney Museum of American Art's Independent Study Program exhibition catalogue.[2] The ISP brought Julia and me together, and we've been in close dialogue ever since. I believe it was the first thing Julia read that I had written, and she told me, to my delight, that she thought it was good. I was honored when she asked me to write about the work she presented for her Studio Museum in Harlem residency in 2017, and again, five years later, to contribute to this monograph.

It's funny but not surprising to come full circle to the notion of *looking* in this essay. A dirty look, stink eye, lookalook, cut your eye, bad eye, glare, look daggers—just a handful of ways to describe a perceived displeasure in looking and being looked at. You may wonder: How can an object, an artwork, look? Back then, I argued that artworks are imbued with the energies, belief systems, and symbols of their creators and the viewers who read and interpret and engage with them. The dirty look can function as a way of critically regarding a situation—a rupture, a break with the codes of looking and being watched that are ingrained within consumerism and specifically capitalism, with its attendant rules of misogyny and racism and classism. And also a moment of relief from physical and virtual carceral geographies such as CCTV and facial recognition software. Perhaps the promise, and the ideal, of art is in the moment of looking and being with work that takes us outside of these structures of surveillance and consumption. Perhaps it relieves us of our hypervisibility as women artists and curators (or other professionals) of color. A dirty look, a critical look, is what we expect when we walk into an exhibition, to have our moment analyzed, seen through different eyes, and be presented with a new way of seeing. These questions are all at play in Phillips' sculptural explorations of how we look and how we are seen. Power and vulnerability are two sides of the same coin of visibility. Within our global societies, shaped as they are by

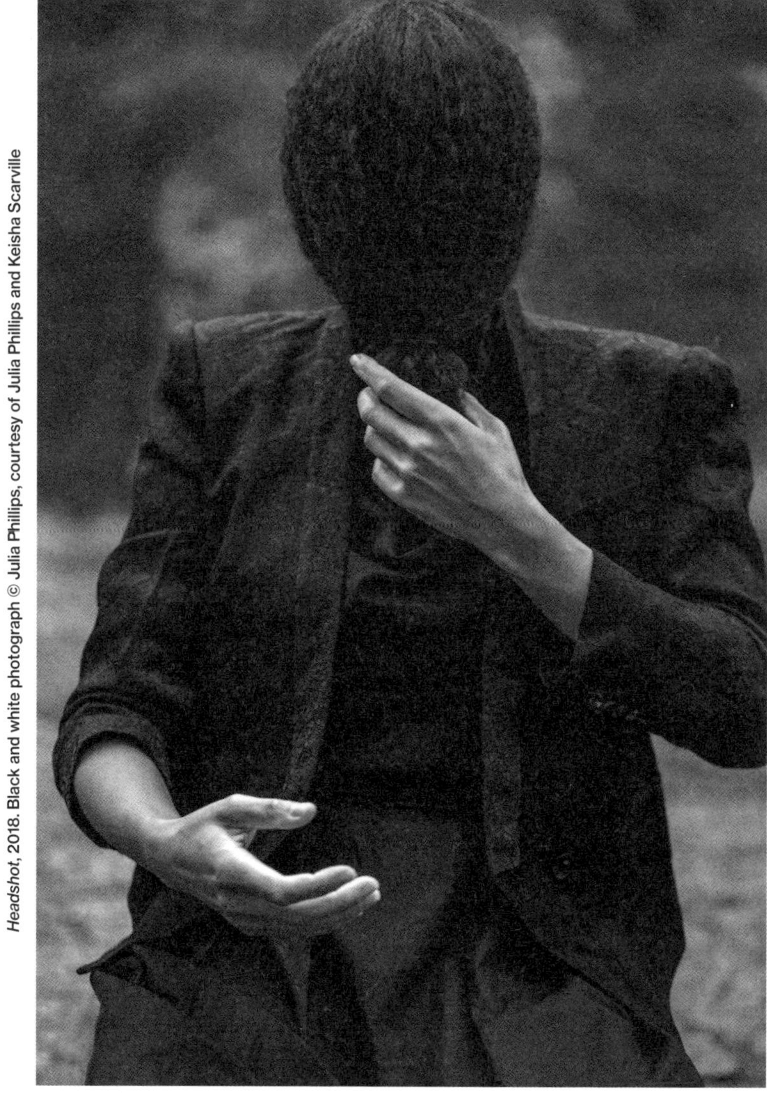

Headshot, 2018. Black and white photograph © Julia Phillips, courtesy of Julia Phillips and Keisha Scarville

colonialism, patriarchy, and racial capitalism, the politics of looking and being looked at are inextricably linked to these histories. Phillips' explorations of anonymity, recognition, and the universal body are tied to this critique of the politics or ethics of looking. For visibility is not a level playing field; it is more extractive, controlling, and deadly for some communities than for others. And it is no accident that social media, internet cultures, and our heightened visibility online have been co-opted by hegemonic forces to collect, monetize, monitor, and influence our behaviors, beliefs, and even means of identification.

What does it mean to be instantly identifiable and Google-able, as an artist? What did Agnes Martin or Sol LeWitt look like? What does it matter? We know what their *work* looks like. Phillips interrupts the smooth ease of knowing-by-looking, pushing back against absorption into circuits of celebrity and fame. There isn't an image of her face online. To know her, you must actually meet her, see her. The image she submits for administrative purposes is a collaboration with the artist Keisha Scarville. In the black-and-white portrait *Headshot* (2018), Phillips' hair completely covers her face and only her hands and clothed body are legible. So, certain phenotypes of gender, taste, class, and ethnicity are shared with the viewer, but her face, and specifically her eyes, are invisible. While casts of her face appear as masks throughout her earlier works, they are taken only from its lower half, never the eyes, the source of recognition and recognizing. Like a decommissioned passport or censored file where a black strip over the eyes conceals identity, this inaccessibility removes the real chance of true recognition, or full consumption, perhaps. This concern for the possibility of anonymity, and the importance of the eyes in this practice, becomes a recurring, multiplicitous theme within Phillips' work.

(p. 08)

Early Works

Returning to Phillips' earliest video pieces, one notes the emergence of her visual lexicon of looking. In each of these works, including *Shake (A Choreography for Flying Hair)* (2013), *Becoming (the Hunter, the Twerker, the Submitter)* (2015), and *Burdened* (2018), the artist establishes a denial of the eyes. In each work she appears, each time with her eyes obfuscated. Either her face is visible from the nose downward, the frame cuts her eyes out of the shot, or she is backlit, with her closed eyes essentially disappearing into a silhouette. This concealment becomes an anonymizing, censoring, blinding, disidentifying gesture, a jarring denial of visual consumption against the controlling gaze that exemplifies our culture.

(p. 11) (p. 19) (p. 16)

In *Becoming (the Hunter, the Twerker, the Submitter)*, clay stands in for gendered bodies, and two figures—the artist and an older woman ("a matriarchal figure," in the artist's words)—embody the trifecta of titular nouns (that is, the hunter, twerker, and submitter) through discreet and overt gestures performed within one of Phillips' constructions, a tiled circular stage, a cage of sorts. Subtitles overlaid onto the image narrate a monologue:

> She tells me, if the female body is a vessel, she is a vessel with agency. And as opposed to this object transgressing the boundaries of that object, *this* object places herself around this object. She says the question is not if, but *how* she gets her prey. She believes that if matter is particularly flexible in her nature, the matter is asking her to find her full potential within self-determined limitations.

Playing with quick cuts and a suggestive use of clay and props, the video is an ambiguous exploration of the politics of desire, power, and consumption. Like Phillips' consideration of Josephine Baker in the sculptures *Exoticizer (Josephine Baker's Belt)* and *Exoticizer, Worn Out (Josephine Baker's Belt)*, both from 2017 and each formed of a circular, encompassing belt, the encircling stage seems concerned with the ambiguity of the performance of the female body, by Baker and others, in a world that is openly, systemically, and intimately hostile and abusive toward it. The stage is at once a site of observation, a space of becoming, a site of production and economic labor, and a means of projecting one's interior self, offering oneself up for observation. The tension between watching and being watched is suggested by the title and the text component of the video, as are different aspects of this tension, including submission, display, and predation. The *becoming* is the unstable state of these complex, competing modalities. Further, the capacity of the body to perform these critiques—to use sex, submission, and desire for protection, pleasure, and survival—is key to Phillips' investigation of looking and being seen. Here we are drawn to notice the imperfect transgressions as radical possibilities for looking and being looked at.

(p. 62)

In *Becoming (the Hunter, the Twerker, the Submitter)*, a dancing figure, its body isolated and separated into parts as a torso, arms, legs, and bottom, provides a visual narration, as in *Burdened*, in which a truncated body, shown from calves to shoulders, struggles under the weight of an ever-growing (clay) burden, stomping on a malleable floor, squelching and churning up the ground and leaving deep footprints. *Burdened* is a metaphor for the endless balancing act of inhabiting bodies and interacting with others and the world around us. As with *Shake (A Choreography for Flying Hair)*, the protagonist is dynamic, shaking and flicking their head around the screen in an endless loop, performing the quintessential circulatory hair flip of a rock/pop star or dancer. The hair flip is itself caught up in racialized and gendered tropes and histories, as it necessitates a certain length and texture of hair, whether achieved naturally or through treatments or wigs. Here, the subject has close-cut hair, so, nothing to suggestively flip. The gesture becomes absurd, highlighting and parodying the movement itself. Like the twerk, it is a convoluted gesture—cycled through popular culture, marred by appropriation, and filtered down to a trope. In Phillips' videos, these movements and gestures are mined for their cultural legibility and ability to communicate multiple modes of looking and signaling.

Scenes, Tools, Objects

The dynamic, sometimes frenetic movements displayed in Phillips' video works find their contemporary counterpart in the ghostly stillness of her sculptures, described as scenes, tools, and objects. In *Positioner* (2016), a metal archway features two ceramic hand grips positioned on either side of a suspended partial cast that captures the space between the artist's nose and neck. The face's mouth is agape, and the white ceramic tiles that form the base of the structure reveal footprints and blue droplets of glaze. The title and the configuration of disparate elements suggest to the viewer that this structure would place a body in an awkward kneeling position, where they become vulnerable and subservient, in many ways compromised. Leaving the eyes out of the mask anonymizes the subject, creating an absence that speaks to the missing body in the scene and amplifies the sense of loss. This act of censorship denies our ability to fully identify the subject, yet at the same time allowing for a stronger sense of empathy or self-identification within the structure. A similar eyeless face mask, this time positioned as an absent body on all fours with a pipe entering its mouth, is employed within the mise-en-scène of *Extruder* (2017). Here we see how the complex modalities (p. 64) of the gaze—of watching, being watched, and imagining the subject behind the mask as well as a potential third party—are delicately, viscerally embodied within the ambiguous architectures of Phillips' sculptural work.

It's in the Eyes

Put simply, my work deals with relations and relationships.
—Julia Phillips, 2022

Observer I (2016) is Phillips' first work to feature such explicit reference to the eyes. These ceramic binoculars, fixed atop a metal telescoping pole and footed by a square base of nine ceramic tiles, are, we imagine, used to spy on the viewer, or at least on someone or something just over their head. It is a stark and spare sculpture, certainly an abstraction of a body, whose minimal offerings—height, tool—engender our imagination to populate the scene with a body. Phillips' binoculars here concretize the gaze. As a mechanism for extending and optimizing looking, with their more nefarious connotations

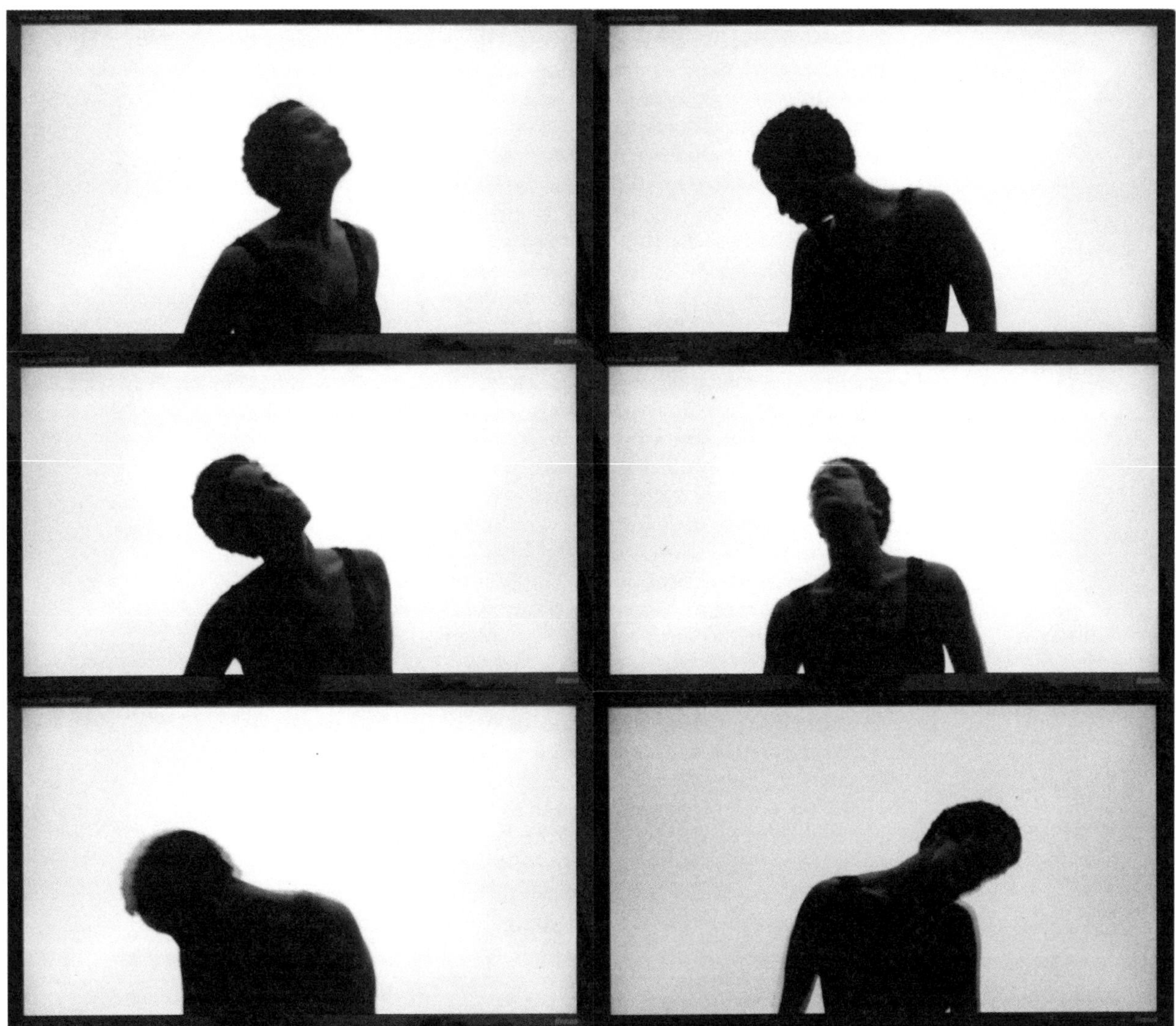

Shake (A Choreography for Flying Hair), 2013. Single-channel HD video: black-and-white, no sound, 7 second loop © Julia Phillips, courtesy of the artist. Collection of MUSEUM MMK für Moderne Kunst

as instruments for surveillance, invasive observation, or sexual exploitation, the binoculars are a loaded and powerful cipher. *Observer II* (2020) continues in this vein, with binoculars, this time atop a circular quartzite base, that are angled downward and eye pieces glazed in tones that suggest flesh. Phillips' binoculars, like the absent eyes throughout her work, are an obsolete instrument and serve to put the observer on display within the gallery space. The gaze is again defeated. This ambiguity, the shifting presence and absence, is at the core of Phillips' work. It is an oscillating relation, constantly in flux, power moving and morphing between observer and observed, positioner and positioned.

(p. 141-143)

The next phase in Phillips' exploration of the schemas of looking is *Observer, Observed* (2022), her first public project, a complex multimedia work commissioned for New York's High Line. In it, bronze binoculars allow the viewer to zoom in to whatever they like from their position on 26th Street. But as soon as eyes are detected looking through the binoculars, a camera inside captures a livestream and projects those eyes onto a ten-foot-wide screen nearby. This mechanism, the two-way or double-sided binoculars, is designed to suggest the vacillating, interactive power dynamics of looking. Further, it is, in the artist's words, a way of proposing that there "is a price to pay for looking"—and that price, of course, is being looked at. It also conceptualizes her concerns with our culture of anonymous observation and invasive lurking on social media. What are the ethics of looking? What would an ethics of observation look like?

(p. 145)

The arc of Phillips' work across the past decade is notable in form, material, and content. From highly intimate, one-to-one relations seen in earlier works, in which the power dynamic seems more overt and fixed, to more nuanced, almost imperceptible registers of discord and struggle in institutionalized negotiations and relations, the artist's recognizable body and face casts have steadily fallen away, replaced by partial casts and further bodily abstractions that seek out anonymity and an imagined universal body. In the negative spaces of her installations, the viewer imports their own form or body, imagining how one would stand/negotiate (see *Negotiator (#1)*, 2020) and enact/interact with the sculpture, thus completing the work. Over time, Phillips has become more concerned with the formal aspects of the works, their intimate mechanisms as metaphors for the body and relationships to the body. Stripping away the traces of her own corporeality to the most essential referents, she has found new, minimal ways of making the work legible to the viewer in the precise proportions, measurements, scales, and other inconspicuous visual markers.

(p. 95)

Headshot

Returning to *Headshot*: Phillips conceived this collaboration in response to overwhelming requests for an image of herself, a fixed representation for the purposes of websites, catalogues, conference programs, and other outputs. Phillips seized it as an opportunity to enact a personal politics and a chance to collaborate with her respected colleague Keisha Scarville, who in her own work in black-and-white photography expresses a careful sensibility for textures and amplifying tactility. Influenced, too, by Lorraine O'Grady's important video work *Landscape (Western Hemisphere)* (2010–11), *Headshot* considers the multitudes that a Black woman's hair communicates as "a metaphor for the miscegenation of the Western Hemisphere, its objective correlative."[3] Phillips' hands, caught in motion while adjusting her hair, offer up, alongside the phenotype of hair, further markers of her identity as a sculptor and a person of color.

The politics of the gaze have been a fixture, a central concern, of Phillips' work across mediums. To "feel seen" is in common parlance to feel acknowledged and visible, beyond one's visual attributes. In patois, "seen?" is a question of understanding among the community. Phillips' exploration of the gaze, as an individual and an artist sited within intersectional identities, has created an entire world of possibilities for feeling seen, seeing otherwise, and questioning the assumed and inherited power dynamics of the gaze.

1 See for instance Roser Cañigueral and Antonia F. de C. Hamilton, "The Role of Eye Gaze during Natural Social Interactions in Typical and Autistic People," *Frontiers in Psychology* 10 (2019): https://www.frontiersin.org/articles/10.3389/fpsyg.2019.00560/full: "For instance, when we see a pair of eyes we can gather information about what other people are looking at, and how they feel or think. At the same time, we can use our eyes to strategically cue another's attention. Depending on the duration and direction of our gaze, we are also able to perceive and signal a variety of meanings, such as desire to communicate, threat and dominance, attractiveness, or seeking for approval."

2 Daniella Rose King, *On Limits: Estrangement in the Everyday* (New York: Whitney Independent Study Program, 2016).

3 Lorraine O'Grady in conversation with the author, November 10, 2017.

Wir teilen so viel durch den Blick.
— Julia Phillips, 2022

Man kann nicht durch das Auge nehmen, ohne zugleich zu geben.
— Georg Simmel, 1921

Unsere Augen haben eine Doppelfunktion, die in der Wissenschaft bislang häufig übersehen wurde: denn der Blick nimmt nicht nur Informationen wahr, sondern kommuniziert sie gleichzeitig nach außen (Cañigueral/Hamilton, 2019)[1]. Betrachten und Betrachtetwerden sind das Ergebnis einer multisensorischen, erlernten Erfahrung, eines Hin und Hers, einer Beziehung zwischen Licht, Auge, Gehirn und Kultur der jeweiligen Person, die betrachtet oder/und betrachtet wird. Ein Blick kann intensive, unerwartete physiologische Reaktionen hervorrufen. Mit dem Austausch von Blicken gehen mehr oder weniger subtile und offenkundige Signale einher, die nicht nur die Sprache der Augen, sondern auch Mimik, Tonfall und Gestik umfassen. Betrachten und Betrachtetwerden finden aber nicht nur auf der Ebene des Sehens, sondern auf sprachlicher und sensorischer Ebene statt: Sie sind olfaktorisch, räumlich und von Erinnerung und Wahrnehmung geprägt. Sie sind also das Ergebnis eines äußerst komplizierten Zusammenspiels von Faktoren.

Seen: Augen, Blicke und Julia Phillips' skulpturale Politik des Betrachtens

Daniella Rose King

Julia Phillips' Skulpturen, Installationen, Videos und Arbeiten auf Papier beschäftigen sich mit komplexen Modalitäten, die bestimmen, wie wir aussehen, sehen und gesehen werden. Die Augen, Mittel des Betrachtens, rücken als Instrument des Sehens und des Erkennens in den Fokus ihrer künstlerischen Arbeit. Andere Phänotypen werden durch Größe, Proportion, Textur und Farbe sowie durch Körperabgüsse der Künstlerin dargestellt, um auf erkennbare Merkmale wie Körperhöhe, Hautton und Geschlecht hinzuweisen – von der Anatomie bis hin zur Art und Weise, wie Personen auftreten, wie Körper sich bewegen. Diese Markierungen bestimmen unsere Existenz und wie wir in der Welt wahrgenommen werden.

Julia und ich kennen uns seit 2015, als wir beide am Independent Study Program (ISP) des Whitney Museum of American Art teilnahmen, und stehen seitdem in engem Kontakt. Im gleichen Jahr verfasste ich für den Ausstellungskatalog des ISP einen Essay mit dem Titel „Dirty Looks". Wenn ich mich richtig erinnere, war „Dirty Looks" das Erste, was Julia von mir las, und es war mir eine große Freude, dass ihr mein Essay gefiel – und eine ebenso große Ehre, als sie mich bat, über ihre Arbeiten zu schreiben, die sie 2017 im Rahmen der Künstler_innenresidenz im Studio Museum in Harlem präsentierte. Fünf Jahre später nun freue ich mich, einen Beitrag für diese Monografie zu schreiben. Es ist witzig, aber nicht überraschend, dass ich mich auch in diesem Essay mit dem Thema *Betrachten* auseinandersetze und sich damit ein Kreis schließt. Ein böser Blick, ein mieser Blick, ein beißender Blick, ein stechender Blick, ein Dolchblick – eine Handvoll Ausdrücke, um die Wahrnehmung von Unmut beim Betrachten und Betrachtetwerden zu beschreiben. Vielleicht kommt jetzt die Frage auf: „Wie kann ein Objekt, ein Kunstwerk, einen Blick erteilen?" Damals argumentierte ich, dass Kunstwerke durchdrungen sind von den Energien, Glaubenssystemen und Symbolen der Künstler_innen, die sie geschaffen haben, und der Betrachter_innen, die sie erörtern, interpretieren und sich mit ihnen auseinandersetzen. Ein böser Blick kann eingesetzt werden, um eine Situation kritisch zu betrachten. Er kann zu einem Bruch mit den Kodierungen des

Betrachtens und Beobachtetwerdens führen, die im Konsumismus, insbesondere im Kapitalismus mit seinen Regeln der Misogynie, des Rassismus und Klassismus, verankert sind. Ein böser Blick kann aber auch einen Moment der Befreiung bedeuten aus physischen und virtuellen Gefangenenschafts-Geografien, die Gesichtserkennungssoftware und Videoüberwachung einsetzen. Viel-

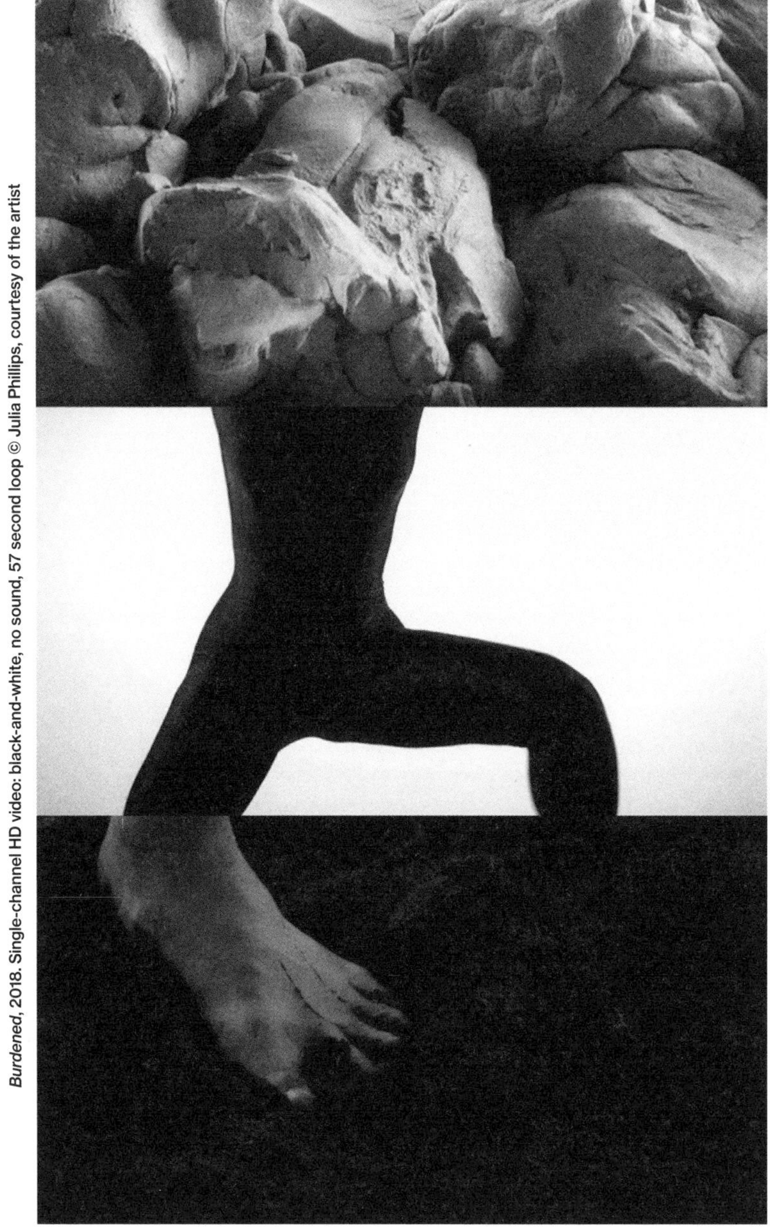

Burdened, 2018. Single-channel HD video: black-and-white, no sound, 57 second loop © Julia Phillips, courtesy of the artist

leicht macht dies gerade die Verheißung der Kunst, ihr Ideal aus, dass die Betrachtung und Reflexion von künstlerischen Arbeiten uns aus den Strukturen der Überwachung und des Konsums herausführen. Vielleicht befreit es uns von unserer Hypervisibilität als BIPoC-Künstlerinnen, Kuratorinnen und Kulturschaffende. Wir rechnen mit einem bösen Blick, einem kritischen Blick, wenn wir eine Ausstellung betreten, und damit, dass dieser Moment, der unserer ist, analysiert wird. Wir sind darauf vorbereitet, dass er durch andere Augen wahrgenommen wird und somit eine neue Sichtweise aufgezeigt wird. All diese Fragen spielen eine Rolle in Phillips' skulpturalen Erkundungen darüber, wie wir aussehen und wie wir gesehen werden.

Macht und Verletzlichkeit sind zwei Seiten derselben Medaille der Sichtbarkeit. In unseren historisch von Kolonialismus,

Patriarchat und rassistischem Kapitalismus geprägten globalen Gesellschaften ist die Politik des Betrachtens und Betrachtetwerdens untrennbar mit dieser Geschichte verbunden. Phillips' Auseinandersetzung mit Anonymität, Erkennbarkeit und dem Körper als etwas Universellem nimmt Bezug auf den kritischen Diskurs zur politischen und ethischen Ebene des Betrachtens. Denn Sichtbarkeit bedeutet nicht für alle das Gleiche. Für manche Communities ist Sichtbarkeit ausbeuterischer, kontrollierender und tödlicher. Es ist kein Zufall, dass soziale Medien, Internetkulturen und unsere erhöhte Sichtbarkeit online von hegemonialen Kräften vereinnahmt wurden, um unser Verhalten, unsere Überzeugungen und sogar unsere Selbstidentifizierung zu erfassen, zu monetarisieren, zu überwachen und zu beeinflussen.

Was bedeutet es, als Künstler_in unmittelbar identifizierbar und googelbar zu sein? Wie sahen Agnes Martin oder Sol LeWitt aus? Warum ist das überhaupt wichtig? Wir wissen, wie ihre Werke aussehen. Phillips unterbricht die Leichtigkeit, mit der wir durchs Betrachten Wissen erlangen, und widersetzt sich der Einspeisung in die Kreisläufe von Prominenz und Ruhm. Es gibt kein Bild von ihrem Gesicht im Internet. Um die Künstlerin zu kennen, muss man sie real kennen, sie treffen, sie sehen. Das Bild, das sie für administrative Zwecke einreicht, ist eine Zusammenarbeit mit der Künstlerin Keisha Scarville. Auf dem Schwarz-Weiß-Porträt (p. 08) *Headshot* (2018) ist Phillips' Gesicht vollständig von ihren Haaren verdeckt, nur ihre Hände und ihr bekleideter Körper sind erkennbar. Bestimmte Phänotypen, die auf Geschlecht, Modestil, soziale Herkunft und ethnische Zugehörigkeit hinweisen, werden mit den Betrachtenden geteilt, aber das Gesicht der Künstlerin, insbesondere ihre Augen, bleiben verborgen. Zwar tauchen in ihren früheren Kunstwerken immer wieder Abgüsse ihres Gesichts in Form von Masken auf, doch zeigen diese nur die untere Gesichtshälfte, nie die Augen, die als Repräsentanten des Erkennens und Wiedererkennens dienen würden. Wie bei einem ungültigen Pass oder einer zensierten Akte, bei der ein schwarzer Streifen über den Augen die Identität verbirgt, wird die Abbildung unzugänglich gemacht und somit ein reales Erkennen oder gar ein Konsumieren verhindert. Das Anliegen, Anonymität zu wahren, und die bedeutende Rolle, die die Augen in diesem Prozess spielen, sind ein wiederkehrendes, vielschichtiges Thema in Phillips' Arbeit.

Frühe Werke

Phillips' früheste Videoarbeiten bilden zusammengenommen ein visuelles Lexikon des Betrachtens. In jeder dieser Arbeiten, dar- (p. 11) unter *Shake (A Choreography for Flying Hair)* (2013), *Becoming (the* (p. 19) *Hunter, the Twerker, the Submitter)* (2015) und *Burdened* (2018), (p. 16) verweigert sich die Künstlerin der Augen als Mittel der Erkennung – sie erscheint zwar im Bild, aber nie werden ihre Augen sichtbar: Abgebildet ist etwa nur die untere Gesichtshälfte, oder die Augen sind durch den Rahmen abgeschnitten oder die Künstlerin wird von hinten beleuchtet, wobei ihre geschlossenen Augen in einer Silhouette verschwinden. Das Verbergen wird zu einer anonymisierenden, zensierenden, versperrenden, desidentifizierenden Geste, zu einer heftigen Verweigerung des visuellen Konsums gegenüber dem kontrollierenden Blick, der ein Kennzeichen unserer Kultur ist.

In *Becoming* wird Keramikton als Metapher für geschlechtsspezifische Körper eingesetzt. Zwei Figuren – die Künstlerin und eine ältere Frau, laut Phillips „eine matriarchale Figur" – verkörpern das Dreiergespann der titelgebenden Wörter (d. h. die Jägerin, die Twerkerin und die Unterwerfende). Subtile Bewegungen und offensichtlichere Gesten werden auf einer von Phillips konstruierten runden Bühne mit gefliestem Boden, einer Art Käfig, ausgeführt. Die Untertitel eines Monologs überlagern das Bild:

> Sie sagt mir, wenn der weibliche Körper ein Gefäß ist, dann eines mit Handlungsmacht. Und anstatt, dass dieses Objekt die Grenzen des anderen Objekts überschreitet, *stülpt* sich das andere Objekt um dieses herüber.

Sie sagt, die Frage sei nicht ob, sondern *wie* sie an ihre Beute kommt. Sie glaubt, eine besonders flexibel beschaffene Materie fordert dazu auf, ihr volles Potenzial innerhalb selbstbestimmter Grenzen zu entfalten.

Das Video, das mit schnellen Schnitten und dem Einsatz von Keramikton und Requisiten spielt, ist eine mehrdeutige Erkundung der Politik des Begehrens, der Macht und des Konsums. Bei (p. 62) den Skulpturen *Exoticizer (Josephine Baker's Belt)* und *Exoticizer, Worn Out (Josephine Baker's Belt),* beide von 2017, bezieht Phillips Josephine Baker mit ein. Beide Skulpturen bestehen aus einem kreisförmigen, umschließenden Gürtel; die umlaufende Bühne scheint sich mit der Vieldeutigkeit der Performance des weiblichen Körpers durch Baker und andere zu befassen, in einer Welt, die ihnen öffentlich, systematisch und auf intime Weise feindselig begegnet und sie missbraucht. Die Bühne ist gleichzeitig ein Ort der Beobachtung, ein Raum der Entfaltung *(Becoming)*, ein Ort der Produktion und der wirtschaftlichen Tätigkeit. Sie ermöglicht es, das Innere nach außen zu projizieren und sich dem Blick der anderen, der Betrachtung, auszusetzen. Die Spannung zwischen Beobachten und Beobachtetwerden wird durch den Videotitel und -text angedeutet sowie verschiedene Aspekte dieser Spannung, beispielsweise Unterwerfung, Zurschaustellung und Prädation. Die *Entfaltung* ist der instabile Zustand dieser komplexen, miteinander konkurrierenden Modalitäten. Darüber hinaus gibt es einen weiteren zentralen Aspekt zu Phillips' Auseinandersetzung mit der politischen Dimension des Betrachtens und Betrachtetwerdens: die Fähigkeit des Körpers, biologische Triebe wie Sex, Unterwerfung und Begehren für die Sicherstellung von Schutz, das Erleben von Lust und das Überleben einzusetzen. Wir werden dazu angehalten, unvollkommene Grenzüberschreitungen wahrzunehmen und ihnen als radikale Momente des Betrachtens und Betrachtetwerdens zu begegnen.

Becoming ist eine visuelle Erzählung durch eine tanzende Figur, deren Körper isoliert und in Torso, Arme, Beine und Gesäß gegliedert ist. Ähnlich auch in *Burdened*: ein von den Waden bis zu den Schultern ausschnitthaft gezeigter Körper kämpft unter dem Gewicht einer immer größer werdenden Lehmlast. Der Körper stapft auf einem matschigen Boden herum, mischt ihn auf und hinterlässt tiefe Fußspuren. *Burdened* ist eine Metapher für den endlosen Balanceakt, den wir vollziehen, indem wir unseren Körpern innewohnen, während wir mit unseren Mitmenschen und unserer Umwelt interagieren. Auch im Video *Shake (A Choreography for Flying Hair)* ist die Protagonistin animiert, schüttelt und wirft ihren Kopf in einer endlosen Schleife über den Bildschirm und zeigt den typisch kreisenden Haarwurf von Rock-/Popstars oder Tänzer_innen. Der Haarwurf ist selbst in rassistische und geschlechtskategorisierende Stereotypen verstrickt, da er eine bestimmte Haarlänge und -textur voraussetzt, unabhängig davon, ob diese durch die eigenen naturbelassenen Haare, durch Haarbehandlungen oder Perücken gegeben ist. In *Shake* hat die Darstellerin kurzgeschnittenes Haar, also keines, mit dem sie solch einen Haarwurf ausüben könnte. Die Bewegung wird zu einer absurden Geste, die den Bewegungsablauf selbst hervorhebt und parodiert. Wie der „Twerk" handelt es sich um eine behaftete Geste, die durch die Popkultur zirkuliert, durch Aneignung entstellt und auf ein Klischee reduziert ist. In Phillips' Videos werden diese Bewegungen und Gesten auf ihre kulturelle Lesbarkeit hin untersucht sowie auf ihre Fähigkeit, verschiedene Formen des Betrachtens und Signalisierens zu vermitteln.

Szenen, Werkzeuge, Objekte

Den dynamischen, manchmal sehr energischen Bewegungen in Phillips' Videoarbeiten steht die geisterhafte Stille ihrer Skulpturen gegenüber, die die Künstlerin selbst als Szenen, Werkzeuge und Objekte beschreibt. In *Positioner* (2016) sind zwei an einen Metallrah- (p. 57) men montierte keramische Handgriffe jeweils auf einer Seite eines

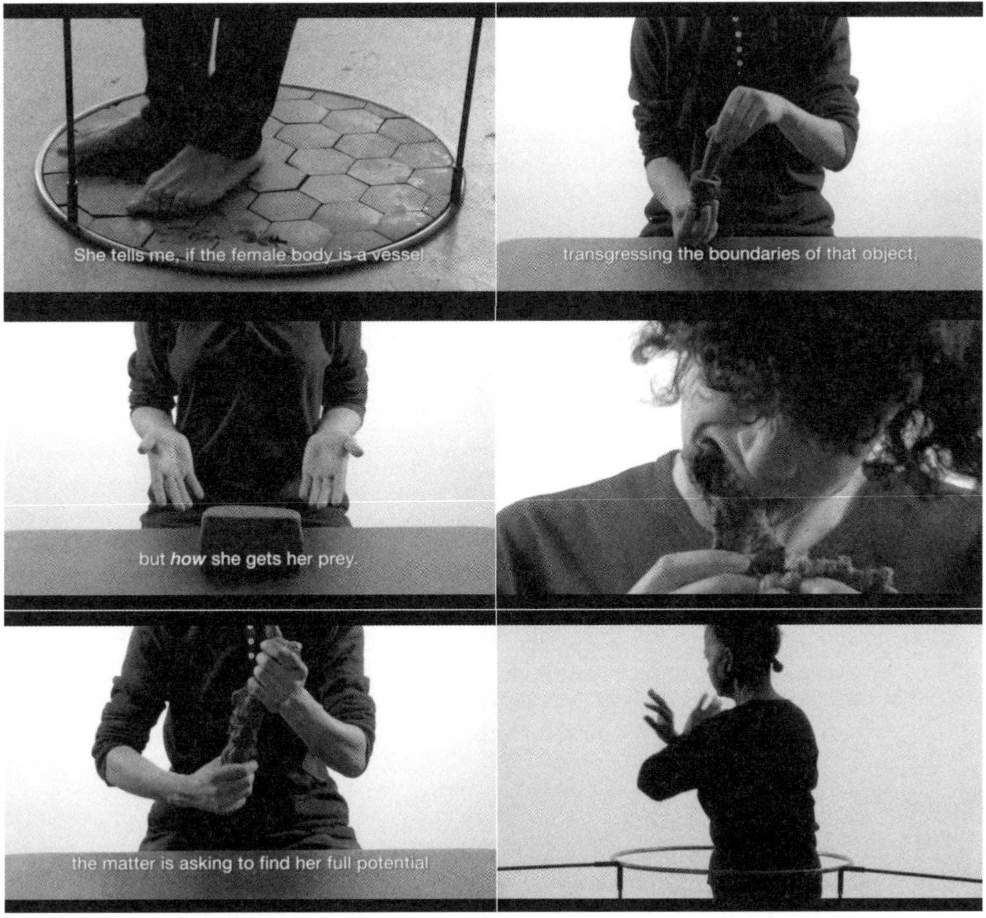

Becoming (the Hunter, the Twerker, the Submitter), 2015. Single-channel HD video: color, no sound, 1 minute, 36 second loop © Julia Phillips, courtesy of the artist

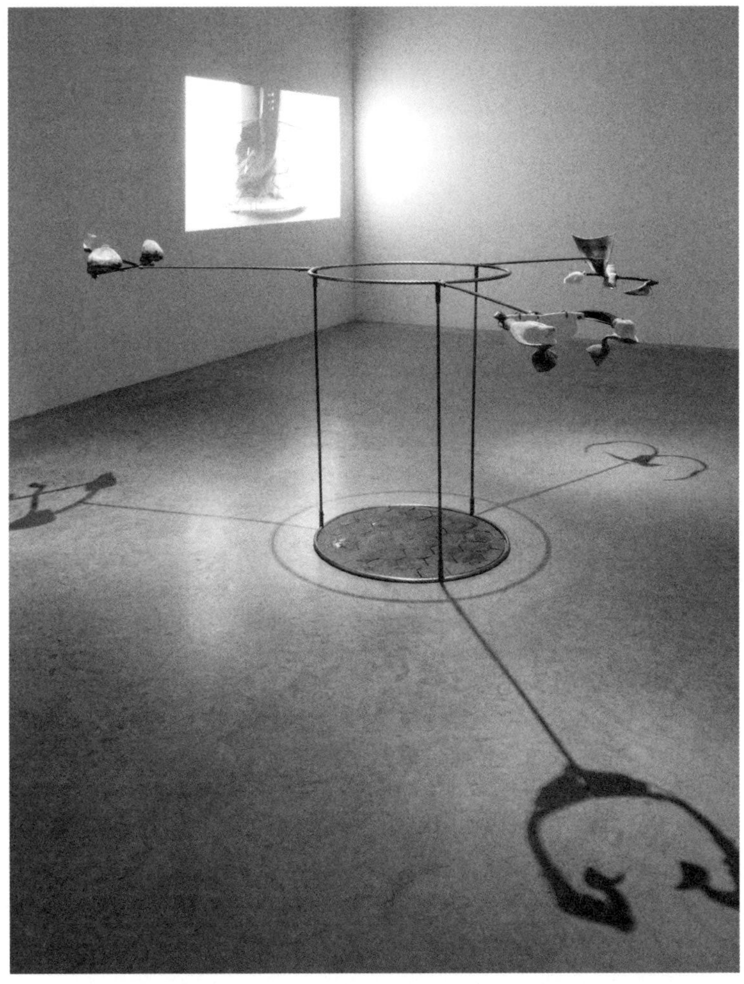

Connecter & Becoming (the Hunter, the Twerker, the Submitter), 2015. Ceramics, metal hardware, steel, sound, speaker, single-channel HD video: color, no sound, 115 × 210 × 210 cm; 45½ × 82¾ × 82¾ inches © Julia Phillips, courtesy of the artist

hängenden Maskenabdrucks angebracht, der den Bereich zwischen Nase und Hals der Künstlerin abbildet. Der Mund in diesem Gesicht ist aufgesperrt, und die weißen Keramikfliesen, die die Plattform der Skulptur bilden, zeigen Fußabdrücke und blaue Glasurtropfen. Der Titel und die Anordnung der verschiedenen Elemente suggerieren den Betrachtenden, dass diese Konstruktion einen Körper in eine merkwürdige, kniende Position bringt, verletzlich, unterwürfig und in vielerlei Hinsicht gefährdet. Die ausgesparten Augen in der Maske anonymisieren das Subjekt und schaffen eine Leerstelle, die auf den verschwundenen Körper in der Szene hinweist und das Gefühl des Verlusts verstärkt. Dieser Zensurakt verwehrt den Betrachtenden die vollständige Identifizierung des dargestellten Subjekts, führt die Betrachtenden aber zu einer stärkeren Empathie oder gar Identifizierung mit ihm. Eine ähnliche augenlose Gesichtsmaske, diesmal als abwesender Körper auf allen Vieren, dessen Mund ein (p. 64) Rohr durchdringt, wird in der Mise en Scène von *Extruder* (2017) verwendet. Hier verkörpert Phillips' in mehrdeutigen Skulpturenarrangements feinfühlig und sinnlich die komplexen Modalitäten des Blicks – das Betrachten, das Betrachtetwerden, die Vorstellung des Subjekts hinter der Maske sowie einer möglichen dritten Person.

Im Auge der Betrachtenden

Observer I (2016) ist die erste Arbeit von Phillips, die sich explizit auf Augen bezieht. Das aus Keramik modellierte, an einer eisernen Teleskopstange befestigte Fernglas, das auf einer quadratischen Plattform aus neun Keramikfliesen steht, dient unserer Vorstellung nach dazu, die Besucher_innen des Ausstellungsraumes oder etwas leicht höher Liegendes näher in Augenschein zu nehmen. Es handelt sich um eine prägnante, reduzierte Skulptur, die Abstraktion eines Körpers, deren minimale Ausstattung – Höhe, (Aussichts-)Gerät – unsere Vorstellungskraft dazu anregt, die Szene mit einem Körper zu besetzen. Phillips' Fernglas konkretisiert den Blick. Das Fernglas als Werkzeug zur Erweiterung und Optimierung der Sicht ist eine vieldeutige, mächtige Chiffre, ein tendenziell skrupelloses Instrument, das mit Überwachung, invasiver Beobachtung und sexueller Ausbeutung in Verbindung steht. Dieser Gedanke wird in *Observer II* (2020) (p. 141-143) fortgesetzt, diesmal mit einem auf einem runden Quarzitsockel stehenden keramischen Fernglas, dessen Okular- und Objektivseiten in Fleischtönen glasiert sind. Phillips' Fernglas ist ein nichtfunktionales Instrument und dient, wie die abwesenden Augen in ihrem gesamten Werk, dazu, die Betrachtenden in den Vordergrund zu stellen. Der Blick erfährt erneut eine Niederlage. Diese Mehrdeutigkeit, die schwankende An- und Abwesenheit, bildet den Kern von Phillips' Kunst, eine Wechselbeziehung, die ständig im Fluss ist und in der sich die Macht zwischen Beobachtenden/Beobachteten, Positionierenden/Positionierten bewegt und formt.

(p. 145) Die nächste Phase in Phillips' Auseinandersetzung mit dem Betrachten ist *Observer, Observed* (2022), ein komplexes, multimediales Kunstwerk. Das von der New Yorker High Line Art in Auftrag gegebene Projekt ist ihr erstes im öffentlichen Raum. Darin ermöglicht ein bronzenes Fernglas den Betrachtenden, von der 26th Street aus einen näheren Blick auf ihr Umfeld zu werfen. Sobald sich jedoch ihr Blick dem Fernglas nähert, werden ihre Augen von Kameras in den Objektiven des Fernglases erfasst und das Bild wird via Livestream auf einen drei Meter breiten öffentlich sichtbaren Bildschirm übertragen. Dieser Mechanismus des zweiseitigen beziehungsweise doppelseitigen Fernglases soll auf die schwankende, interaktive Machtdynamik des Blicks aufmerksam machen. Die Künstlerin möchte, wie sie selbst sagt, mit ihrer Arbeit ein Bewusstsein dafür schaffen, dass „das Betrachten einen Preis" hat, nämlich das Betrachtetwerden. Auch Phillips' Beschäftigung mit unserer Kultur des anonymen Beobachtens und des invasiven Onlinestalkings in den sozialen Medien hat Eingang in diese Arbeit gefunden, die der Frage nachgeht, wie eine Ethik des Betrachtens und des Beobachtens aussehen könnte.

*Einfach ausgedrückt, geht es in meiner Arbeit um Verhältnisse und
Beziehungen.*
– Julia Phillips, 2022

Mit ihrem Werk hat Phillips in den letzten zehn Jahren einen in Form,
Material und Inhalt bemerkenswerten Bogen geschlagen: von den
intimen Beziehungen zwischen zwei Akteur_innen in den frühen
Arbeiten, in denen eine offenkundige und verfestigte Machtdynamik
zu herrschen scheint, bis hin zu nuancierten, fast unmerklichen
Registern von Unstimmigkeit und Kampf in institutionalisierten Ver-
handlungen und Verhältnissen. An die Stelle der bekannten Körper-
und Gesichtsabdrücke der Künstlerin treten zunehmend abstrakte
und immer abstrakter werdende Körperabschnitte, tastende Versuche nach Anonymität und einem imaginierten universellen Körper.
Die Betrachtenden importieren ihre eigenen Vorstellungen beziehungsweise ihren eigenen Körper in die Hohlräume von Phillips'
Installationen. Die Skulpturen laden die Betrachtenden ein, sich
vorzustellen, wie man auf ihnen Fuß fasst, mit ihnen (ver)handelt
(siehe *Negotiator (#1)*, 2020) und interagiert, und sie auf diese Weise (p. 95)
zu vervollständigen. Im Laufe der Zeit hat sich Phillips mehr mit den
formalen Aspekten ihrer Kunstwerke beschäftigt, mit den intimen
Mechanismen als Metaphern für den Körper und die Beziehungen
zum Körper. Indem sie die Spuren ihrer eigenen Körperlichkeit auf
die wesentlichsten Elemente reduziert, hat sie neue, minimale Möglichkeiten gefunden, das Werk für die Betrachtenden in den genau-
en Proportionen, Maßen, im Umfang und in unscheinbaren anderen
visuellen Markierungen lesbar zu machen.

Headshot

Zurück zu *Headshot*: Entstanden ist dieses Gemeinschaftswerk mit
Keisha Scarville in Reaktion auf die Nachfragen nach einem Foto
von sich, mit denen Phillips immer wieder konfrontiert wurde, etwa
für Websites, Kataloge, Konferenzprogramme und andere Veröf-
fentlichungen. Phillips nutzte diese Forderung nach einem Portrait
für eine politische Auseinandersetzung mit ihren administrativen
Prozessen und für eine Kollaboration mit der von ihr geschätzten
Kollegin Keisha Scarville, einer namhaften Fotografin und Künstlerin,
die in ihren Schwarz-Weiß-Fotografien eine Sensibilität für Texturen
und deren Haptik betont. *Headshot* ist zudem von Lorraine O'Gra-
dys bedeutender Videoarbeit *Landscape (Western Hemisphere)*
(2010–11) beeinflusst und betrachtet die Vielfältigkeit, die die Haare
einer Schwarzen Frau als „Metapher für die Vermischung der Völker
im Westen, ihr objektives Korrelat" repräsentieren.[2] Phillips' Hände,
die sich beim Zurechtmachen ihrer Haare bewegen, bieten neben
dem Phänotyp der Haare weitere Aspekte ihrer Identität als Bild-
hauerin und Person of Color.

  Die Politik des Betrachtens ist ein fester Bestandteil und ein
zentrales Anliegen von Phillips' medienübergreifenden Arbeiten.
Sich „gesehen zu fühlen" bedeutet alltagssprachlich, über die eigenen visuellen Merkmale hinaus anerkannt zu werden und sichtbar
zu sein. In Patois ist „gesehen?" („seen?") eine Frage, bei der es um
Verstehen innerhalb der Community geht. Phillips' Erkundung des
Blickes als individuelle Person und Künstlerin, positioniert innerhalb
intersektionaler Identitäten, hat eine ganze Welt von Möglichkeiten
geschaffen, sich gesehen zu fühlen, anders zu sehen und die nor-
mative und über Generationen weitergegebene Machtdynamik des
Blickes zu hinterfragen.

Übersetzt von Melody Makeda Ledwon

1 Vgl. Cañigueral, Roser und Hamilton, Antonia F.de C.: The Role of Eye Gaze During Natural Social
Interactions in Typical and Autistic People, in Frontiers in Psychology, Bd. 10, 2019, S.2. https:// www.
frontiersin.org/articles/10.3389/fpsyg.2019.00560/full. Dort heißt es: „Wenn wir beispielsweise ein
paar Augen sehen, erhalten wir Informationen darüber, wo andere Personen hinschauen, wie sie sich
fühlen und was sie denken. Gleichzeitig können wir unsere Augen einsetzen, um die Aufmerksamkeit
eines anderen strategisch zu lenken. Je nach Dauer und Richtung unseres Blicks ist es uns möglich,
eine Bandbreite an Bedeutungen wahrzunehmen und zu signalisieren, etwa einen Kommunikation-
swunsch, Bedrohung und Dominanz, Attraktivität oder die Suche nach Anerkennung." (Übs. M.M.L.)

2 Lorraine O'Grady im Austausch mit der Autorin, 10. November 2017.

JANET DEES   The titling of your artworks is so precise, with astute and careful attention to language. You use words such as "intruder," "mediator," "destabilizer," and "distancer," which are both mechanical and relational, providing the viewer with a conceptual frame. Would you discuss your titling process and the function of your titles in relation to the objects?

JULIA PHILLIPS   My work almost always starts with a title, and these titles describe relations, a role, a person, a function, all at once. Language is a powerful tool for analyzing and laying bare the mechanisms behind interpersonal relationships, but also behind more structural and political relations. So, with titles like *Intruder, Mediator, Destabilizer,* and *Distancer,* there is always a mechanical metaphor at play, but also a bodily one. The tools that the mechanisms are embedded in relate to the body and often put two bodies, two interacting agents, in relation.

JANET   It's interesting to hear that you start with the title and then develop the object.

The Tension between Specificity and Indeterminacy:

Julia Phillips in Conversation with Janet Dees

JULIA   Sometimes I know I want to make a work about a specific experience or relation. For instance, I've been carrying around the title *Supporter* for years, but I haven't yet made the work because it's still not clear to me what it's going to look like. The same goes for the title *Isolator*—which, I should say, became an idea way before the pandemic. It feels almost like I'm pregnant with certain titles, and the gestation periods of the works are just really long.

Once I write the title down in my sketchbook, for example *Supporter,* I walk through life looking at moments of experiencing support or providing support in a more conscious way. It's about experiencing both sides of the doer/done-to dynamic of these titles, functions, relations, or interactions. And I'm hoping for the nuances and complexities to eventually feed into the making of a sculpture.

Sometimes the inspiration also comes from encountering (p. 84) a piece of mechanical hardware. With *Distancer* (2019), for instance, I think the work actually started with my coming across a turnbuckle, which is the little mechanism I used to connect the two partial masks. A turnbuckle comes into play in all kinds of construction situations to create tension. It introduces two rods of opposing directions such that the rods either move toward or apart from each other at the same pace, because they're operated by the same threading of the shared turnbuckle. I found it so metaphorical for interpersonal relationships and the dichotomy of mutually moving toward or away from each other. So, in this case, I think the mechanical hardware came first, then the title, and then the sculpture.

JANET   Sometimes you use the same title several times so that there is a serialization of the sculptures. For example, *Purifier I* and *II* (2021) and *Intruder, Misused I* and *II* (2019). What compels you to return to the same title and revisit similar forms?

(p. 101-103) (p. 71-73)

JULIA   Often the seriality allows for different versions, meaning slight variations in functionality. In the case of the two *Purifier* works, one part of both sculptures is a forehead cast with a mouth/funnel piece attached to it that leads into a handle. The handle on *Purifier I* is an object similar to a broomstick. It's unclear who would hold that device, whether the person fitting into the forehead shield or a second interacting agent who would hold the device onto another person's body. When I completed that sculpture, I was interested in being more specific about who is holding the device, so I made a second version with grips. Grips are a recurring element in my work and have this great property of positioning the body in a clear way. In *Purifier II*, I positioned the hand grips to suggest that the device is being held by the person who applies it to their own forehead. That's a new trajectory in my work: a tool for self-usage, a single user.

JANET   Cast forms like the back of the head or the top of the shoulders are motifs that appear in a few of your works, for example in the 2019 installation *Fake Truth (Witness I–III)* (p. 87-89) (2019). They communicate the shape of the human body while also evading the particularity of the face, which can be a holder of details that we use to interpret identity— to ascribe gender and ethnicity, for example. There's a beautiful metaphor in these forms for the tension I perceive in your work between specificity and indeterminacy.

JULIA   Yes, it is true that casts of these forms, or what I call masks, are a recurring element. But it is only more recently, basically since *Fake Truth (Witness I–III)*, that I've used the juxtaposition of a partial mask with shoulders to create a bust-like presence. Busts historically are the sculptural approach to portraiture. But I think in my work, I'm doing quite the opposite, in that I'm never interested in portraying one specific identity or subjectivity. I'm intending to portray an identity that can be projected onto, meaning that different viewers can somehow find themselves in it. That's part of the reason why I usually avoid the eye area, because eyes are the identifying marker of a person's face. The face also represents four out of the five senses. It's equipped with mouth, nose, eyes, and ears, and therefore represents the ability to take things in, but also the ability to relate. The bust-like presence is also a way to show posture, the way we carry ourselves and navigate through different moments. This is really evident in the installation *Oppressor* (p. 96-99) *with Soul, In Treatment & Suppressor with Spirit, In Treatment* (2020), which I can talk about in a moment.

But to go back to the tension between specificity and indeterminacy, I have the wish for my sculptural forms to be unspecific, somewhat general, and universal, although I know that's completely impossible. I made a decision years ago not to cast different bodies, because in my mind that becomes portraiture. Instead, I always cast my own body in the hope that when seen in juxtaposition and in seriality, it will read as more general than if I were to cast different bodies, different people in my life, highlighting different features of their bodies.

JANET   By only using your own body and not representing facial features, you're emphasizing the structures of human relation that might be more universal rather than the specificity of human identity. I think this is partly what your work is investigating.

JULIA   Right. But, of course, it runs into problems of norms and normality, like, "What is a shoulder?" and so forth. I think this is a familiar experience when interacting with functional devices—the way hands fit into scissors or how the body situates on a bicycle saddle and so forth. It also brings up questions of ableism and the tolerances within the norm. What deviation from the norm is accounted for in functional devices? What requires a custom-built device? But I think that's a whole different discourse.

JANET   I want to return to the installation *Oppressor with Soul, In Treatment & Suppressor with Spirit, In Treatment* as one of the works in which this bust-like form is incorporated. I think the installation brings together several strands that your practice explores. You investigate the physical constructions of devices and how these devices ask for particular kinds of bodily interactions, but they also have metaphorical implications. You explore the medical and the physiological but also the spiritual, the psychoanalytic, and the relational. I find this specific work so interesting for many reasons. One is the way in which it rather directly seeks to give form to immaterial notions. There are these specimen trays that hold forms that seem fleshy, and also ruptured. Might they read as containers for the immaterial soul and spirit of the title?

JULIA   Yes, it's great to be speaking about that work, because it's quite a heady installation and a lot of idiosyncratic ideas brought it to the form it now has. The installation stages a personal proposition that the soul and the spirit are separate, as you say, immaterial or imaginary organs. I find it fascinating that both the soul and the spirit are accounted for in the arts and the sciences. In psychology, for instance there's a book titled *Soul Murder: The Effects of Childhood Abuse and Deprivation* (1989), written by Leonard Shengold. Interestingly enough, Shengold, for five decades, was the psychoanalyst of the neurologist and writer Oliver Sacks, whose research I'm interested in and who has included descriptions of the spirit in his case studies. Sacks is one of the few scientists I have come across who uses the term "spirit." While the term "soul" makes regular appearances in the field of psychology, I find "spirit" more present in the arts than in the sciences. I think especially within the lineage of gospel music. In house music as well, there's a lot of mentioning of the spirit—an entity to be cared for, something that can be broken or uplifted.

I wanted to bring shape and form to these imaginary organs. *Soul* (part of *Oppressor with Soul, In Treatment & Suppressor with Spirit, In Treatment*) is a vessel-like object with one opening, somewhat of a lifelong container of experiences. There are two outgrowths that merge into one opening, a vessel with two enclosures. One of the two enclosures represents our actual lived experiences, and the other our guiding principles and value systems. There is a question of balance and imbalance, what our experiences turn out to be and what we ideally would like them to be.

Spirit (another part of that work) borrows its form from a spiritual metaphor. When I was researching the symbolic meanings of colors, I asked Swami Ishatmananda from my Vedanta study circle about the color orange. He, as the swami, dresses in orange and explained to me that it represents the flame that daily concerns and desires have been cast into on the path to the monastic life to which swamis devote themselves. I found it so interesting to learn about colors in the context of symbolism and metaphor. The spirit, to me, also represents the ability to transcend. In spiritual and meditation practices, there is a lot of mentioning of transcendence and getting beyond one's own body, one's own daily concerns and states of mind—a disassociation and disidentification with one's thoughts. In *Spirit,* that ability to transcend is represented by two openings. It's a crown-like object, the lower rim of which follows the shape of a head and the curves of the ears, as if fitting right above them. The upper rim has a flame-like edge that goes back to the orange flame metaphor I mentioned.

In this installation I'm presenting both imaginary organs—soul and spirit—in a ruptured state that symbolizes a need for treatment. They are placed in what I call medical trays. I'm proposing that the two organs require different forms of treatment for their well-being, which could be psychotherapy for the soul, and spiritual practice for the spirit.

And then there are the two head-shoulder casts in the installation. *Oppressor* is mounted facing downward drastically, as if a force were pressing down, literally oppressing the body. *Suppressor* is drastically looking upward, as if in avoidance. I should note that English is my second language and maybe I mistitled the work. Perhaps it should be called *Repressor*. I'm actually interested in your opinion about that, Janet. What I was trying to get at is the avoidance of something right in front of you, the inability to face something difficult within oneself. Is that repression or suppression?

JANET   In English, and specifically in psychology, "repress" and "suppress" have similar definitions. But then suppression has this additional connotation that's about, say, suppressing something like a revolt. For example, you wouldn't say you repressed the protestors, but that you suppressed them.

JULIA   Well, I meant the German word *Verdrängung*. Just now I'm realizing *die Verdrängung* actually also can be applied to the situation of protests. How interesting. There's a lot to say. I could get more into the sculptural details. For example, in *Oppressor* the ear hole is going inward as if there's an outside force intruding into the body and causing that ruptured hole. But in *Suppressor,* the direction of the hole is going outward, meaning the residue of that pierced hole accumulates outside, as if an inner force from within the subject is pushing it out. This all sounds very metaphysical, I'm realizing.

JANET   It is, but it's great. It's also very rooted in the form of the sculpture.

JULIA   The head-shoulder casts are attached to adjustable tension poles that span the entire height of the space. This is somewhat of a metaphor for universally present forces like oppression or suppression that can be found in any space.

JANET   From your perspective, what do you see as the distinction between the soul and the spirit? Some people see them as interchangeable, but you're thinking of them as two distinct immaterial organs.

JULIA   Coming across these terms in the arts and the sciences, I intuitively understood them as separate. I understood the soul as something that contains and continues accruing more and more—think of the way it's used in English, as in "soul to be filled" or "I carry something in my soul." The way I came across an understanding of the spirit was through spiritual practice, in particular my engagement with Vedantic thought. While the soul contains experiences, the spirit equips the mind to transcend them—guides the mind to, not necessarily higher spheres but other spheres to exist within. I do see them as connected and codependent. I think without the spirit, the soul would potentially be pretty lost. This is all very unscholarly and intuitive, but maybe worth a spontaneous answer.

JANET   I wouldn't say it's unscholarly. It's intuitive, but it's also based on a spiritual tradition, Vedanta, that has its own scholarly tradition dating back thousands of years with very detailed and serious debates and explorations around these matters.

Is there anything you would like to add about how your study of spiritual practices impacts the development of your work? I'm particularly interested in how your work so poetically links physical and psychological states. The fact that the physical and the psychological influence each other has long been a part of spiritual practices and is now being

increasingly explored in fields like psychology and
neurobiology.

JULIA The body of work I created for the 2022 Venice
Biennale is probably the most clearly influenced by these
studies. The suite of works consisting of *Bower, Veiled
Purifier,* and *Stabilizer* already reflects that in the titles,
I think. There is a lot of symbolism—the act of bowing, the veil,
the idea of a pendulum as an indicator of stability, a reliable value.

(p. 107) In *Bower* there is an implied movement, the act of lean-
(p. 104) ing forward, lowering one's head and ego. *Veiled Purifier*
revisits the shape of *Purifier I* and *II,* but in this iteration it's
wall mounted with a mauve veil draping to the ground
from eye level down—a gesture of introspection and focus.

(p. 109) *Stabilizer* is presented in a glass case, referencing an object
of worship found on church walls and other sacred places.
It resembles a cane, with a wire hanging down from the handle with a pendulum marking its end. I came across the
shape through plumbs found in the construction industry,
where a clear identification of the vertical line—the plumb
line—is required. I find this plumb a beautiful metaphor for
a value that does not change, that is stable and firm, always
pointing to the center of the Earth, no matter where you
are on this globe. I consider it a reliable value. Something
I wish there were more of.

JANET DEES Die Titel Deiner Arbeiten sind immer sehr präzise, sprachlich klug und sorgfältig gewählt. Du verwendest Begriffe wie „intruder", „mediator", „destabilisator" und „distancer", die ebenso eine technische wie eine relationale Bedeutung haben und den Betrachtenden einen konzeptionellen Rahmen bieten. Kannst Du uns erklären, wie Du bei der Benennung Deiner Werke vorgehst und welche Funktion Deine Titel für die Objekte haben?

JULIA PHILLIPS Meine Arbeiten gehen fast immer von einem Titel aus, und diese Titel bezeichnen gleichzeitig Beziehungen, Rollen, Personen und Funktionen. Sprache ist ein mächtiges Werkzeug, um die Funktionsweise von zwischenmenschlichen, aber auch von strukturellen oder politischen Beziehungen zu analysieren und offenzulegen. Bei Titeln wie *Intruder, Mediator, Destabilizer* und *Distancer* ist also immer sowohl eine technische als auch eine körperliche Metapher im Spiel. Die Geräte, die diese Funktionen haben, beziehen sich auf den Körper und stellen häufig einen Bezug zwischen zwei Körpern, zwei interagierenden Akteur_Innen her.

Die Spannung zwischen Bestimmtheit und Unbestimmtheit.

Julia Phillips im Gespräch mit Janet Dees

JANET Es ist interessant, dass Du mit dem Titel anfängst und daraus dann das Objekt entwickelst.

JULIA Manchmal weiß ich schon, dass ich eine Arbeit zu einer bestimmten Erfahrung oder Beziehung machen möchte. Zum Beispiel trage ich seit Jahren den Titel *Supporter* mit mir herum und habe immer noch keine Arbeit mit diesem Titel gemacht, weil mir noch nicht klar ist, wie sie aussehen soll. Dasselbe gilt für den Titel *Isolator* – eine bereits lange vor Ausbruch der Pandemie entstandene Idee. Es fühlt sich fast an, als wäre ich mit diesen Titeln schwanger, und bei manchen Arbeiten dauert die Tragezeit einfach sehr lange.

Wenn ich einen Titel in mein Skizzenbuch schreibe, behalte ich ihn im Hinterkopf und begegne meinem Alltag aufmerksamer. Zum Beispiel bin ich bei *Supporter* auf der Suche nach Augenblicken, in denen ich Unterstützung erfahre oder leiste. Dabei geht es darum, sowohl die aktive als auch die passive Seite in der Dynamik dieser Titel, Funktionen, Beziehungen oder Interaktionen zu erleben. Und ich hoffe, dass die verschiedenen Nuancen und Facetten anschließend in die Gestaltung einer Skulptur einfließen.

(p. 84) Manchmal inspiriert mich auch die Begegnung mit einem technischen Gegenstand. *Distancer* (2019) zum Beispiel begann damit, dass ich zufällig auf ein Spannschloss stieß, die kleine Vorrichtung, mit der ich dann die beiden Maskenteile verband. Ein Spannschloss wird in den verschiedensten Konstruktionsbereichen verwendet, um Spannung zu erzeugen. Es verbindet zwei Stangen mit entgegengesetzter Gewinderichtung und bringt sie durch die Drehung dazu, sich synchron aufeinander zu oder voneinander weg zu bewegen. Für mich war das eine sehr treffende Metapher für zwischenmenschliche Beziehungen und die Dichotomie des Sich-aufeinander-zu- oder voneinander-weg-Bewegens. In diesem Fall kam zuerst der technische Gegenstand, dann der Titel und dann die Skulptur.

JANET Gelegentlich verwendest Du denselben Titel mehrfach, sodass einige Skulpturen als Serie auftreteten. Zum Beispiel *Purifier I* und *II* (2021) oder *Intruder, Misused I* und *II* (2019). Was bringt Dich dazu, einen Titel oder eine skulpturale Form wieder aufzugreifen?

(p. 101-103) (p. 71-73)

JULIA   Die Serialität erlaubt oft verschiedene Versionen, also leichte Variationen in der Funktionalität. So bestehen die beiden *Purifier*-Arbeiten jeweils zum Teil aus einer Stirnabformung mit einem Mundstück/Trichterteil, die in einen Griff übergeht. Der Griff von *Purifier I* ähnelt einem einfachen Besenstiel. Es ist unklar, ob die Person, die in das Stirnschild passt, dieses Gerät halten soll oder eine zweite, interagierende Person, die das Gerät an den Körper einer weiteren Person hält. Nachdem ich diese Skulptur fertiggestellt hatte, wollte ich genauer darstellen, wer das Gerät hält, also habe ich eine zweite Version mit einem Doppelgriff aus zwei Handabdrücken gemacht. Handabdrucksgriffe tauchen in meiner Arbeit immer wieder auf und haben die schöne Eigenschaft, den Körper klar zu positionieren. Bei *Purifier II* habe ich die Handgriffe so angebracht, dass sie den Eindruck erwecken, das Gerät würde von einer Person gehalten, die es an ihre eigene Stirn anlegt. Das ist eine neue Entwicklungsrichtung in meiner Arbeit: ein Werkzeug für die Selbstanwendung einer einzelnen Person.

(p. 87-89)

JANET   Abformungen wie etwa eines Hinterkopfes und der Schultern sind ein Motiv, das in manchen Deiner Werke auftaucht, zum Beispiel in *Fake Truth (Witness I–III)* (2019). Sie zeichnen die Form des menschlichen Körpers nach und weichen dabei der Besonderheit des Gesichts aus, anhand dessen wir Identität deuten, also zum Beispiel geschlechtliche und ethnische Zugehörigkeiten zuschreiben könnten. Diese Formen sind eine wunderbare Metapher für das Spannungsverhältnis zwischen Bestimmtheit und Unbestimmtheit, das ich in Deiner Arbeit sehe.

JULIA   Stimmt, diese Abformungen oder Masken, wie ich sie nenne, sind ein wiederkehrendes Element. Aber erst in letzter Zeit, vor allem seit der Installation *Fake Truth (Witness I–III)*, habe ich den Teil einer Maske und Schultern zusammengesetzt, um einen büstenartigen Eindruck zu schaffen. Historisch betrachtet sind Büsten der bildhauerische Ausdruck eines Porträts. Aber ich mache mit meiner Arbeit genau das Gegenteil, denn es interessiert mich nicht, eine bestimmte Identität oder ein bestimmtes Individuum zu porträtieren. Ich möchte eine menschliche Gestalt darstellen, die sich für Projektionen eignet, in der sich also verschiedene Betrachtende in irgendeiner Weise wiederfinden können. Das ist einer der Gründe, warum ich in der Regel die Augenpartie ausspare, denn die Augen sind letztlich das wichtigste Identifikationsmerkmal im Gesicht eines Menschen. Im Gesicht sind außerdem vier von fünf Sinnen vertreten. Mit dem Mund, der Nase, den Augen und den Ohren steht es für die Fähigkeit, Dinge wahrzunehmen, aber auch für die Fähigkeit, Beziehungen herzustellen. Die büstenartige Form verdeutlicht außerdem die Körperhaltung, die Art und Weise, wie wir auftreten und uns durch verschiedene Situationen manövrieren. Das wird besonders in der Installation (p. 96-99) *Oppressor with Soul, In Treatment & Suppressor with Spirit, In Treatment* (2020) deutlich, zu der ich gleich ausführlicher komme.

Aber um noch einmal auf die Spannung zwischen Bestimmtheit und Unbestimmtheit zurückzukommen: Ich möchte, dass meine skulpturalen Formen unspezifisch, irgendwie allgemein und universell sind, und ich weiß, dass das vollkommen unmöglich ist. Ich habe mich vor Jahren dazu entschieden, nicht die Körper von anderen abzuformen, weil das meiner Meinung nach wirklich Porträtcharakter hätte. Stattdessen forme ich immer meinen eigenen Körper ab und hoffe, dass er in der Serie allgemeiner wirkt, als wenn ich verschiedene Körper, verschiedene Menschen in meinem Leben abforme und verschiedene Merkmale ihrer Körper hervorheben würde.

JANET   Indem Du nur Deinen eigenen Körper einsetzt und keine Gesichtszüge abbildest, betonst Du die Strukturen menschlicher Beziehungen, die vielleicht universeller sind als das spezifische menschliche Individuum. Ich denke, darum geht es in Deiner Arbeit zum Teil auch.

JULIA Richtig. Aber natürlich ergeben sich daraus Fragen nach Abweichung und Norm, wie zum Beispiel „Was ist eine Schulter?". Ich denke, das ist eine bekannte Frage beim Umgang mit Gebrauchsgegenständen. Die Art und Weise, wie die Hand in eine Schere passt oder der Körper auf einen Fahrradsattel und so weiter. Und das wirft Fragen zum Thema körperlicher Abweichungen und zum Toleranzbereich einer Norm auf. Welche Abweichungen von der Norm werden bei Gebrauchsgegenständen berücksichtigt und welche nicht? Wann braucht man eine Sonderanfertigung? Aber das ist noch einmal ein ganz anderer Diskurs.

JANET Ich möchte noch einmal auf die Installation *Oppressor with Soul, In Treatment & Suppressor with Spirit, In Treatment* zurückkommen, eine der Arbeiten, die diese büstenartige Form enthält. Ich glaube, die Installation vereint mehrere Stränge Deines künstlerischen Schaffens. Du untersuchst die materielle Konstruktion von Geräten und inwiefern diese Geräte bestimmte Arten körperlicher Interaktionen erfordern, doch sie haben auch metaphorische Bedeutung. Du erforschst medizinisches und physiologisches, aber auch spirituelles, psychoanalytisches und relationales Denken. Ich finde diese spezielle Arbeit aus vielen Gründen sehr interessant. Einer dieser Gründe ist die Art und Weise, wie sie versucht, immateriellen Begriffen eine unmittelbare Form zu geben. Zum Beispiel sind da diese Laborschalen mit fleischig wirkenden Formen darin, die etwas beschädigt und eingerissen sind. Könnte man sie als Behälter für die immaterielle Seele und den Geist des Titels verstehen?

JULIA Ich freue mich sehr, dass wir über diese Arbeit sprechen, denn es ist eine ziemlich verkopfte Installation, und eine Reihe recht eigenwilliger Ideen hat zu ihrer jetzigen Form geführt. Die Installation stellt meine persönliche These dar, dass die Seele und der Geist getrennte immaterielle, wie Du es nennst, oder imaginäre Organe sind. Ich finde es faszinierend, dass sowohl die Seele als auch der Geist in den Künsten und Wissenschaften thematisiert werden. Der Begriff „Seele" wird zum Beispiel in der Psychologie verwendet. Es gibt ein Buch mit dem Titel *Seelenmord – die Auswirkungen von Missbrauch und Vernachlässigung in der Kindheit* von Leonard Shengold. Interessanterweise war Shengold fünf Jahrzehnte lang der Psychoanalytiker des Neurologen und Schriftstellers Oliver Sacks, für dessen Forschung ich mich interessiere und der in seinen Fallstudien auch Beschreibungen des Geistes liefert. Oliver Sacks ist allerdings einer der wenigen Wissenschaftler_innen, die mir begegnet sind, die den Begriff „Geist" verwenden. Während der Begriff „Seele" in der Psychologie regelmäßig auftaucht, scheint mir der Begriff „Geist" in den Künsten präsenter zu sein als in der Wissenschaft. Ich glaube, das gilt besonders für die Gospelmusik. Auch in der House-Musik wird der Geist häufig erwähnt – als etwas, das kultiviert und gehegt werden muss, das gebrochen und wieder aufgerichtet werden kann.

Ich wollte diesen imaginären Organen Gestalt und Form verleihen. *Soul* ist ein gefäßartiges Objekt mit einer Öffnung, eine Art Behälter für die Erfahrungen, die man im Laufe des Lebens macht. Er besteht aus zwei Ausbuchtungen, die zu einer Öffnung verschmelzen, zu einem Gefäß mit zwei Kammern. Eine der beiden Kammern steht für unsere tatsächlichen Erfahrungen, die andere für unsere Leitprinzipien und Wertesysteme. Dabei geht es um Gleichgewicht und Ungleichgewicht, um die Frage, wie unsere Erfahrungen tatsächlich aussehen und wie wir sie idealerweise gerne hätten.

Spirit verdankt seine Form einer spirituellen Metapher. Als ich die symbolische Bedeutung von Farben recherchierte, fragte ich Swami Ishatmananda aus meinem Vedanta-Studienkreis nach der Farbe Orange. Er als Swami kleidet sich orange und erklärte mir, die Farbe symbolisiere eine Flamme: Ein Symbol für das Verbrennen der alltäglichen Sorgen und Bedürfnisse, die Swamis auf dem Weg ins klösterliche Leben hinter sich lassen.

Ich fand es sehr interessant, etwas über die Symbolik und Metaphorik von Farben zu erfahren. Der Geist steht für mich auch für die Fähigkeit zur Transzendenz. Bei spirituellen und meditativen Praktiken ist sehr häufig die Rede von Transzendenz und davon, über den eigenen Körper, seine täglichen Sorgen und Befindlichkeiten hinauszuwachsen – sich von den eigenen Gedanken zu lösen und sich nicht mit ihnen zu identifizieren. Bei *Spirit* wird diese Fähigkeit zur Transzendenz durch zwei Öffnungen dargestellt. Es handelt sich um ein kronenähnliches Objekt, dessen unterer Rand der Form eines Kopfes und den Rundungen der Ohren folgt, als würde er genau darauf passen. Die Oberkante ist flammenförmig, was auf die Metapher der orangefarbenen Flamme zurückgeht, von der ich eben sprach.

In dieser Installation präsentiere ich die beiden imaginären Organe – Seele und Geist – in einem zerrissenen Zustand, der die Notwendigkeit einer Behandlung symbolisiert. Sie liegen in „chirurgischen Schalen", wie ich sie nenne. Ich behaupte, dass beide Organe für ihr Wohlergehen unterschiedliche Formen der Behandlung benötigen. Für die Seele könnte eine Psychotherapie diese Behandlungsform sein und für den Geist ein spirituelles Engagement.

Außerdem gibt es in der Installation noch die beiden Kopf-Schulter-Abformungen. *Oppressor* ist sehr stark nach unten geneigt, wie von einer Kraft nach unten gepresst, die den Körper buchstäblich unterdrückt. *Suppressor* hingegen blickt fast senkrecht nach oben, wie um etwas auszuweichen. Ich muss dazusagen, dass Englisch meine zweite Sprache ist und ich die Arbeit womöglich falsch betitelt habe. Vielleicht müsste sie eher *Repressor* heißen. Mich würde Deine Meinung zu dieser Frage interessieren, Janet. Ich wollte auf die Vermeidung von etwas hinaus, das direkt vor einem liegt, auf die Unfähigkeit, sich etwas Schwierigem zu stellen. Ist das „repression" oder „suppression"?

JANET   Im Englischen und insbesondere in der Psychologie werden die Begriffe „repress" und „suppress" ähnlich verwendet, denke ich. Aber „suppression" hat noch eine weitere Bedeutung, nämlich etwas zu unterdrücken, etwa eine Revolte. Um zu sagen, dass ein Protest unterdrückt wurde, würde man nicht „repress", sondern „suppress" verwenden.

JULIA   Ich meinte das deutsche Wort „Verdrängung". Dass „Verdrängung" auch auf Proteste anwendbar ist, wird mir erst jetzt klar. Wie interessant.

Es gäbe wirklich noch viel dazu zu sagen. Ich könnte etwa näher auf die bildhauerischen Details eingehen. Bei *Oppressor* zum Beispiel öffnet sich das Ohrloch nach innen, als würde sich eine Kraft von außen in den Körper drängen und das Loch aufreißen. Bei *Suppressor* hingegen öffnet sich das Ohrloch nach außen: das von der Bohrung verdrängte Material lagert sich außerhalb der Ohrmuschel ab, als würde sich eine innere Kraft durch das Ohr aus dem Körper drängen. Ich merke gerade, dass das alles ziemlich metaphysisch klingt.

JANET   Stimmt, aber es ist großartig. Es ist auch stark in der Form der Skulptur angelegt.

JULIA   Noch etwas kommt hinzu, nämlich dass diese Kopf-Schulter-Abformungen an verstellbaren Spannstangen befestigt sind, die sich über die gesamte Höhe des Raumes erstrecken. Das ist so etwas wie eine Metapher für die Kräfte der Unterdrückung oder Verdrängung, die in jedem Raum vorhanden sind.

JANET   Worin besteht aus Deiner Sicht der Unterschied zwischen Seele und Geist? Manche Menschen halten sie vielleicht für austauschbar, aber Du verstehst sie als zwei unterschiedliche immaterielle Organe.

JULIA   Als ich in der Kunst und der Wissenschaft auf diese Begriffe stieß, fasste ich sie intuitiv als voneinander getrennt auf. Ich verstand die Seele als etwas, das immer mehr mit Inhalten gefüllt wird – so wie es im Englischen in Formulierungen wie „soul to be filled" („zu erfüllende Seele") oder „I carry something in my soul" („Ich trage etwas in meiner Seele") zum Ausdruck kommt.

Zu meinem Verständnis vom Geist kam ich über die spirituelle Praxis, insbesondere durch meine Beschäftigung mit dem vedantischen Denken. Während die Seele Erfahrungen enthält, ermöglicht der Geist dem Verstand, diese zu transzendieren, und führt ihn nicht unbedingt in höhere, aber in andere Sphären. Ich betrachte sie als miteinander verbunden und voneinander abhängig. Ich glaube, ohne den Geist wäre die Seele wahrscheinlich ziemlich verloren. Das ist alles sehr unwissenschaftlich und intuitiv, aber vielleicht eine spontane Antwort wert.

JANET Ich würde das nicht als unwissenschaftlich bezeichnen. Es ist intuitiv, basiert aber auf einer spirituellen Tradition, dem Vedanta, der eine eigene Jahrtausende alte wissenschaftliche Tradition hat, in der diese Dinge sehr ausführlich und ernsthaft diskutiert und erforscht werden.

Möchtest Du noch etwas über den Einfluss Deiner Beschäftigung mit spirituellen Praktiken auf die Entwicklung Deiner Arbeit sagen? Mich interessiert insbesondere die poetische Art und Weise, mit der Du in Deiner Arbeit eine Verbindung zwischen physischen und psychischen Zuständen herstellst. Die Tatsache, dass sich das Körperliche und das Psychische gegenseitig beeinflussen, ist schon seit langem Bestandteil dieser spirituellen Verfahren und wird heute beispielsweise in der Psychologie und Neurobiologie zunehmend erforscht.

JULIA Die Werke, die ich für die Venedig Biennale 2022 angefertigt habe, sind wahrscheinlich am eindeutigsten von dieser Auseinandersetzung beeinflusst. Ich denke, diese Reihe von Arbeiten spiegelt das bereits in ihren Titeln wider: *Bower*, *Veiled Purifier* und *Stabilizer*. (p. 107) (p. 104) (p. 109) Darin ist sehr viel Symbolik enthalten – der Akt des Verbeugens, der Schleier, die Idee eines Pendels als Gradmesser für Stabilität, einen verlässlichen Wert.

Bower impliziert eine Bewegung, das Vorbeugen, das Senken des Hauptes und des Egos. *Veiled Purifier* nimmt die Form von *Purifier I* und *II* wieder auf, allerdings ist er dieses Mal an der Wand befestigt und mit einem purpur-/mauvefarbenen Schleier versehen, der ab Augenhöhe zum Boden hängt – eine Gebärde der Introspektion und Konzentration. *Stabilizer* wird in einem Glaskasten präsentiert und verweist auf sakrale Objekte, wie sie an den Wänden von Kirchen und an anderen heiligen Orten zu finden sind. Er ähnelt einem Gehstock, von dessen Griff ein Draht mit einem Pendel am Ende herunterhängt. Dieser Form bin ich im Baugewerbe begegnet, wo Lote für die eindeutige Identifizierung der vertikalen Linie, der Lotrechten, benötigt werden. Ich finde, dieses Lot ist eine schöne Metapher für einen Wert, der sich nicht verändert, der stabil und fest ist und immer auf den Mittelpunkt der Erde zeigt, egal wo auf diesem Globus man sich befindet. Ich betrachte ihn als einen verlässlichen Wert. Davon würde ich mir mehr wünschen.

Übersetzt von Sylvia Zirden

JAMIESON WEBSTER   I wanted to start by reading you a couple of quotes from Sigmund Freud in *Findings, Ideas, Problems* from 1938, published posthumously in 1941. They're often thought of as the last things Freud wrote—scribblings, but they're very charming. The first is, "A sense of guilt also originates from unsatisfied love. Like hate. In fact, we have been obliged to derive every conceivable thing from that material: like economically self-sufficient states with their Ersatz or substitute products." The second is, "Space may be the projection of the extension of the psychical apparatus. No other derivation is possible. Instead of Kant's a priori determinants of our psychical apparatus, psyche is extended; knows nothing about it."

JAMIESON   The reason I thought of these was sculpture, and the fact that from the material relationship between affect, the body, and psyche, we derive products that are substitute satisfactions, and we create space in general as an extension of the body. So much of your work, I think, speaks to that, and to the nature of sculpture as a working and reworking of that ground.

Like Changing One's Own Voice:

JAMIESON   I think it's a way of playing with the extension of psyche. Freud said, "The ego is first and foremost a body ego. It's the extension of the surface of the body." But you don't just project the surface. On the one hand, when we

JULIA PHILLIPS   Very nice, very poetic.

Julia Phillips in Conversation with Jamieson Webster

JULIA   When hearing the quote about unsatisfied love and substitute products, I thought of relationships that end unreconciled, which I see as resonant with the idea of unsatisfied love. My titles refer to a role, a function, and sometimes a specific person who ends up being somewhat interchangeable. Almost like in a dream, where I start dreaming about one person, but then in a later part of the dream the role gets carried out by another person. Interpersonal expression can be very limited. And art making is a way to continue an expression about a relationship—by portraying it. So, to some degree, I would say that my work can even be revenge, a way to get even.

I remember in the piece you wrote about Louise Bourgeois, you listed all of the things that psychoanalysis meant for her.[1] One of them is duty. She describes her relationship to analysis in similar ways to how I would describe art making: an access to the unconscious, a kind of sane-keeping.

Bourgeois also speaks about the main formal gestures of sculpting—joining and separating—and the psychic space that she is ideally in when working in the studio, something I can relate to. My sculpting technique is self-developed and self-taught. I don't take actual casts in the traditional sense using a plaster mold, but instead I prepare clay slabs, then push a slab onto my body and wait until the clay hardens enough to roughly hold its shape. When I take it off, I immediately have to support it. Then there's a lot of reworking and mending. In traditional casting, the negative form (the cast) picks up textural details that result on the surface of the positive. But the way my molds work is that the most detailed information is actually on the inside of the sculpture, in the negative space, because there is no negative process. The sculpture is negative and positive at the same time, in a weird way.

think of our visual image, that's all we see. But there are so many aspects of the body and its extension. Freud says the best organs are quiet organs, because when our organs are loud, we suddenly pay attention to them. There is something to me about your work that goes beyond the surface projection of space. I didn't know about your casting technique, but that makes a lot of sense to me in the way that I was thinking about what you do.

I wanted to ask about the *Intruder* series (2017), and its exploring of the exploitative and questions of power and abuse. You mentioned Dianne Elise's paper on male fantasies of intrusion.[2] Maybe you could tell me a little bit about that. You identify as a woman. Was it interesting for you to read about the male fantasy from an analyst, or was this already your experience, as a woman, of men? How did you approach that?

(p. 70)

JULIA   I came across the essay when searching for the intersection of certain keywords. I think my search words were "penetration," "psychoanalysis," and "postcolonialism." The only reason why the essay came up with "postcolonialism" as a keyword is because Elise quotes Robert M. Friedman, who speaks about the psyche as the dark continent.[3]

JAMIESON   Freud used the phrase "dark continent" in the context of the psyche, but also to speak of women. It's been brought up that there's something misogynistic about that, and there's also obviously something racial about it.

JULIA   Racial and potentially colonial and exploitative. The hidden resource, and the attempt of going in and taking out. There's much to say, but it's not what the essay is about. The title of Elise's paper is "Unlawful Entry: Male Fears of Psychic Penetration." I was interested in the articulations about paternal law and a denied access to the mind and emotional landscape.

JAMIESON   I was thinking of your work as not simply from the male perspective but about a penetration between parties—something can be more ambiguous there. It's not necessarily so gendered: male penetrator or perpetrator. Although we have to think of the violent historical aspects of it. But anybody can assume that position.

JULIA   The essay speaks about penetration in very abstract terms. It was certainly a source of inspiration for some works. During the time of reading it, I discovered an agricultural auger in a thrift store, basically an oversize corkscrew at what I found to be an uncomfortable scale. I remember thinking, "What could this possibly be used on?" The answer is the earth (Mother Earth!). Augers are used to penetrate the ground for planting seedlings. One of the works that (p. 64) was inspired by both Elise's essay and the auger is *Extruder* (2017), an installation with an auger of phallic diameter as part of a larger exploitative apparatus. I also made augers (p. 71-73) with bent threads, the *Intruder, Misused* series (2019). The title suggests that their bent state is the result of them being used with too much force—overused—which implies that intrusion can also happen appropriately: *not* misused. I was thinking about the intrusive nature of psychoanalysis as a form of treatment that requires consensual intrusion of the psyche.

JAMIESON   It can be hard for patients, or students, to think of the relationship between analyst and patient and what is intrusive or violent about it. Importantly, there is this prohibition on touch in relation to the body in psychoanalysis; everything that's going to be exchanged is words.

This reminds me of your sculptural shift to horizontal power dynamics. These are your *Mediator* (2020/21) (p. 90-93) and *Observer* (2016/20) sculptures, which involve the shapes (p. 141-143) of microphones and binoculars. I don't assume that you know this, but Jacques Lacan mapped out the objects of the body. While the very classical objects in Freud are the oral object and the anal object and then the genitals, Lacan adds to the series the gaze and the voice. We can't hear ourselves while we are speaking, and when we do hear ourselves speaking, it's shocking. I saw this shift in your work. I know that you've thought about it as a move from vertical to horizontal relations, but it's also a shift from material objects of the body to immaterial objects. We don't see the fact that we look vigorously at some things and not others. We don't hear the modulations of our voice. There can be a violence in the gaze and the voice at the same time that there can be incredible tenderness. There's an amplitude between these different registers that we're unaware of, in comparison to, say, oral hunger and devouring feelings, or our anal expulsion, or hoarding, or penetrating-penetrative dimensions of experience.

JAMIESON　Something containing and/or neutral has disappeared in this post-truth world. We have a spectacle of aggressive speech dominating culture, and it's interesting to think of your sculptures as trying to bring people to an experience where they see or hear themselves as they interact with your work.

JULIA　The first work I made using microphones was *Fake Truth (Witness I–III)* (2019) for the *Fake Truth* exhibition. (p. 87-89) It's an installation with three sculptures suspended from the ceiling, each equipped with microphones and hidden speakers, and a gravel floor filling the exhibition space. The cardioid microphone in each of the three sculptures filters the viewer's voice in a different way, rendering it with effects. So the sculptures almost speak back, reflecting the viewer in altered ways.

It's interesting what you said about not hearing oneself as one speaks and the shock and rejection toward one's voice. The installation deals with recognition of the self, but also with recognition of an event, the question of truth. I made the work in 2019 with Donald Trump in office and was thinking about the destabilization of our relationship to the media and to objectivity and truth. Fake news seems like an abuse of the notion of subjectivity. By abuse, I mean that the claim to subjectivity was taken so far as that one can say, "Well, it didn't happen in my perception." Doing that with facts is really dangerous.

JULIA　Going back to the immaterial, both the gaze and the voice are so open to interpretation, which is always subjective—the "reading into something," a gaze or the tone. In *Observer*, a sculpture that looks like binoculars, both vertical sides (the viewer side and the lens side) resemble a face cast, where a person's eyes could fit. There's a suggestion of the gaze going both ways—that there is an Other on the opposite side, looking back. An Other in front of the lens that is not just objectified but "subjectified." I developed *Observer* further for my first public sculpture, *Observer,* (p. 145) *Observed* (2022), made for the New York High Line. The moment the viewer looks through the binoculars and gets a privileged close-up view of the surroundings, they are giving away part of their own identity by having their eyes on public display. It's my first work that deals explicitly with the idea of anonymity, showing eyes as an identifying physical element. The work addresses the public politics of looking, also having social media in mind, and the idea of anonymous lurking and surveillance.

In Alfred Hitchcock's *Rear Window* (1954), there's a beautiful scene toward the end, where the protagonist asks himself what his responsibility is for lurking around and seeing what his neighbors are engaged in. In the movie he accidentally witnesses a crime in an adjacent apartment building and struggles with his position as a silent observer. The movie concludes with the question of responsibility and the politics around the position of the observer.

JAMIESON   What's aggressive about the gaze is that you don't include yourself in what you see. You don't include yourself as the person looking. Lacan brings up the picture plane, because to understand that there's a perspective that you're taking, you have to include yourself as the observer of it, and you have to include the space behind your own head.

JULIA   Yes, the picture plane informing your subject position, the picture plane as the literal "surroundings." This brings up the idea of postcolonial theory and the gaze as dominating, exoticizing, and objectifying. But I think observation can happen "horizontally," and power dynamics can shift, for instance in the experience of motherhood. I am thinking about the position of the parent or the mother observing the infant, and the infant gazing back.

JAMIESON   Yes, with the infant, there's so much room to play with the gaze, looking at each other, different intonations with the eyes. We lose so much of that. And something can get rigidified through customs, whereas it's so open with children.

JULIA   There's so much to learn and get inspired from with children. This unapologetic staring that is so nonjudgmental at the same time.

JAMIESON   Yes, that doesn't have that feeling of obscenity, which is very beautiful. That brings me to the spirituality in your work. There's something about the internal gazing, as opposed to the external gazing, that you explore. And I just wanted to read one more thing from Freud's final notes. He writes: "Mysticism is the obscure self-perception of the realm outside the ego, of the id." Amazing that Freud's last note is on mysticism. I know this is an important turning point in your work.

JULIA   Yes, my interest in spiritual practices has recently informed my work. I turned my focus from external relations to internal relations, relationships with the self.

JAMIESON   This brings me back to what you brought up about Louise Bourgeois. I think of spiritual practices a lot like Bourgeois thinks about sculpture: a way of joining and breaking differently within oneself than what the world perhaps permits us.

JULIA   Right, breaking with something. For a while I wanted to change the tone of my work, and I found it very hard to actually do it. I wanted to change a violent, exploitative, abusive, and forceful tone to something more reconciling. And I realized that an internal shift had to happen. I couldn't just dream up a peaceful sculpture; I needed to rethink the values that govern my decision making and how to navigate relationships and life events in order to change that tone. Almost like changing one's own voice.

JAMIESON   It is one of the things that changes—as we like to call it, with the very elegant phrase, late-stage analysis, termination-stage analysis. It's the moment when the patient's tone changes. We think about the literal voice that you produce, but this also has to do with change to the voices inside, the allowance of more affect in the voice, more singsonginess, less constriction. Things that feel sedimented in the psyche, as if these suddenly open up at the very end of analysis. There's also something about internalizing the voice of the analyst such that you can leave them. You carry with you something of their voice or their quality of speaking to you.

Maybe that helps bring me to the last thing I wanted to ask you about, your latest show, *Me, Ourself & You* (2022),

on motherhood, on conception. I love the *Conception Drawings.* (p. 124-133)
And I'm so happy we were featured together in the
New York Review for my essay "A Child Is Being Aborted."[4]
One thing that struck me is the fact that conception, fetal
development, is sculptural. Lacan was a doctor and was fascinated by embryology, which led him to his investigation
of topological forms. The way something holds together
without being a closed surface, because a body isn't a closed
surface. And he felt that if the analyst was going to work
on a deeper level, they had to play around with these things.
Psychoanalysts need to be sculptors!

JULIA   As an artist thinking about pregnancy, it was almost
obvious for me to try and give form to exactly what I don't
know. Conception, despite the research on it, is still quite
mysterious. I have never even seen a photo of an actual
uterus. Only as an illustration on a tampon box or something.
It's really under-depicted. In those *Conception Drawings,*
I was trying to illustrate something that I could only imagine. I almost had to dream it up, as I was anxious about
conceiving. There was no way that I could physically understand it and "get it right," because we're speaking about
not just organs but also the moment of chance and the biomaterial of the impregnator.

JAMIESON   That brings me nicely to my last question, which
is about female sexuality. I noticed that, on the one hand,
there was an investigation of power and how that takes
place within relationships. And some of that could be in the
male-female intersection, or dominant versus the object of
that dominance. And then your work moves more and more
toward spirituality, mysticism, motherhood. A woman is
often put into one of two categories—either the object or the
mother, the mystic—and her sexuality, her particular subjective sense of her sexuality, is often lost. Did you see yourself
as wanting to evoke that duality? Where do you make room
for female sexuality? I've done work on different artists,
and Louise Bourgeois, I think, does amazing work with this
same split. And then you have sculptors like Tracey Emin
or Sarah Lucas who go hard-core for the sexuality. How do
you imagine yourself in that lineage of women sculptors?

JULIA   I appreciate that and those artists' work as well.
Where do I make room for sexuality? In 2013 I had just ended
work with two different feminist collaboratives and did
a letter project, where I asked women to anonymously send
me letters about their sexual fantasies, imaginations, frus-
trations, and so forth. And I got a few pieces back. So there
was that exploration for a certain time. My thesis work
in 2015 concluding grad school was also looking at female
desire and sexuality. It's an installation consisting of a video
(p. 19) and a sculpture. The video is called *Becoming (the Hunter,
the Twerker, the Submitter)* and the sculpture is called
Connecter. In the video, I'm creating these three characters
who all have different attributes that represent different
types of desires. For the show you saw that deals with conception, motherhood, and reproductive rights, *Me, Ourself
& You,* I very consciously left out two obvious aspects: birth
(because I don't like the spectacle of it) and sex. There are
(p. 118-123) the two works, *Impregnator* and *Aborter* (2022), but they don't
represent the sexual act and desire. Instead, they read
as medical devices and are getting into the mechanics
of impregnation and abortion. So with this question about
female sexuality, I'm not sure if I have an answer for you
other than: I acknowledge that.

JAMIESON   Well, I think it's interesting to mark its absence.
And maybe there's something important about that, insofar
as the way in which female sexuality has been portrayed
is often a problem—it has to be immediately political.

And to make it the space around your work, because you cannot say that it's not there, to make it sort of within and between, I think, is maybe where I'll say "I can see it" without being directly addressed as such.

JULIA   Yes. And the moment you put bodies and tools together, you're immediately in the department of kink. There have been several opportunities to show my work in the context of BDSM and such, but I have resisted that. I acknowledge that there are aspects of the work that can take you there, and in fact I don't mind it. But I don't want to be formally placed in that context because so much of my work addresses involuntary power dynamics that have nothing to do with consent. And consent is one of the main aspects of kink, if I understand correctly; there's a whole product industry and insider vocabulary around it.

JAMIESON   Yes. And I think that your work is more on the side of ambiguity than what kink tries to do in terms of reducing that ambiguity.

JULIA   Exactly. And the ambiguity is the reason for all the absences in the work. Everything that is not shown is up to the viewer. I'm just hoping to give hints with what I am showing. And then, in that negative space, I'm hoping the viewer will complete the work for themselves and fit their realities.

1   Jamieson Webster, "A Dangerous Method," *Artforum*, July 28, 2021, https://www.artforum.com/slant/jamieson-webster-on-louise-bourgeois-and-psychoanalysis-86266, referring to Louise Bourgeois, Philip Larratt-Smith, and Elisabeth Bronfen, *The Return of the Repressed* (London: Violette Editions, 2012).
2   Dianne Elise, "Unlawful Entry: Male Fears of Psychic Penetration," *Psychoanalytic Dialogues* 11, no. 4 (August 15, 2001): 499–531.
3   Robert M. Friedman, "The Role of the Testicles in Male Psychological Development," *Journal of the American Psychoanalytic Association* 44, no. 1 (February 1996): 201–53.
4   Jamieson Webster, "A Child Is Being Aborted," *New York Review*, September 21, 2022, https://www.nybooks.com/online/2022/09/21/a-child-is-being-aborted.

JAMIESON WEBSTER   Ich möchte Dir erst einmal ein paar Zitate aus Sigmund Freuds „Ergebnisse, Ideen, Probleme" von 1938 vorlesen, das 1941 posthum veröffentlicht wurde. Sie gelten meist als das Letzte, was Freud geschrieben hat, und sind zwar nur Notizen, aber sehr interessante. Insgesamt möchte ich Dir drei davon vorlesen, aber zunächst die ersten beiden: „Schuldbewusstsein entsteht auch aus unbefriedigter Liebe. Wie Hass. Wirklich haben wir aus diesem Stoff alles mögliche herstellen müssen wie die autarken Staaten in ihren ‚Ersatzprodukten'". Und: „Räumlichkeit mag die Projektion der Ausdehnung des psychischen Apparats sein. Keine andere Ableitung wahrscheinlich. Anstatt Kants a priori Bedingungen unseres psychischen Apparats. Psyche ist ausgedehnt, weiss nichts davon."

JAMIESON   Die Skulpturen und die Tatsache, dass wir aus der materiellen Beziehung zwischen den Affekten, dem Körper und der Psyche Produkte entwickeln, die Ersatzbefriedigungen sind, und dass wir den Raum generell als Ausdehnung, als Erweiterung des Körpers begreifen, haben mich auf diese Zitate gebracht. Ich denke, ein Großteil Deiner Arbeit handelt davon und von der Bedeutung der Bildhauerei als Bearbeitung und Überarbeitung dieses Bereichs.

JULIA PHILLIPS   Sehr schön, sehr poetisch.

Als würde man die eigene Stimme verändern.

Julia Phillips im Gespräch mit Jamieson Webster

JULIA   Bei dem Zitat über unbefriedigte Liebe und Ersatzprodukte dachte ich an Beziehungen, die ohne Versöhnung enden und darin der Idee der unbefriedigten Liebe entsprechen. Meine Titel verweisen auf eine Rolle, eine Funktion oder mitunter auch auf eine bestimmte Person, die aber letztlich irgendwie austauschbar ist. Fast wie in einem Traum, in dem ich von einer Person träume, deren Rolle im Verlauf des Traums von einer anderen Person übernommen wird. Die Verständigungsmöglichkeiten zwischen Menschen können sehr beschränkt sein. Und Kunst zu machen ist ein Weg, mehr über eine Beziehung auszudrücken – indem man sie porträtiert. Daher würde ich sagen, dass meine Arbeit bis zu einem gewissen Grad auch ein Racheakt sein kann, eine Form der Vergeltung.

Ich erinnere mich, dass Du in Deinem Aufsatz über Louise Bourgeois[1] alles aufzählst, was Psychoanalyse für sie bedeutet.[2] Eines davon war Pflicht. Sie beschreibt ihre Beziehung zur Analyse ähnlich, wie ich die Kunstproduktion beschreiben würde: als Zugang zum Unbewussten, als eine Art Gesundheitsvorsorge.

Bourgeois spricht auch über die wichtigsten gestalterischen Gesten in der Bildhauerei, das Zusammenfügen und das Trennen, und über den Gemütszustand, in dem sie sich im Idealfall befindet, wenn sie im Atelier arbeitet – alles Dinge, die ich gut nachvollziehen kann. Ich habe meine Abformtechnik selbst entwickelt; ich fertige keine traditionellen Abgüsse mit einer Gipsform an, sondern arbeite mit Tonfladen. Die Fladen drücke ich so lange auf meinen Körper, bis der Ton genügend ausgehärtet ist, um einigermaßen seine Form zu halten. Nach dem Abnehmen muss ich die Form sofort unterstützen. Und schließlich arbeite ich noch einiges nach und bessere aus. Beim traditionellen Gießverfahren nimmt das Negativ (die Gussform) strukturelle Details von der Oberfläche des Positivs auf. Doch weil ich nicht mit einem Negativverfahren arbeite, befinden sich die detailliertesten Informationen bei meinen Abformungen tatsächlich auf der Innenseite der Skulpturen, im negativen Raum. Dadurch ist die Skulptur auf merkwürdige Art und Weise negativ und positiv zugleich.

JAMIESON Ich denke, das ist eine Möglichkeit, mit der Erweiterung der Psyche zu spielen. Freud schrieb: „Das Ich ist vor allem ein körperliches, es ist [...] die Projektion einer Oberfläche." Du projizierst jedoch nicht einfach die Oberfläche. Einerseits ist sie alles, was wir sehen, wenn wir an das visuelle Bild von uns denken. Andererseits gibt es so viele andere Erscheinungsformen des Körpers und seiner Ausdehnung. Freud sagt, die besten Organe sind stille Organe, denn wenn unsere Organe laut sind, richten wir plötzlich unsere Aufmerksamkeit auf sie. Für mich hat Deine Arbeit etwas, das über die Oberflächenprojektion des Raums hinausgeht. Ich kannte Deine Abformtechnik bisher nicht, aber sie erscheint mir für das, was Du meiner Meinung nach tust, sehr sinnvoll.

Ich wollte Dich nach der *Intruder*-Serie (2017) fragen, in der (p. 70) es um Ausbeutung und Fragen von Macht und Missbrauch geht. Du hast einmal Dianne Elises Aufsatz über männliche Fantasien des Eindringens erwähnt. Vielleicht kannst Du mir etwas dazu sagen. Da Du Dich als Frau verstehst: War es für Dich interessant, was eine Analytikerin über männliche Fantasien schreibt, oder hattest Du als Frau bereits diese Erfahrung mit Männern gemacht? Wie bist Du an das Thema herangegangen?

JULIA Ich bin bei der Suche nach Überschneidungen bestimmter Schlüsselbegriffe auf diesen Aufsatz gestoßen. Ich glaube, meine Suchbegriffe waren „Penetration", „Psychoanalyse" und „Postkolonialismus". Der Aufsatz war nur deshalb unter dem Schlagwort „Postkolonialismus" zu finden, weil Elise Robert M. Friedman[3] zitiert, der von der Psyche als dem dunklen Kontinent spricht.

JAMIESON Das ist lustig, weil Freud den Ausdruck „dunkler Kontinent" sowohl in Bezug auf die Psyche als auch auf Frauen verwendet hat. Dazu wurde angemerkt, es sei tendenziell frauenfeindlich, und es hat offensichtlich auch etwas Rassistisches.

JULIA Rassistisch und potenziell kolonialistisch und ausbeuterisch. Die versteckte Quelle und der Versuch, hineinzugehen und sie auszuschöpfen. Es gäbe viel dazu zu sagen, aber darum geht es in dem Aufsatz nicht. Sein Titel lautet „Unlawful Entry. Male Fears of Psychic Penetration" (Unerlaubtes Eindringen. Männliche Ängste vor psychischer Penetration)[4]. Mich interessierten die Äußerungen über das väterliche Gesetz und den verwehrten Zugang zur geistigen, seelischen und emotionalen Welt.

JAMIESON Ich denke, dass Deine Arbeit nicht einfach die männliche Perspektive einnimmt, sondern dass es um eine Penetration zwischen verschiedenen Beteiligten geht – was durchaus mehrdeutig sein kann. Das muss nicht unbedingt so geschlechtsspezifisch sein: der männliche Eindringling oder Täter. Auch wenn wir natürlich die historischen Erscheinungsformen von Gewalt beachten müssen. Aber letztlich kann jede_r diese Position einnehmen.

JULIA Der Aufsatz spricht auf sehr abstrakter Ebene von Penetration. Für einige Arbeiten war er zweifellos eine Inspirationsquelle. Zu der Zeit, als ich den Aufsatz las, entdeckte ich in einem Gebrauchtwarenladen einen Erdbohrer, im Prinzip ein überdimensionaler Korkenzieher in einer, wie ich fand, wirklich beunruhigenden Größe. Ich weiß noch, wie ich dachte: „Wozu ist das wohl gedacht?" Die Antwort ist Erde (Mutter Erde!) – Erdbohrer werden verwendet, um in den Erdboden einzudringen und Setzlinge zu pflanzen. Eine der Arbeiten, die sowohl von Elises Aufsatz als auch von dem Erdbohrer inspiriert (p. 64) wurden, ist *Extruder* (2017), eine Installation mit einem Erdbohrer, der einen phallischen Durchmesser hat und Teil eines größeren Ausbeutungsgeräts ist. Anders habe ich für die Serie (p. 71-73) *Intruder, Misused* (2019) Bohrer mit verbogenen Gewinden angefertigt. Der Titel deutet darauf hin, dass die Verbiegung der Gewinde Folge eines übermäßigen Kraftaufwands bei ihrer Benutzung ist – sie wurden überbeansprucht –, was impliziert, dass ein Eindringen auch auf angemessene Weise erfolgen kann: nicht missbräuchlich. Ich dachte dabei an den eindringlichen Aspekt der Psychoanalyse als Behandlungsform, die ein einvernehmliches Eindringen in die Psyche erfordert.

JAMIESON Für Patient_innen und Auszubildende ist es sehr schwer, sich vorzustellen, was an der Beziehung zwischen Analytiker_in und Patient_in eindringlich oder gewalttätig ist. In diesem Zusammenhang ist die Untersagung der körperlichen Berührung in der Psychoanalyse sehr wichtig; was stattfindet, ist ein jeglicher Austausch von Worten.

Das erinnert mich daran, dass ich Dich nach dem Umschwung Deiner bildhauerischen Praxis auf horizontale Machtdynamiken fragen wollte. Ich meine damit Deine Skulpturen *Mediator* (2020) und *Observer* (2016/20), in denen die Erscheinungen von Mikrofonen und Ferngläsern auftauchen. Ich gehe nicht davon aus, dass Du das weißt, aber Jacques Lacan hat die Objekte des Körpers genau beschrieben. Während die ganz klassischen Objekte bei Freud das orale Objekt, das anale Objekt und die Genitalien sind, fügt Lacan noch den Blick und die Stimme hinzu. Wir können uns selbst nicht hören, wenn wir sprechen, und wenn wir uns sprechen hören, ist es schockierend. Diese Verschiebung sehe ich auch in Deiner Arbeit. Ich weiß, dass Du sie als eine Verlagerung von vertikalen zu horizontalen Beziehungen verstehst, aber es ist auch eine Verschiebung von den materiellen Körperobjekten zu immateriellen Objekten. Wir nehmen nicht wahr, dass wir manche Dinge aufmerksam betrachten und andere nicht. Wir hören den Tonfall unserer Stimme nicht. Im Blick und in der Stimme kann gleichzeitig etwas Gewaltsames und etwas unglaublich Zärtliches liegen. Zwischen diesen verschiedenen Registern gibt es eine Schwankungsbreite, derer wir uns nicht bewusst sind, anders als etwa bei den oralen Gefühlen des Hungers und des Verschlingens, dem analen Ausscheiden oder Zurückhalten oder den Erfahrungsdimensionen des Durch- und Eindringens.

(p. 90-93)
(p. 141-143)

JAMIESON In dieser postfaktischen Welt ist alles Verbindliche und/oder Neutrale verschwunden. Angesichts des aggressiven Getöses, das die Diskurskultur dominiert, ist es interessant sich vorzustellen, dass Deine Skulpturen den Menschen die Erfahrung vermitteln möchten, sich selbst zu sehen oder zu hören, indem sie mit Deiner Arbeit interagieren.

(p. 87-89)

JULIA Die erste Arbeit, für die ich Mikrofone verwendet habe, ist *Fake Truth (Witness I–III)* (2019). Die Installation besteht aus drei von der Decke herabhängenden Skulpturen, die jeweils mit Mikrofonen und versteckten Lautsprechern ausgestattet sind, und einem den gesamten Ausstellungsraum einnehmenden Kiesboden. Die Richtmikrofone der drei Skulpturen filtern die Stimmen der Betrachtenden jeweils auf unterschiedliche Weise und geben sie mit verschiedenen Effekten wieder. Auf diese Weise antworten die Skulpturen dem Publikum sozusagen und spiegeln es auf unterschiedliche Weise wider.

Was Du darüber gesagt hast, dass man sich selbst beim Sprechen nicht hört, dass einen die eigene Stimme schockiert und man sie ablehnt, ist interessant. In dieser Installation geht es um Selbstwahrnehmung, aber auch um die Wahrnehmung und Zeugenschaft eines Geschehens, um die Frage nach Wahrheit. Die Arbeit entstand 2019, als Donald Trump im Amt war und ich über die Destabilisierung unseres Verhältnisses zu den Medien und zu Objektivität und Wahrheit nachdachte. Fake News kommen mir wie ein Missbrauch des Subjektivitätsbegriffs vor. Mit Missbrauch meine ich, dass der Anspruch auf Geltung der subjektiven Wahrnehmung so weit getrieben wird, dass man behaupten kann: „Nun, meiner Wahrnehmung nach ist das nicht passiert." Wenn man so mit Fakten umgeht, wird's wirklich gefährlich.

JULIA   Um noch einmal auf das Immaterielle zurückzukommen: Sowohl der Blick als auch die Stimme bieten so viele Interpretationsmöglichkeiten, die immer subjektiv sind – die in einen Blick oder einen Tonfall „etwas hineinlesen".

Bei der Skulptur *Observer*, die wie ein Fernglas geformt ist, sehen die beiden senkrechten Seiten (die Okularseite und die Objektivseite) wie ein Gesichtsabdruck aus, in den die Augen einer Person passen könnten. Damit wird suggeriert, dass der Blick in beide Richtungen geht – dass es auf der gegenüberliegenden Seite eine andere Person gibt, die zurückblickt. Eine_n Andere_n vor dem Objektiv, die/der nicht nur objektiviert, sondern „subjektiviert" ist. Ich habe *Observer* zu meiner ersten Skulptur im öffentlichen Raum, (p. 145) *Observer, Observed* (2022), für die New Yorker High Line weiterentwickelt. In dem Augenblick, in dem eine Person durch das Fernglas schaut und einen exklusiven Nahblick auf die Umgebung erhält, gibt sie einen Teil ihrer eigenen Identität preis, indem sie ihre Augen der Öffentlichkeit offenbart. Es ist mein erstes Werk, das sich explizit mit der Idee der Anonymität auseinandersetzt und die Augen als körperliches Identitätsmerkmal zeigt. Die Arbeit beschäftigt sich mit der Politik des öffentlichen Blicks, auch hinsichtlich der sozialen Medien, und mit der Idee des anonymen Onlinestalkings und der Überwachung. In Hitchcocks Film *Das Fenster zum Hof* gibt es gegen Ende eine sehr schöne Szene, in der sich der Protagonist fragt, welche Verantwortung er übernimmt, wenn er sich auf die Lauer legt und seine Nachbarn beobachtet. In dem Film wird er zufällig Zeuge eines Verbrechens in seinem Wohnblock und hadert mit seiner Position als stiller Beobachter. Am Ende des Films geht es um die Frage der Verantwortung und die – auch politische – Bedeutung der Beobachterposition.

JAMIESON   Das Aggressive am Blick ist, dass man sich selbst nicht in das einbezieht, was man sieht. Man bezieht sich selbst nicht als Betrachter_in ein. Lacan spricht von der „Bildebene", denn um zu verstehen, dass man eine bestimmte Perspektive einnimmt, muss man sich selbst als Betrachter_in und den Raum hinter dem eigenen Kopf mit einbeziehen.

JULIA   Ja, die Bildebene bestimmt die eigene Subjektposition, die Bildebene als buchstäblicher „Umkreis". Das bringt uns auf postkoloniale Theorien und die Idee des Blicks als dominierender, exotisierender und objektivierender Akt. Ich denke aber, dass Beobachtung auch „horizontal" stattfinden kann und Machtdynamiken sich verschieben können, zum Beispiel bei der Erfahrung der Mutterschaft. Wenn ich mir die Position der Eltern oder der Mutter vorstelle, die den Säugling beobachten, dann blickt der Säugling zurück.

JAMIESON   Ja, bei Säuglingen gibt es sehr viele Möglichkeiten, mit dem Blick zu spielen, sich gegenseitig anzuschauen, verschiedene Intonationen der Augen. Wir verlieren so vieles davon. Und durch Gewohnheiten kann etwas, das bei Kindern noch ganz offen ist, sich verfestigen.

JULIA   Von Kindern lässt sich eine Menge lernen, und sie sind so inspirierend. Dieses interessierte Anstarren, das gleichzeitig völlig unvoreingenommen ist.

JAMIESON   Ja, das hat nichts Obszönes, was sehr schön ist. Das bringt mich auf das Spirituelle in Deiner Arbeit. Sie hat etwas mit dem Blick nach innen im Gegensatz zum Blick nach außen zu tun, den Du erforschst. Dazu möchte ich noch einmal aus Freuds letzten Aufzeichnungen vorlesen. Dies ist seine allerletzte Notiz: „Mystik die dunkle Selbstwahrnehmung des Reiches ausserhalb des Ichs, des Es." Erstaunlich, dass es in Freuds letzter Notiz um Mystik geht. Sie ist ja ein wichtiger Wendepunkt in Deiner Arbeit, wie ich weiß.

JULIA   Ja, mein Interesse an spirituellen Praktiken hat in letzter Zeit meine Arbeit beeinflusst. Ich habe meinen Fokus von den

JAMIESON   Das erinnert mich an das, was Du über Louise Bourgeois gesagt hast. Ich sehe spirituelle Praktiken ganz ähnlich wie Bourgeois die Bildhauerei: als eine Möglichkeit, in sich selbst Brüche und Verbindungen zuzulassen, die anders sind, als es uns die Welt vielleicht zugesteht.

JAMIESON   Das ist eines der Dinge, die sich verändern – wir haben dafür die elegante Bezeichnung „Analyse der Spätphase" oder „Analyse der Endphase" – es ist der Augenblick, in dem sich der Tonfall der Patientin oder des Patienten verändert. Wir denken dabei wortwörtlich an die Sprechstimme, aber es geht auch um die Veränderung der inneren Stimmen, das Zulassen von mehr Emotionen in der Stimme, mehr Singsang, weniger Beengtheit. Dinge lösen sich, die sich in der Psyche abgelagert haben und erst ganz am Ende der Analyse zum Vorschein kommen. Es hat auch damit zu tun, dass man die Stimme der Analytikerin oder des Analytikers so verinnerlicht hat, dass man sich von ihr oder ihm trennen kann. Man trägt etwas von der Stimme oder der Art, wie sie oder er zu einem spricht, in sich.

Das bringt mich möglicherweise zu dem letzten Thema, zu dem ich Dich befragen wollte: Deine letzte Ausstellung *Me, Ourself & You* (2022) über Mutterschaft und Empfängnis. Ich liebe Deine *Conception Drawings*. Und ich freue mich sehr, dass wir anlässlich meines Aufsatzes „A Child Is Being Aborted" (Ein Kind wird abgetrieben) gemeinsam in der New York Review vertreten waren.[5] Was mir plötzlich einleuchtete, ist die Tatsache, dass die Empfängnis, die Entwicklung des Fötus, skulptural ist. Lacan war Arzt und von der Embryologie fasziniert, was ihn zu seiner Untersuchung topologischer Formen brachte, der Art und Weise, wie etwas zusammenhält, das keine geschlossene Oberfläche ist, denn ein Körper ist keine geschlossene Oberfläche. Und er spürte, dass Analytiker_innen mit diesen Dingen spielen müssen, wenn sie auf einer tieferen Ebene arbeiten wollen. Psychoanalytiker_innen müssen Bildhauer_innen sein!

JAMIESON   Das ist eine gute Überleitung zu meiner letzten Frage, bei der es um die weibliche Sexualität geht. Mir ist aufgefallen, dass Du Dich einerseits mit dem Thema Macht und ihrer Rolle in Beziehungen befasst. Sie könnte sich zum Teil aus der Überschneidung von Männlichem und Weiblichem ergeben oder aus

äußeren Beziehungen auf die inneren Beziehungen, die Beziehungen zum Selbst, verlagert.

JULIA   Genau, Brüche zulassen. Eine Weile lang wollte ich den Tonfall meiner Arbeit ändern und fand es sehr schwierig, es tatsächlich zu tun. Ich wollte einen gewaltsamen, ausbeuterischen, missbräuchlichen und energischen Tonfall durch etwas Versöhnlicheres ersetzen. Und ich stellte fest, dass es dazu einer inneren Veränderung bedurfte. Ich konnte mir nicht einfach eine friedfertige Skulptur ausdenken. Um diesen Tonfall zu ändern, musste ich die Werte, die meinen Entscheidungen zugrunde lagen, und meine Art und Weise, mit Beziehungen und Lebensumständen umzugehen, überdenken. Fast so, als würde man die eigene Stimme verändern.

JULIA   Als Künstlerin, die sich mit Schwangerschaft befassen wollte, war es für mich naheliegend zu versuchen genau dem, was ich nicht weiß, Form zu verleihen. Die Empfängnis bleibt trotz aller Forschung darüber immer noch ziemlich geheimnisvoll. Ich habe noch nie ein Foto von einer realen Gebärmutter gesehen. Nur als Illustration auf einer Tamponverpackung oder Ähnlichem. Sie wird viel zu selten abgebildet. Bei diesen *Conception Drawings* versuchte ich etwas darzustellen, das ich mir nur vorstellen konnte. Ich musste es mir regelrecht zusammenfantasieren, während ich unter Anspannung Empfängnis gegenübertrat. Es war unmöglich, die Darstellung physisch zu greifen und „richtig" abzubilden, denn es ging ja nicht nur um die Organe, sondern auch um den entscheidenden Augenblick und das Biomaterial des Inseminators.

(p. 124-133)

der Beziehung zwischen dem dominanten Teil und dessen Objekt. Und dann bewegt sich Deine Arbeit andererseits zunehmend in Richtung Spiritualität, Mystik und Mutterschaft. Eine Frau wird oft einer von zwei Kategorien zugeordnet, entweder der des Objekts oder der der Mutter, der Mystikerin – und ihre Sexualität, ihr spezielles subjektives Gefühl für ihre Sexualität, geht dabei oft verloren. Wolltest Du diese Dualität evozieren? Wo schaffst Du Raum für die weibliche Sexualität? Ich habe ja zu verschiedenen Künstler_innen gearbeitet. Louise Bourgeois macht, denke ich, inspiriert von ebendieser Zweiteilung erstaunliche Arbeiten. Und dann gibt es Bildhauerinnen wie Tracey Emin oder Sarah Lucas, die in Sachen Sexualität wirklich Hardcore sind. Vielleicht möchtest Du Dich in diese Reihe von Bildhauerinnen stellen?

JULIA　Das würde ich gerne tun, und ich schätze auch die Arbeit dieser Künstlerinnen. Wo schaffe ich Raum für Sexualität ...? 2013 habe ich nach dem Abschluss von zwei verschiedenen feministischen Kollaborativen ein Briefprojekt gestartet, bei dem ich Frauen gebeten habe, mir anonym Briefe über ihre sexuellen Fantasien, Vorstellungen, Frustrationen und so weiter zu schicken. Und ich habe darauf einige Beiträge erhalten. Eine Zeit lang habe ich mich also mit diesem Thema auseinandergesetzt. Meine Abschlussarbeit, mit der ich 2015 das Studium beendete, beschäftigte sich ebenfalls mit weiblichem Begehren und Sexualität. Diese Installation besteht aus (p. 19) einem Video und einer Skulptur. Das Video heißt *Becoming (the Hunter, the Twerker, the Submitter)* und die Skulptur *Connecter*. In dem Video stelle ich drei Charaktere mit jeweils unterschiedlichen Eigenschaften dar, die verschiedene Arten von Begehren repräsentieren. In der Ausstellung *Me, Ourself & You*, die Du gesehen hast, habe ich sehr bewusst zwei naheliegende Aspekte ausgelassen: Geburt (weil ich das Spektakel darum meiden möchte) und Sex. Es gab zwar die beiden Werke (p. 118-123) *Impregnator* und *Aborter* (2022), aber sie stehen nicht für den sexuellen Akt und das Verlangen. Vielmehr lassen sie sich als medizinische Geräte lesen und thematisieren Mechanismen der Befruchtung und der Abtreibung. Ich fürchte, auf die Frage nach der weiblichen Sexualität habe ich keine andere Antwort für Dich, als dass ich die Frage als berechtigt ansehe.

JAMIESON　Ich glaube, ihre Abwesenheit ist interessant. Und möglicherweise ist das insofern wichtig, als die Art und Weise, wie weibliche Sexualität dargestellt wird, häufig ein Problem ist – sie wird sofort politisch. Und wenn Du sie als Raum um Deine Arbeit herum betrachtest, weil Du nicht sagen kannst, sie sei nicht da, dann ist das vielleicht der Punkt, an dem ich sagen würde: „Ich kann sie sehen", ohne dass sie direkt als solche angesprochen wird.

JULIA　Ja. Und in dem Moment, in dem Körper und Werkzeuge kombiniert werden, ist man sofort in der Kink-Abteilung. Ich hätte schon mehrfach die Gelegenheit gehabt, meine Arbeit im Kontext von BDSM und Ähnlichem zu zeigen, habe das aber immer abgelehnt. Ich erkenne an, dass es in meiner Arbeit einige Aspekte gibt, die vielleicht Anlass zu dieser Assoziation geben, und das macht mir auch nichts aus. Aber ich möchte nicht explizit in diesen Zusammenhang gestellt werden, denn ein Großteil meiner Arbeit befasst sich mit unfreiwilligen Machtdynamiken, die nichts mit Zustimmung zu tun haben. Und Zustimmung ist einer der Hauptaspekte von Kink, wenn ich es richtig verstehe, und es gibt ja eine ganze Produktindustrie drum herum und ein Insider-Vokabular.

JAMIESON　Ja. Und ich denke, dass Du mit Deiner Arbeit auch eher auf Seiten der Ambivalenz stehst, anders als Kink, der versucht, diese Mehrdeutigkeit zu reduzieren.

JULIA　Ganz genau. Und die Ambivalenz ist der Grund für all die Aussparungen und Auslassungen in meiner Arbeit. Alles, was nicht gezeigt wird, bleibt den Betrachtenden überlassen.

Ich hoffe nur, dass ich mit dem, was ich zeige, Andeutungen machen kann. Und dann hoffe ich, dass die Betrachter_innen diesen negativen Raum nutzen, um das Werk für sich selbst zu vervollständigen und an ihre eigene Wirklichkeit anzupassen.

Übersetzt von Sylvia Zirden

1   Jamieson Webster, „A Dangerous Method", in: *Artforum*, 28. Juli 2021, https://www.artforum.com/slant/jamieson-webster-on-louise-bourgeois-and-psychoanalysis-86266.

2   Louise Bourgeois, Philip Larratt-Smith und Elisabeth Bronfen, *The Return of the Repressed*, London: Violette Editions, 2012.

3   Robert M. Friedman, „The Role of the Testicles in Male Psychological Development", in: *Journal of the American Psychoanalytic Association* 44, Nr. 1 (Februar 1996), S. 201–253.

4   Dianne Elise, „Unlawful Entry. Male Fears of Psychic Penetration", in: *Psychoanalytic Dialogues* 11, Nr. 4 (15. August 2001), S. 499–531.

5   Jamieson Webster, „A Child Is Being Aborted", in: *The New York Review*, 21. September 2022, https://www.nybooks.com/online/2022/09/21/a-child-is-being-aborted.

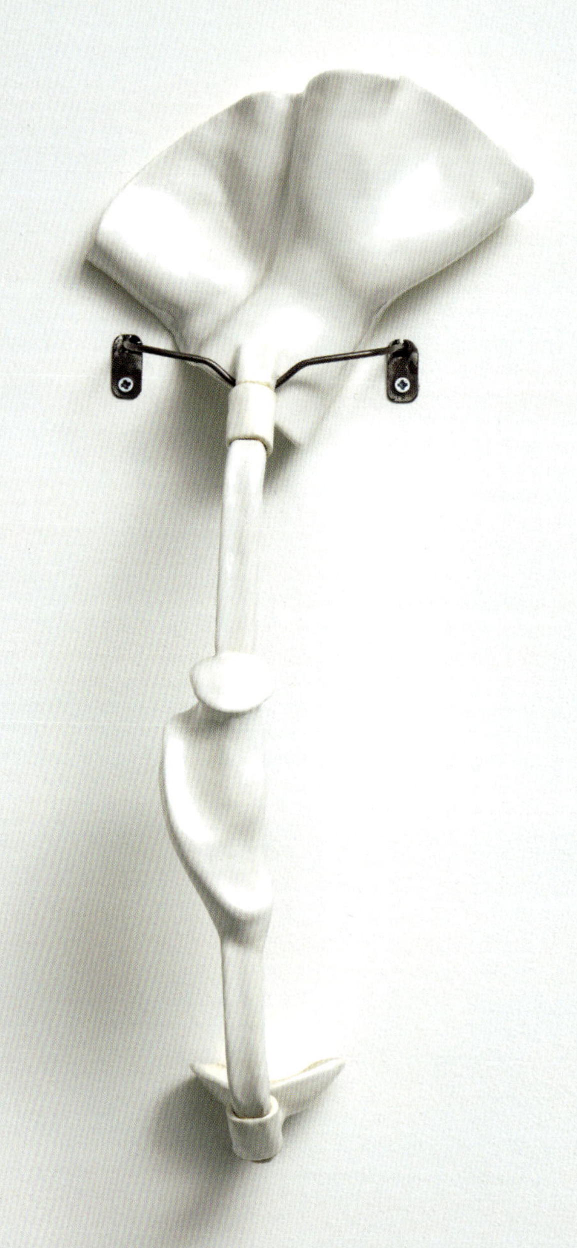

Objectifier II, 2014. Ceramic, steel, 46 × 22 × 18 cm; 18¼ × 8¾ × 7¼ inches

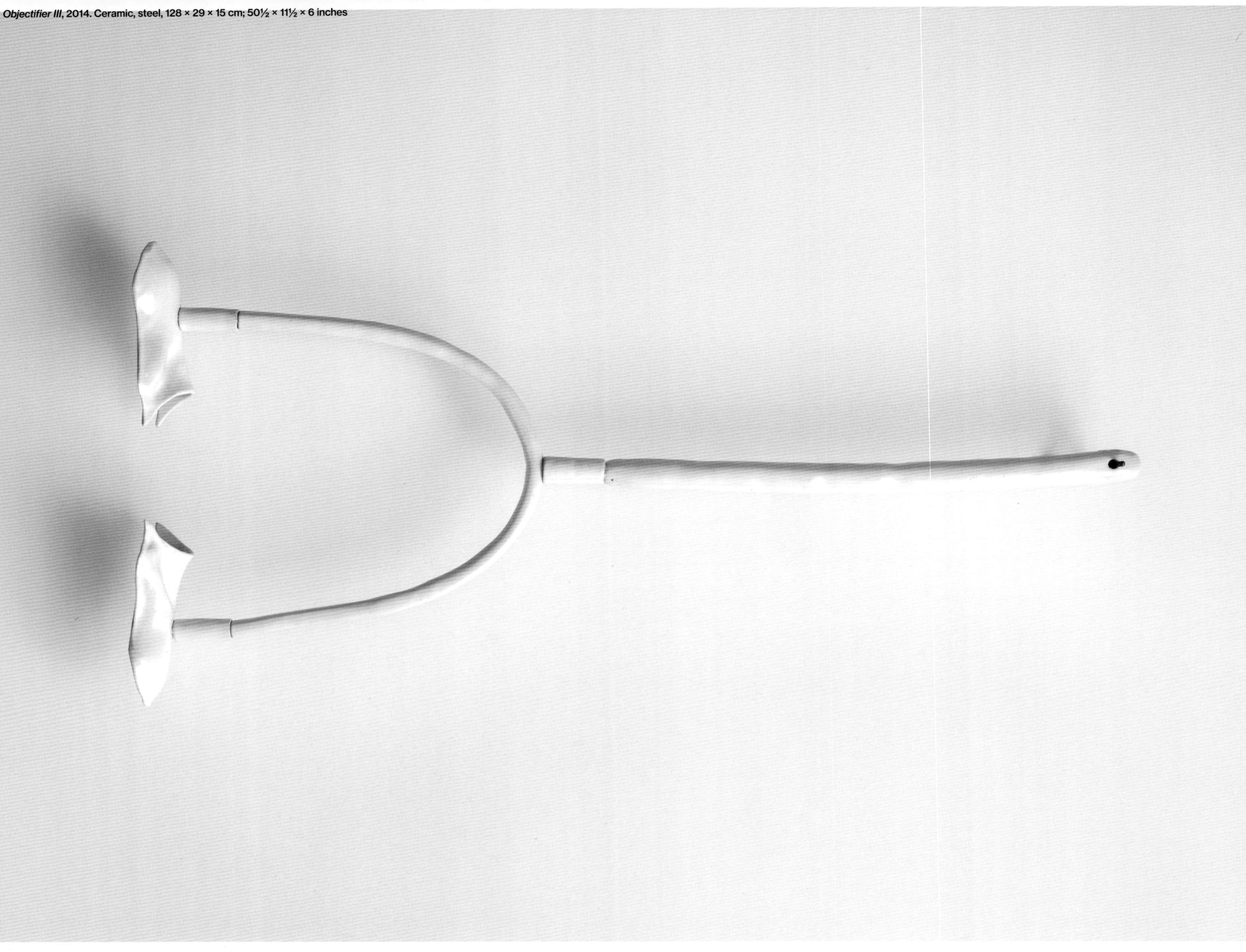

Objectifier III, 2014. Ceramic, steel, 128 × 29 × 15 cm; 50½ × 11½ × 6 inches

Impenetrable Entry, installation view, Campoli Presti, London, 2016

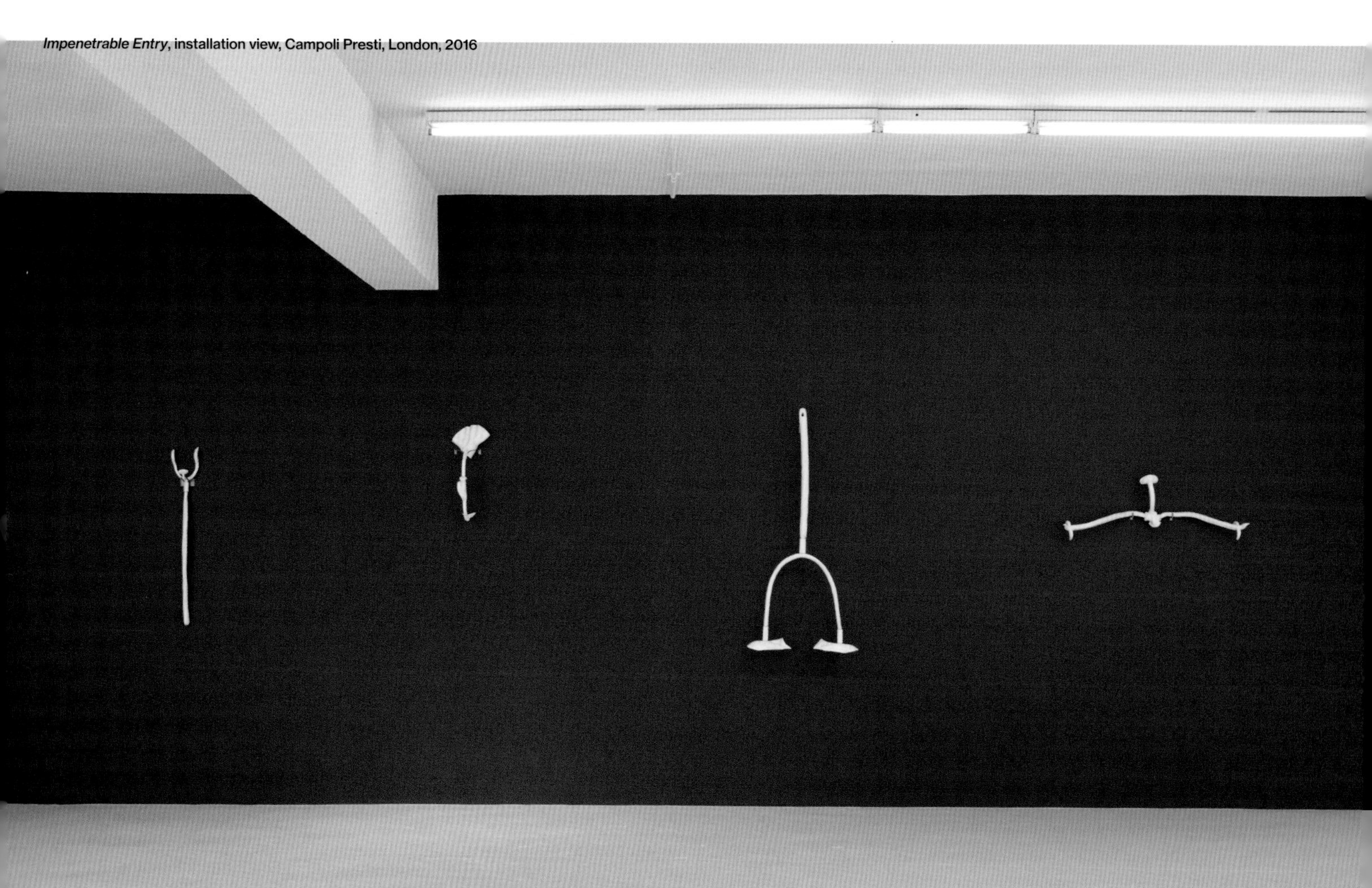

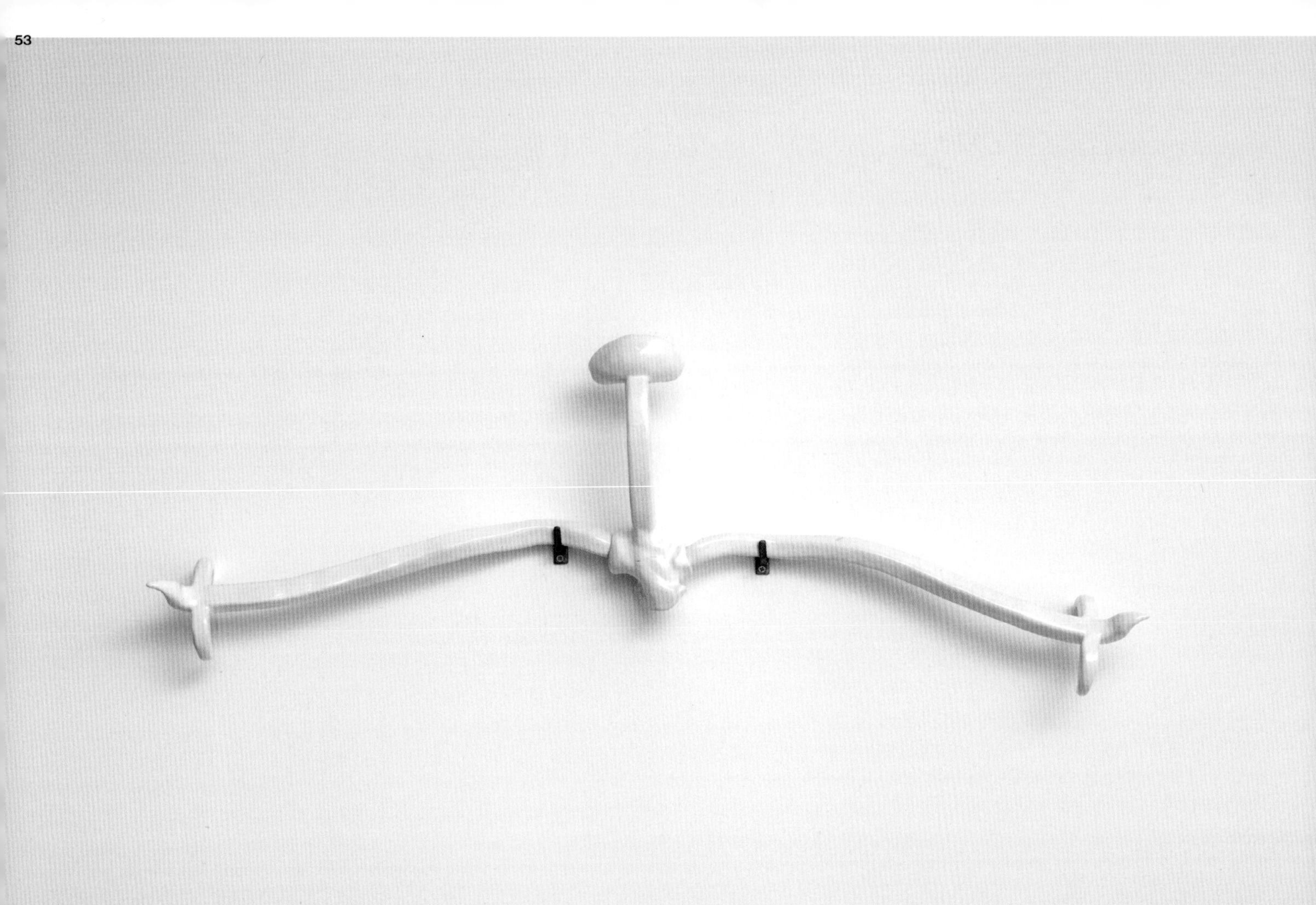

Objectifier IV, 2014. Ceramic, steel, 22 × 103 × 17 cm; 8¾ × 40¾ × 6¾ inches

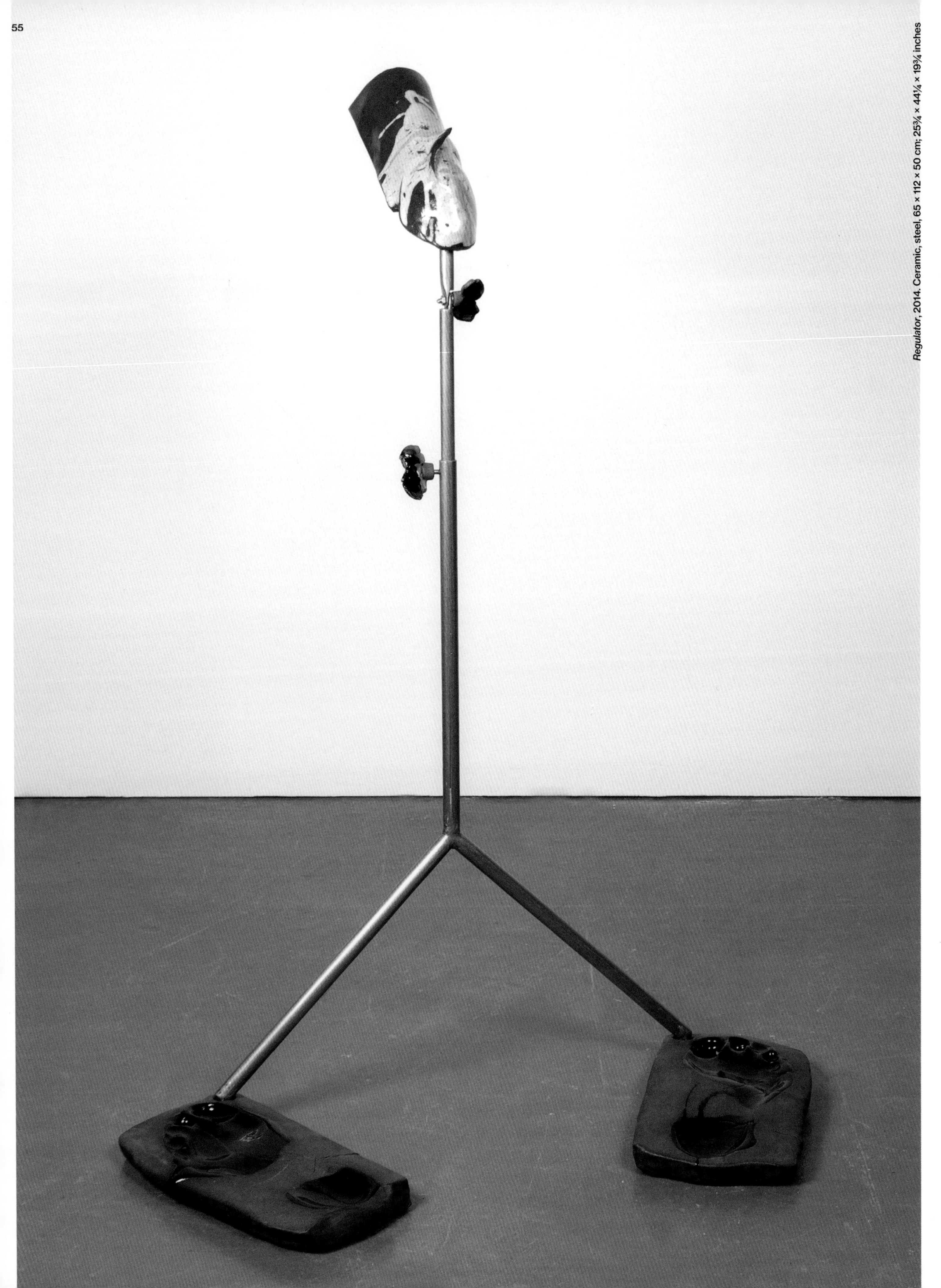

Regulator, 2014. Ceramic, steel, 65 × 112 × 50 cm; 25¾ × 44¼ × 19¾ inches

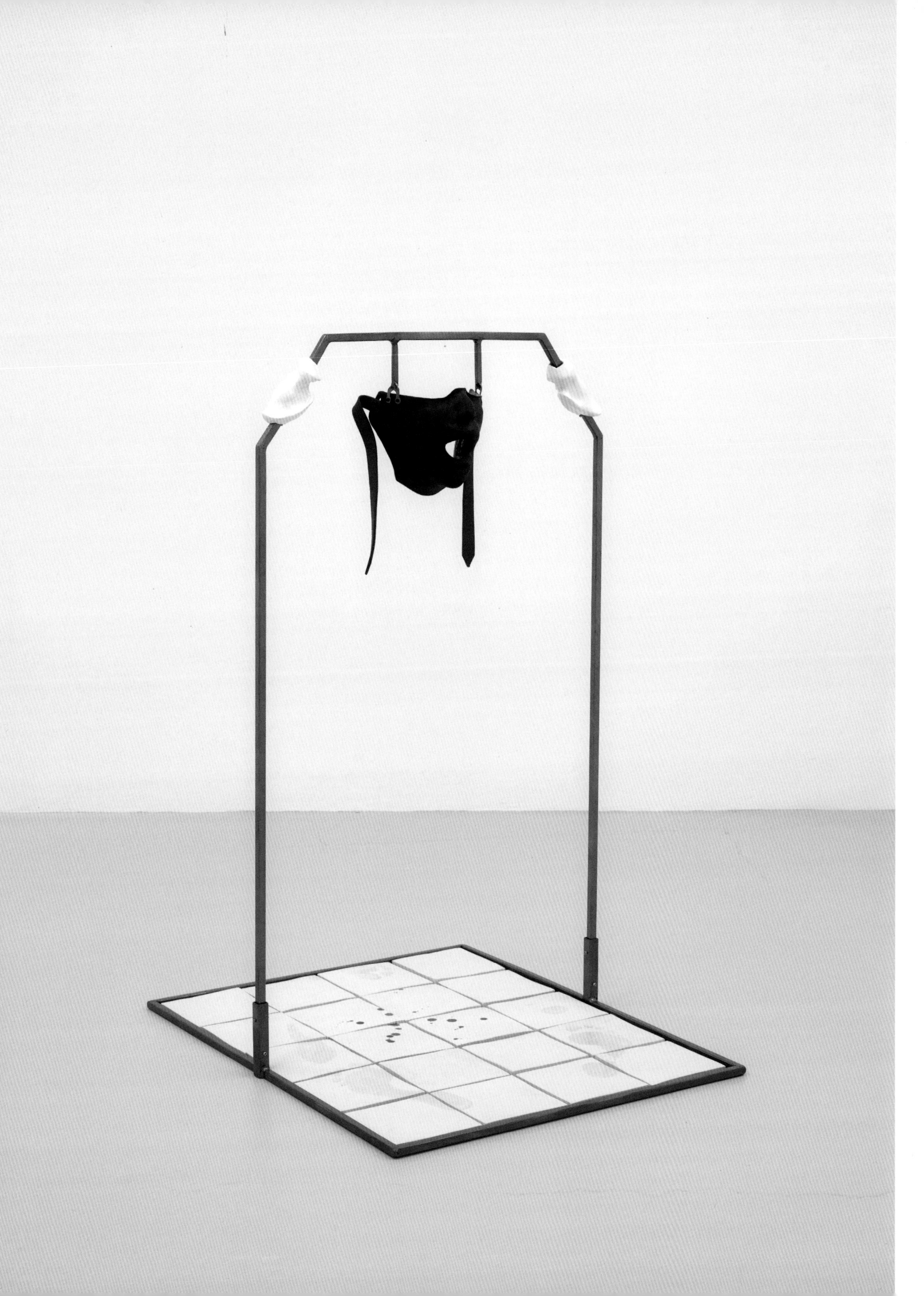

Positioner, 2016. Ceramic, steel, 112 × 62 × 78 cm; 44¼ × 24½ × 30¾ inches

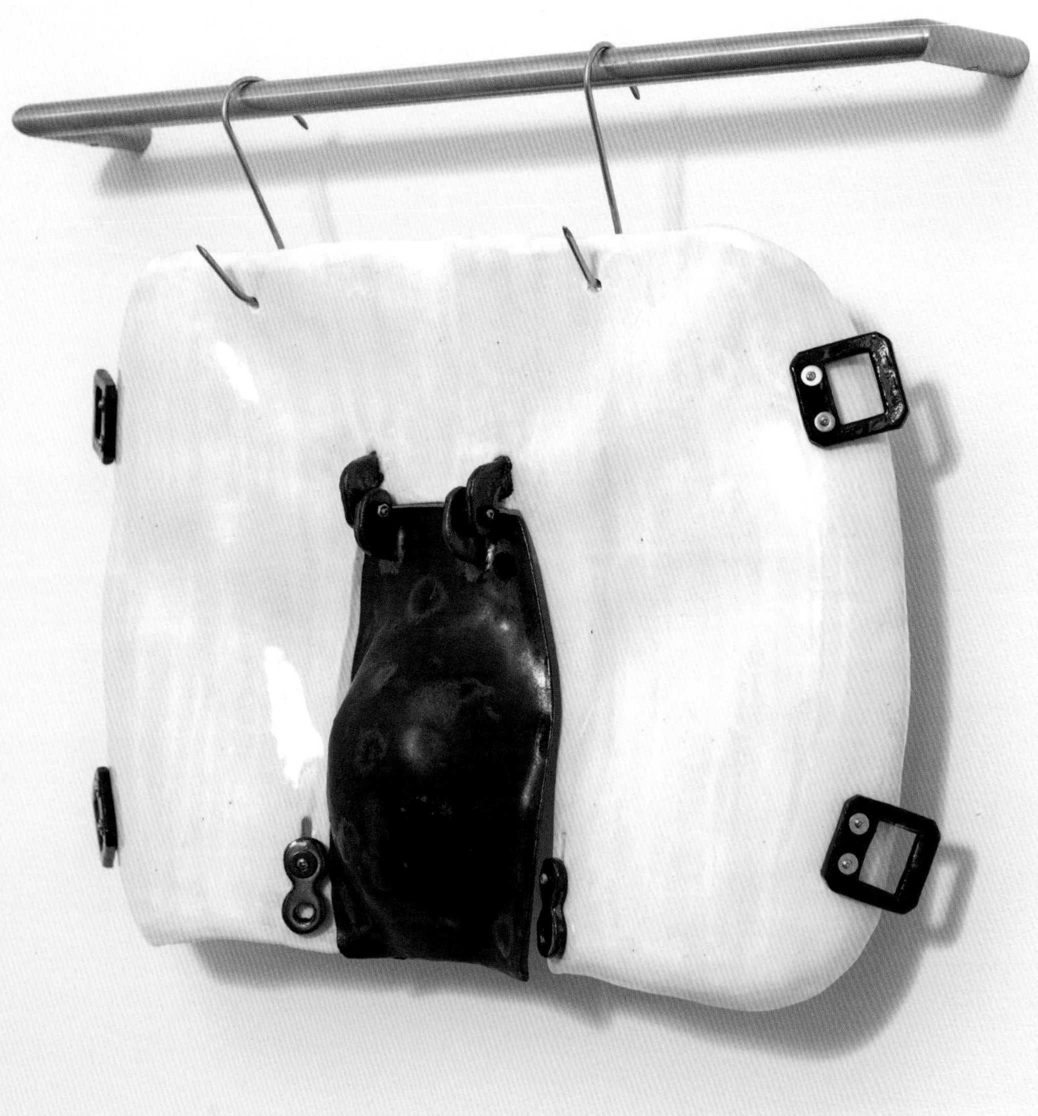

Protector I, 2016/18. Ceramic, metal hardware, stainless steel, 30 × 38 × 6 cm; 12 × 15 × 2½ inches

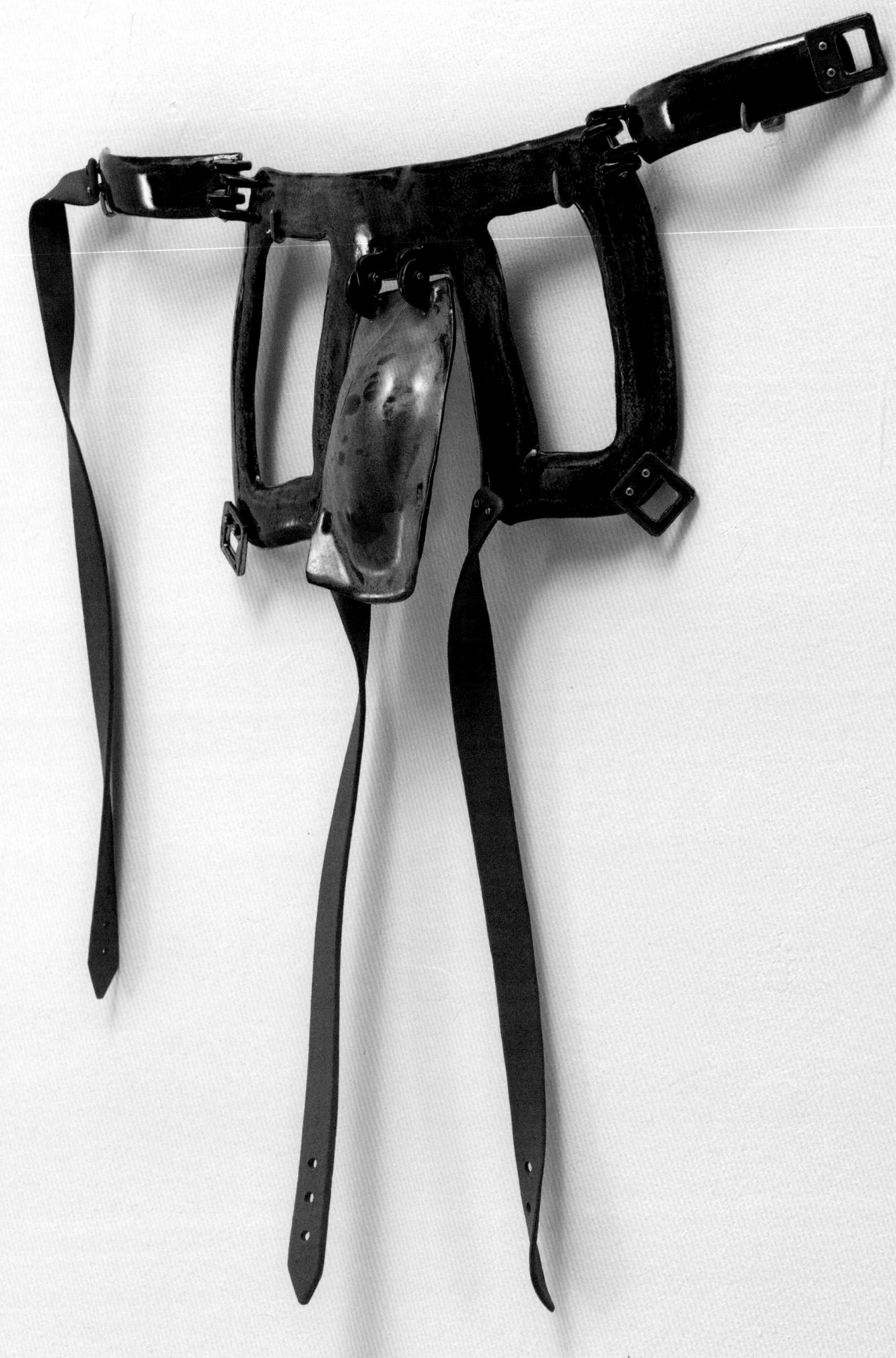

Protector II, 2016. Ceramic, metal hardware, steel, 63 × 57 × 10 cm; 25 × 22½ × 4 inches

Exoticizer, Worn Out (Josephine Baker's Belt), 2017. Ceramic, brass hardware, steel, Sculpture 7 × 33 × 38 cm; 2⅝ × 13 × 15 inches; Pedestal 94 × 41 × 41 cm; 37 × 16 × 16 inches

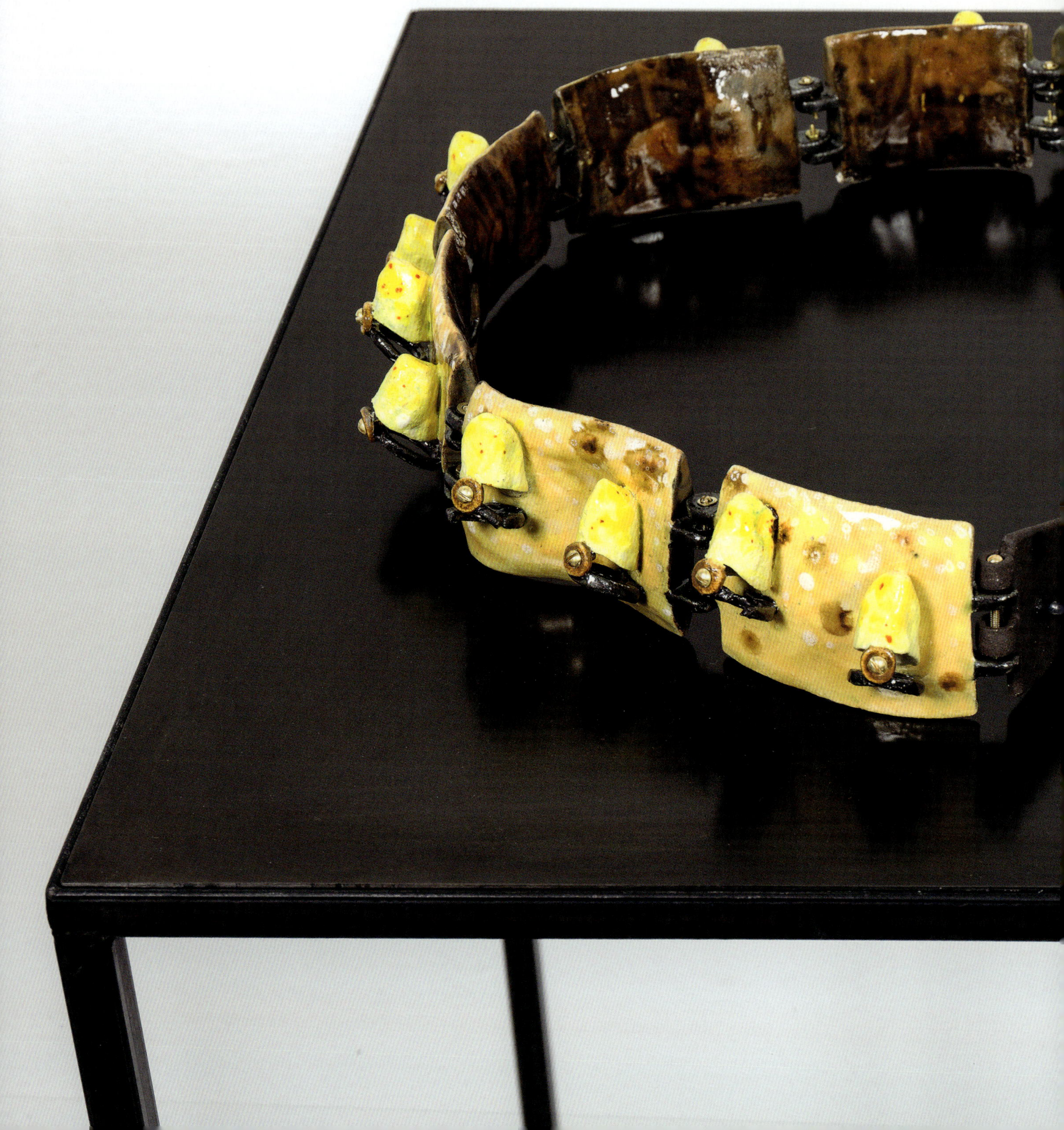

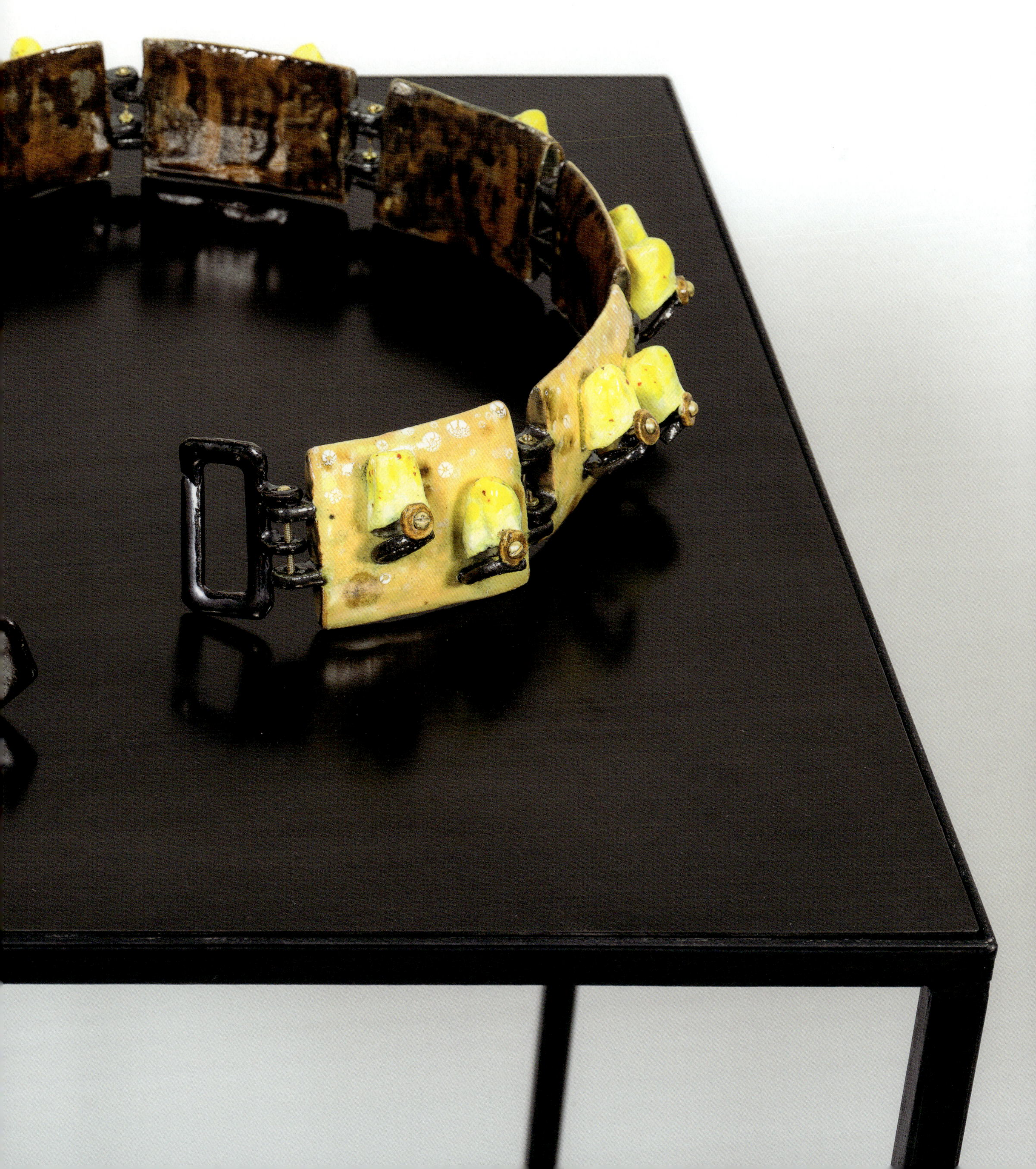

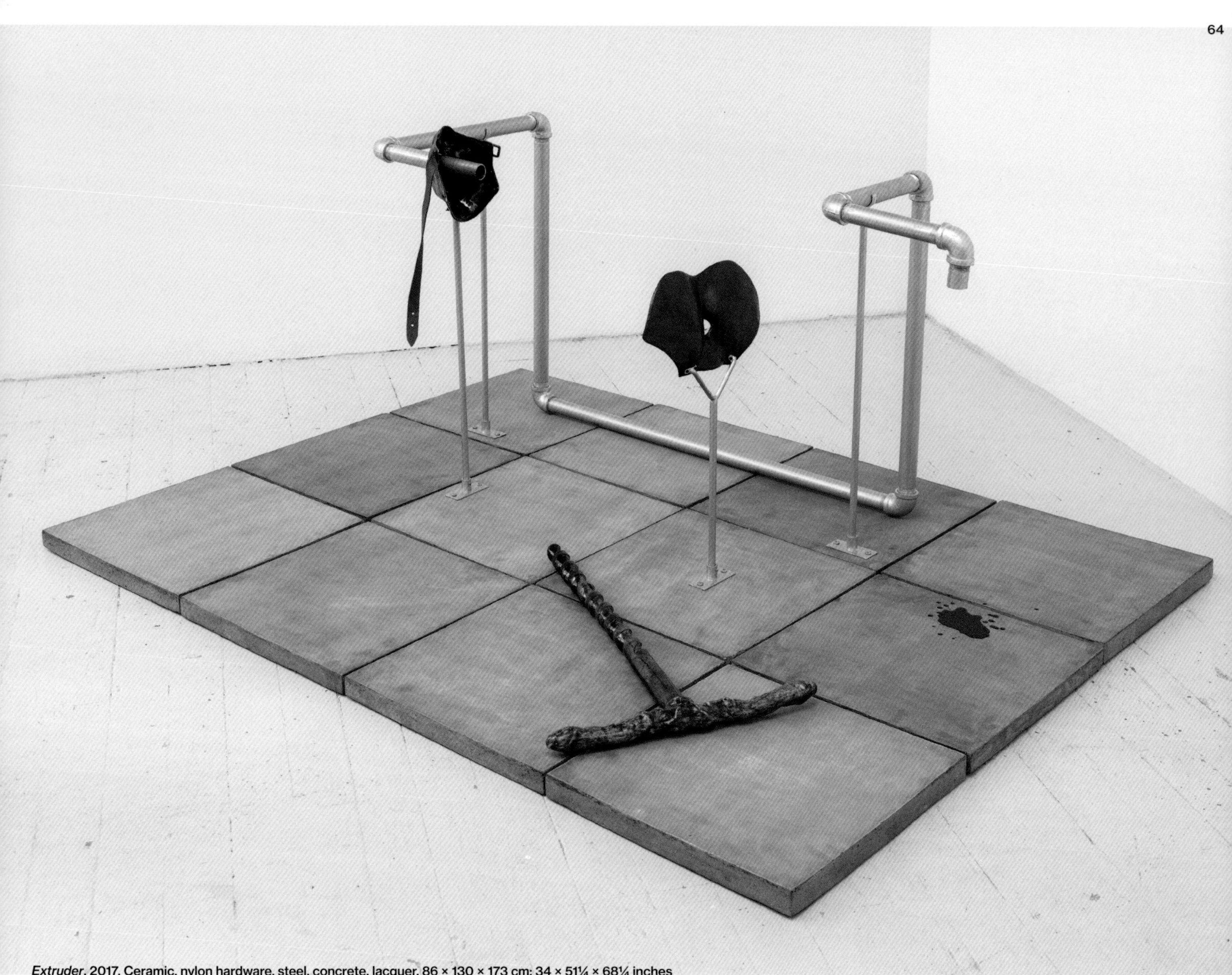

Extruder, 2017. Ceramic, nylon hardware, steel, concrete, lacquer, 86 × 130 × 173 cm; 34 × 51¼ × 68¼ inches

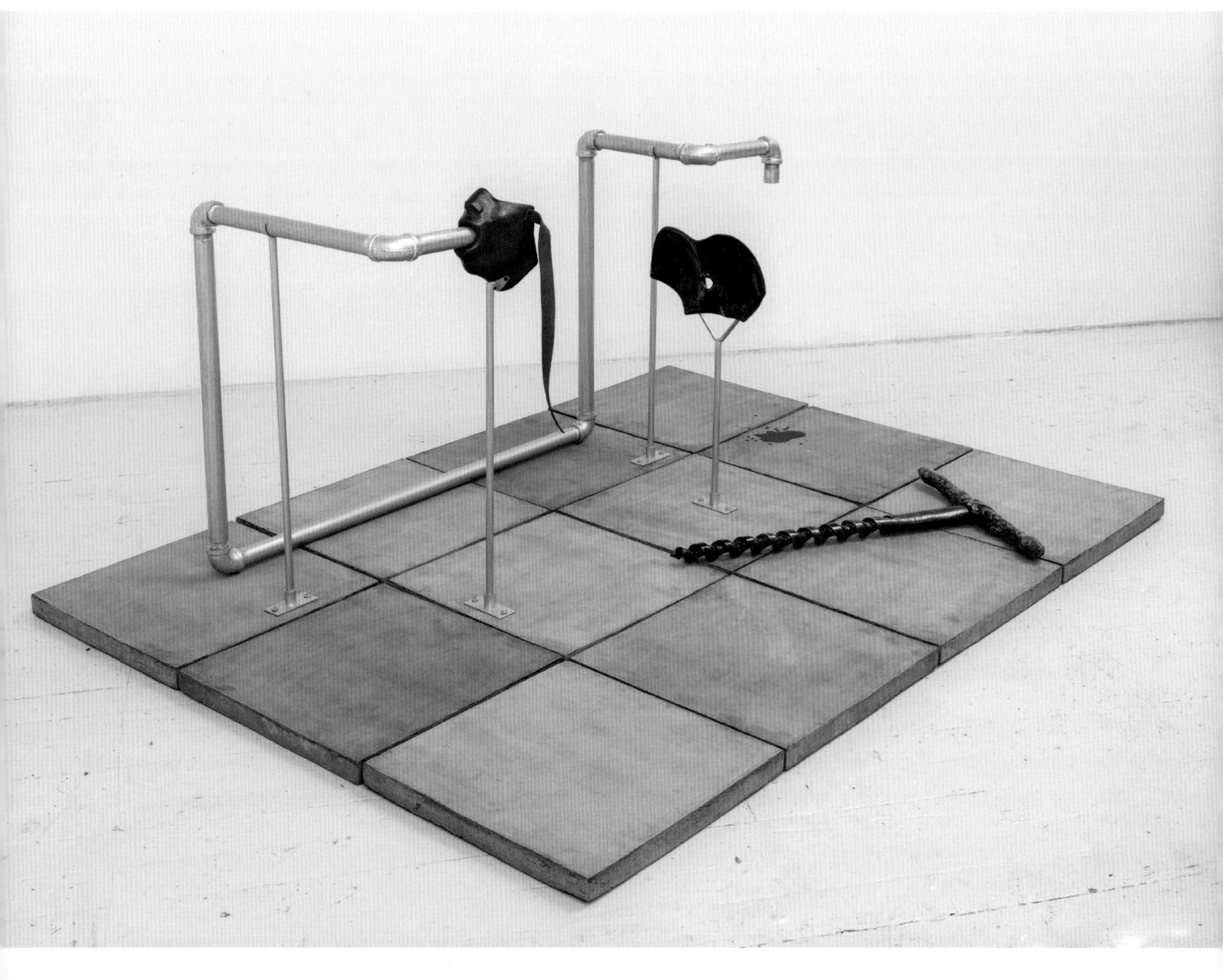

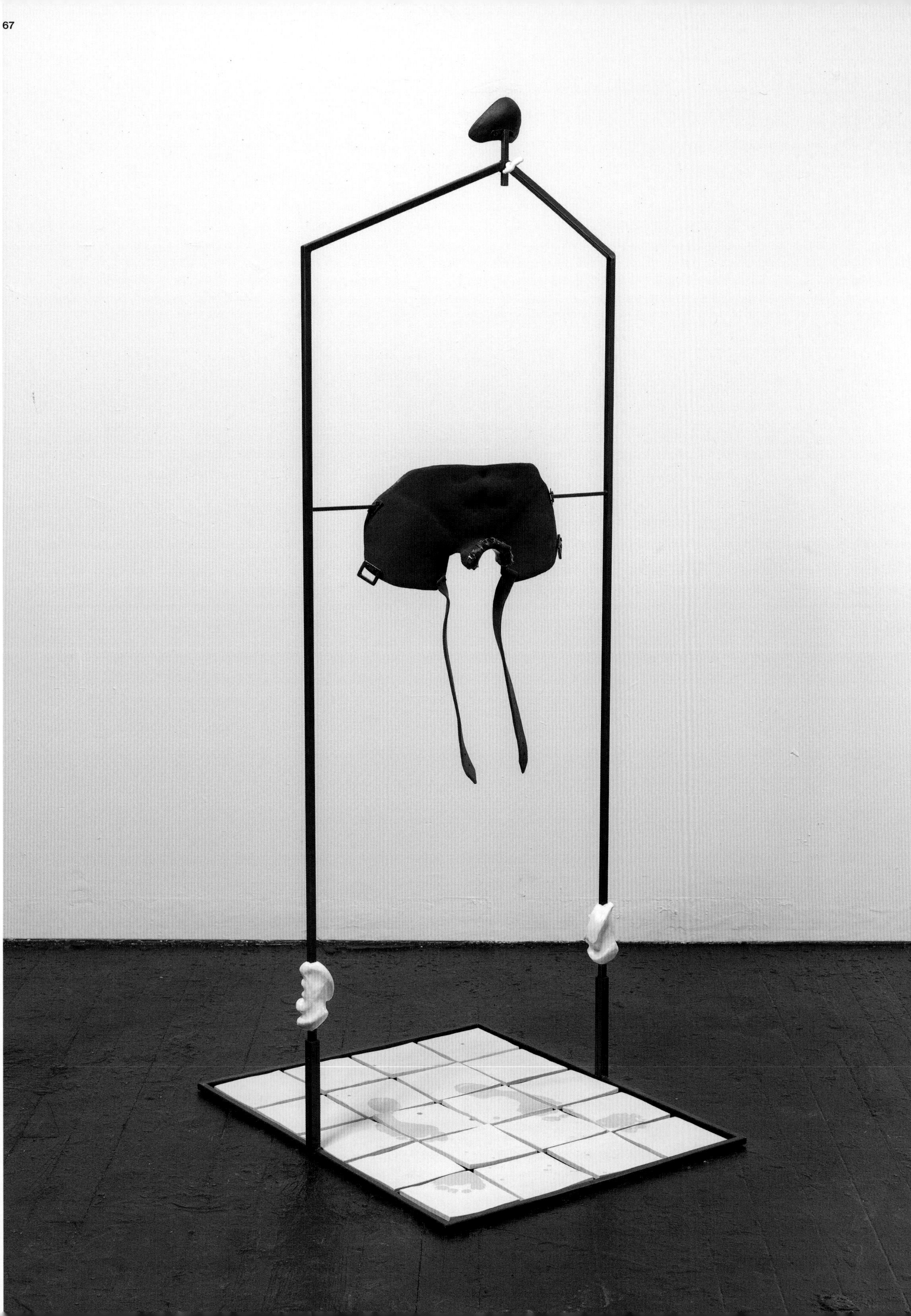

Fixator (#1), 2017. Ceramic, nylon hardware, steel, 177 × 64 × 79 cm; 69¾ × 25¼ × 31¼ inches

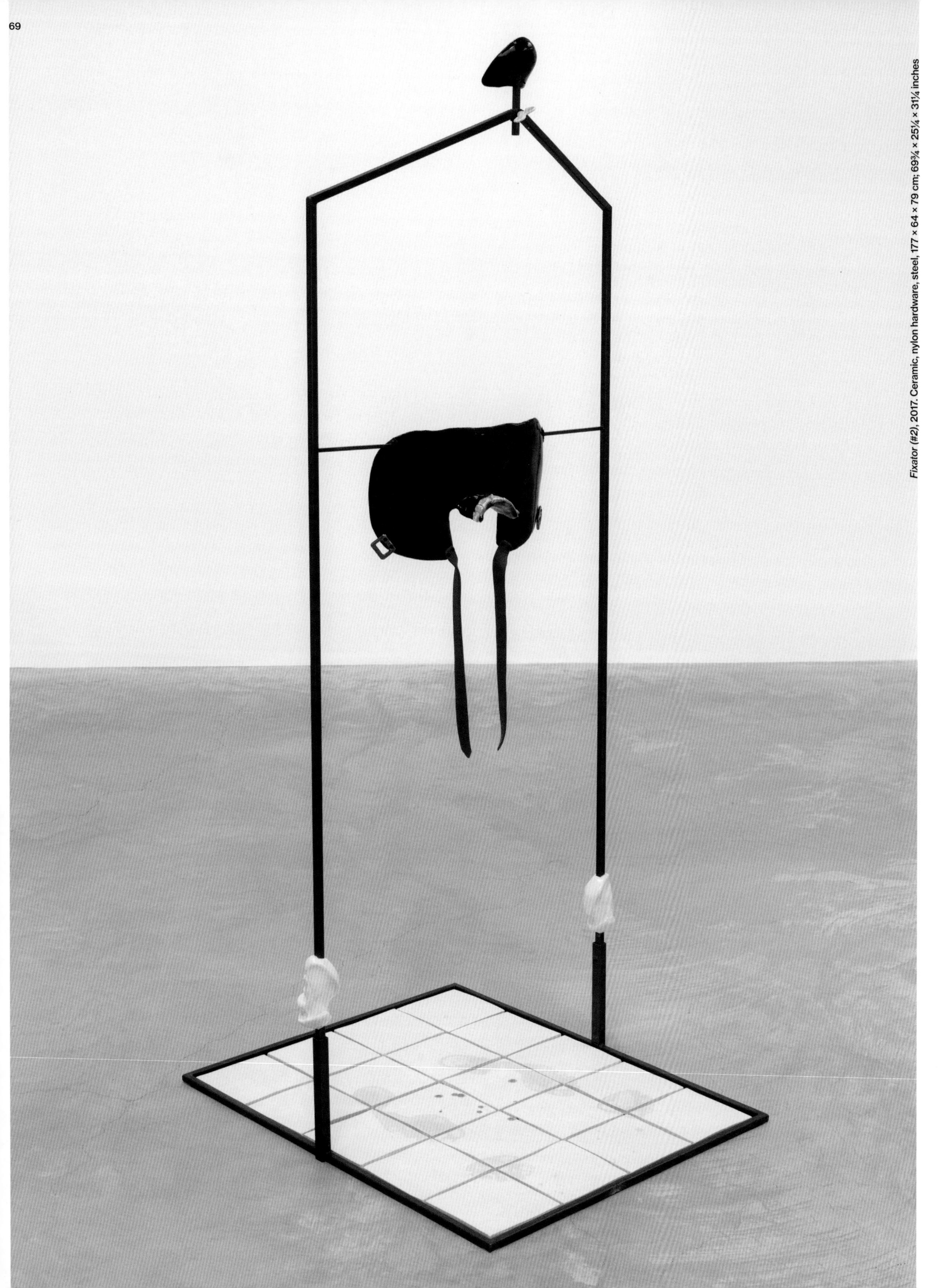

Fixator (#2), 2017. Ceramic, nylon hardware, steel, 177 × 64 × 79 cm; 69¾ × 25¼ × 31¼ inches

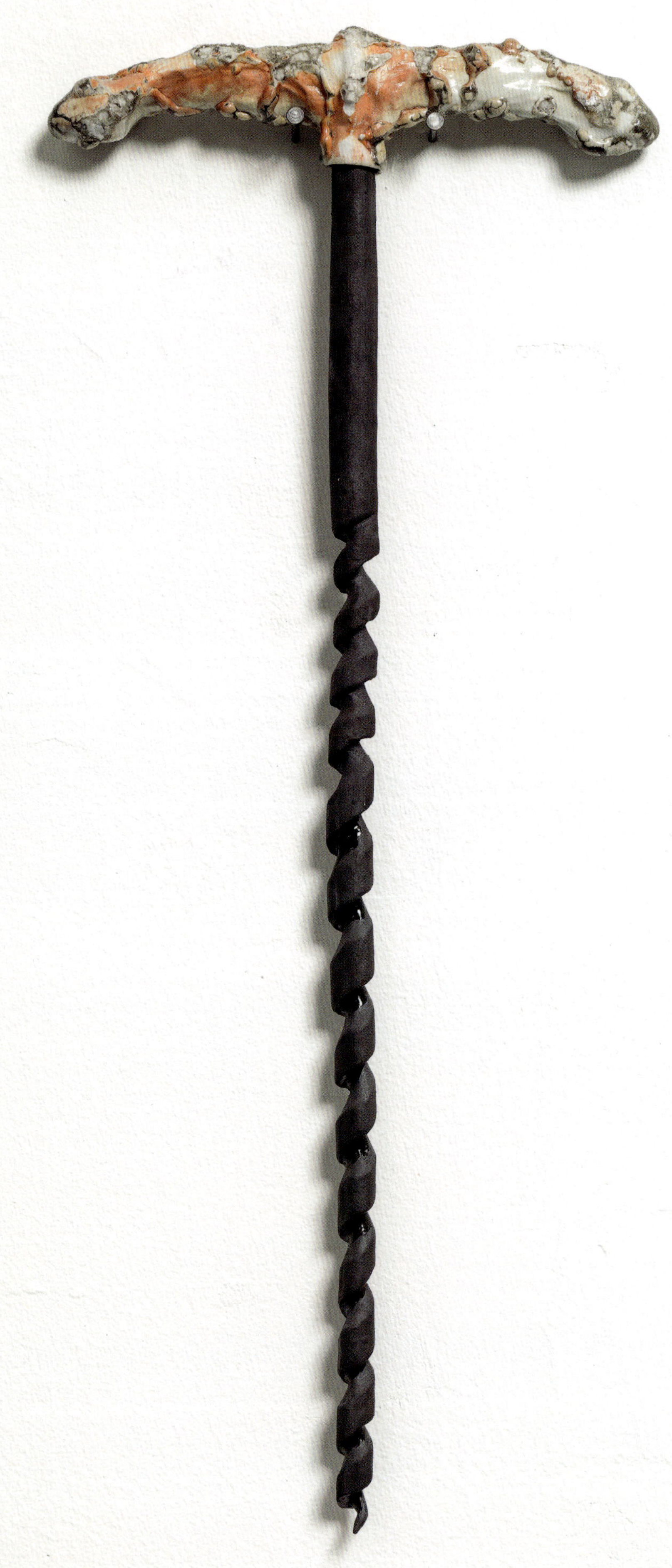

Intruder Study VII, 2017. Ceramic, 62 × 24 × 4 cm; 24½ × 9½ × 1¾ inches

  Intruder, Misused I, 2019. Ceramic, 64 × 36 × 3.5 cm; 25¼ × 14¼ × 1½ inches

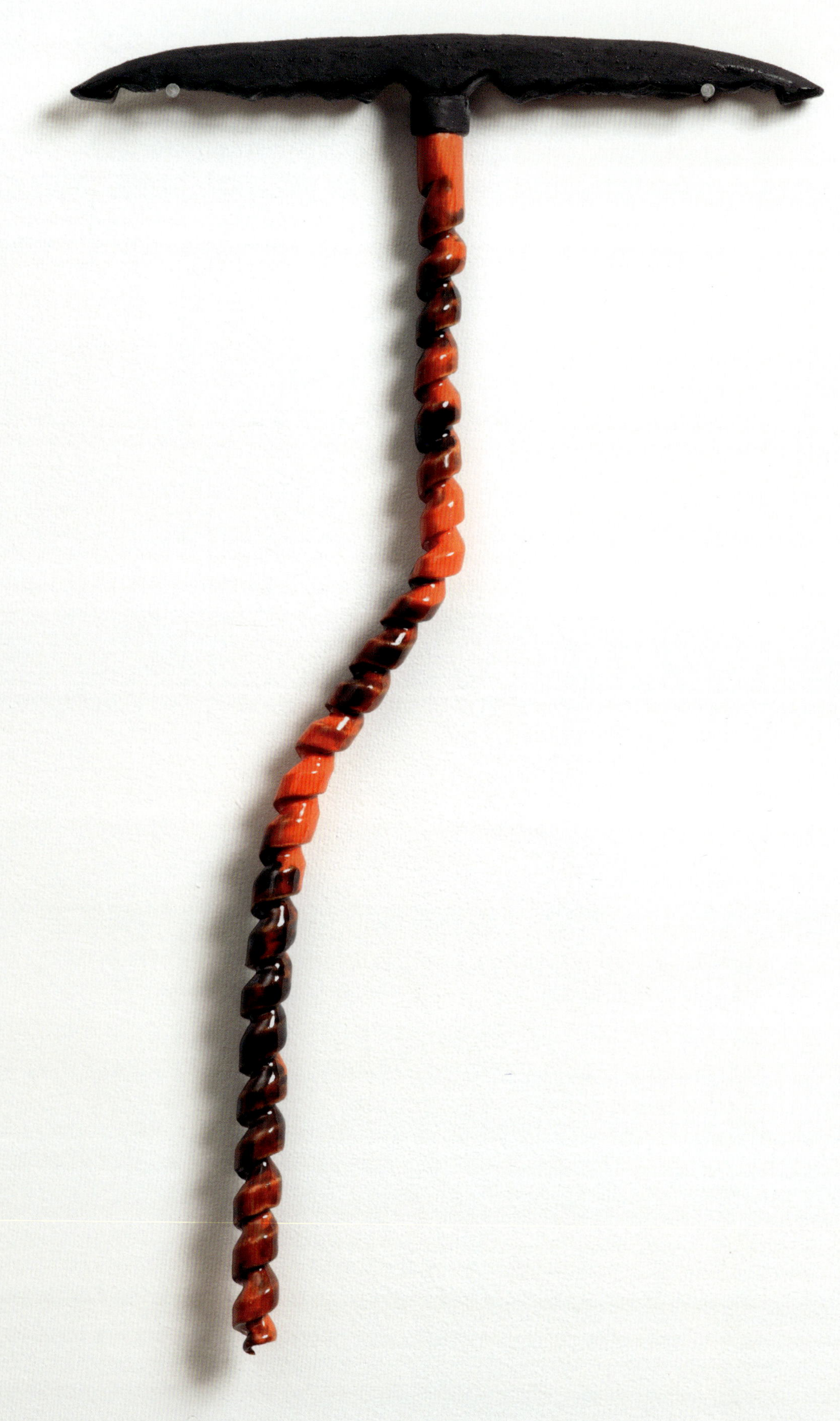

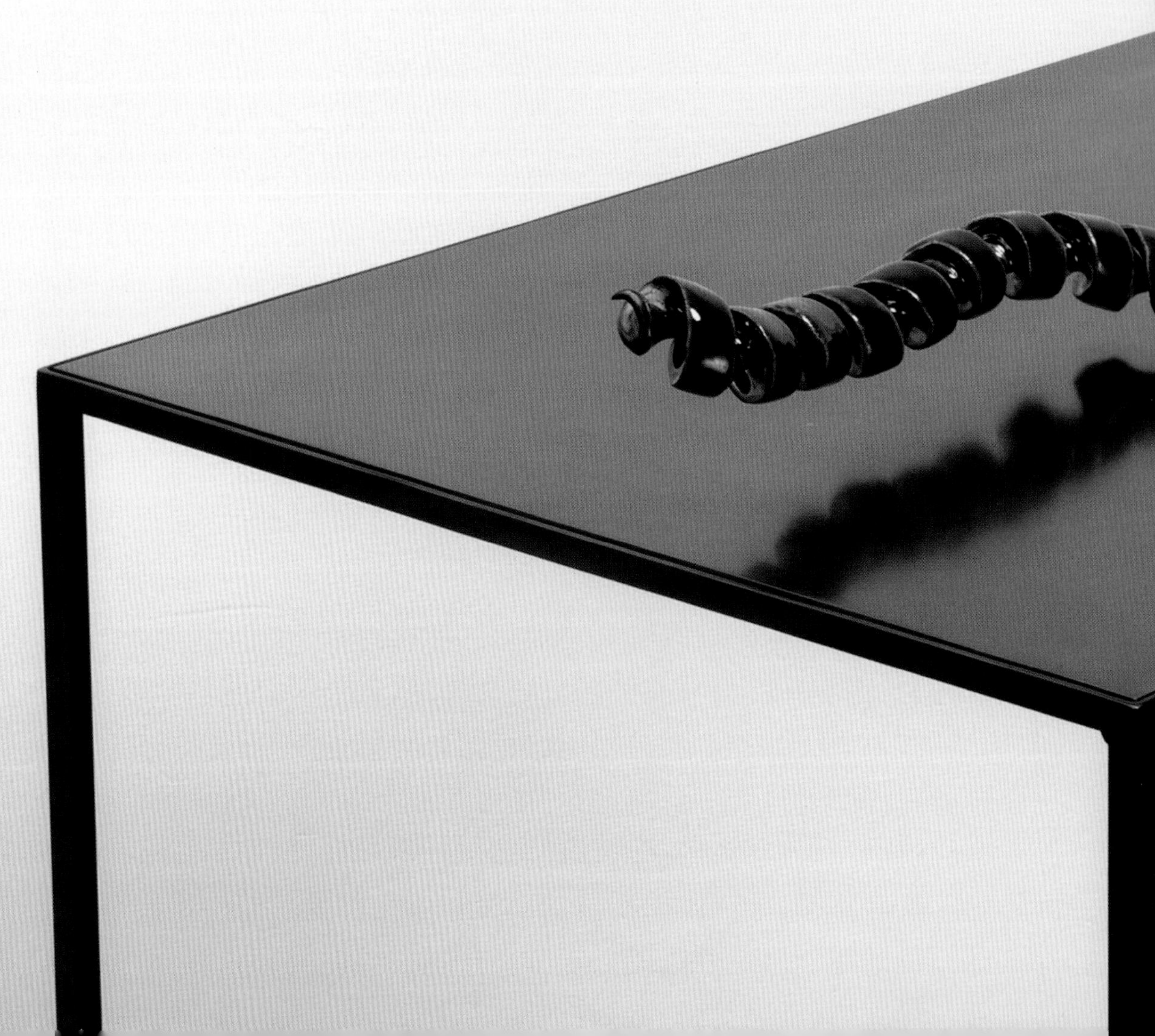

Intruder, Misused II, 2019. Ceramic, steel, Sculpture 8 × 71 × 46 cm; 3¼ × 27¾ × 18¼ inches, Pedestal 94 × 81 × 51 cm; 37 × 32 × 20 inches

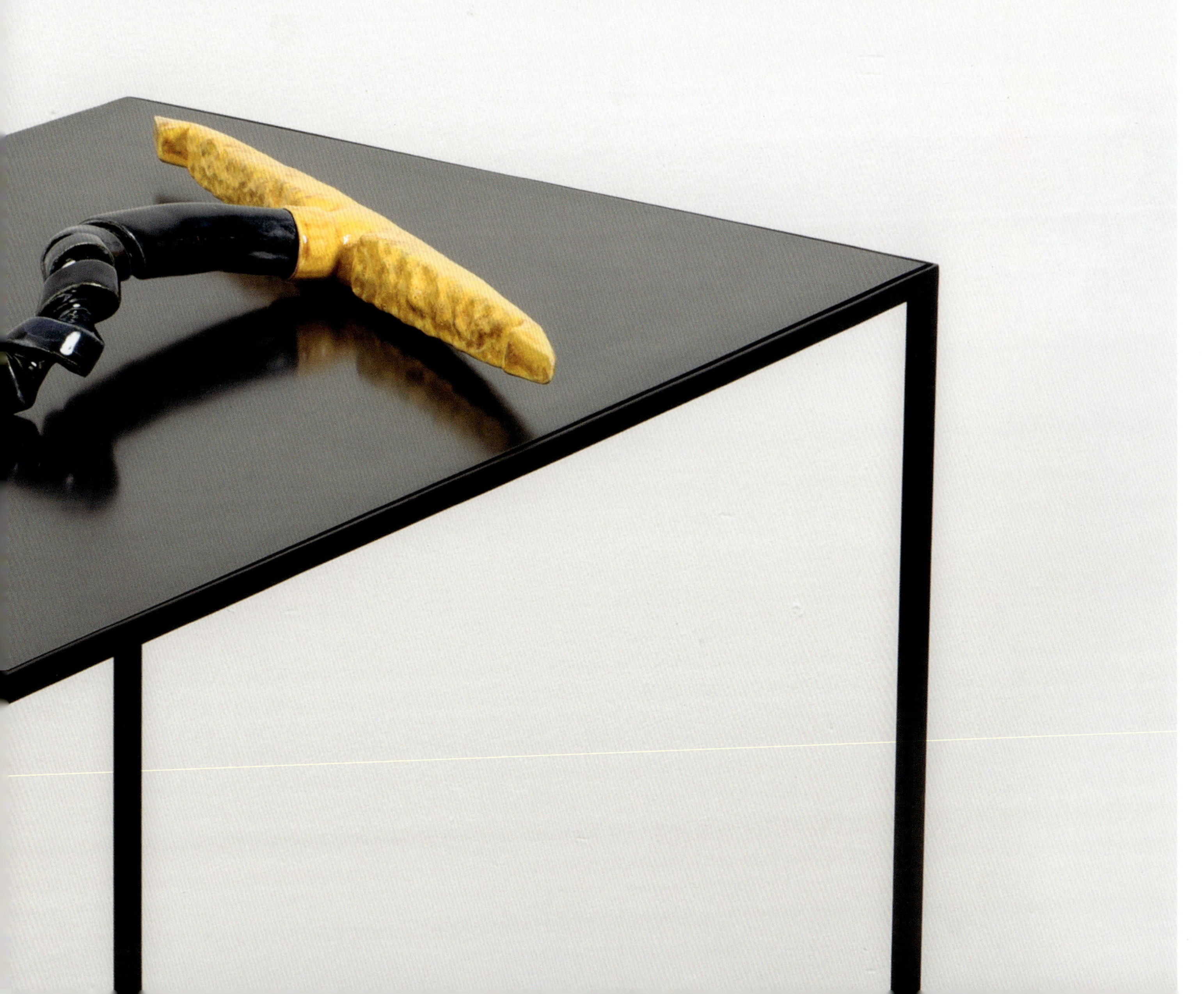

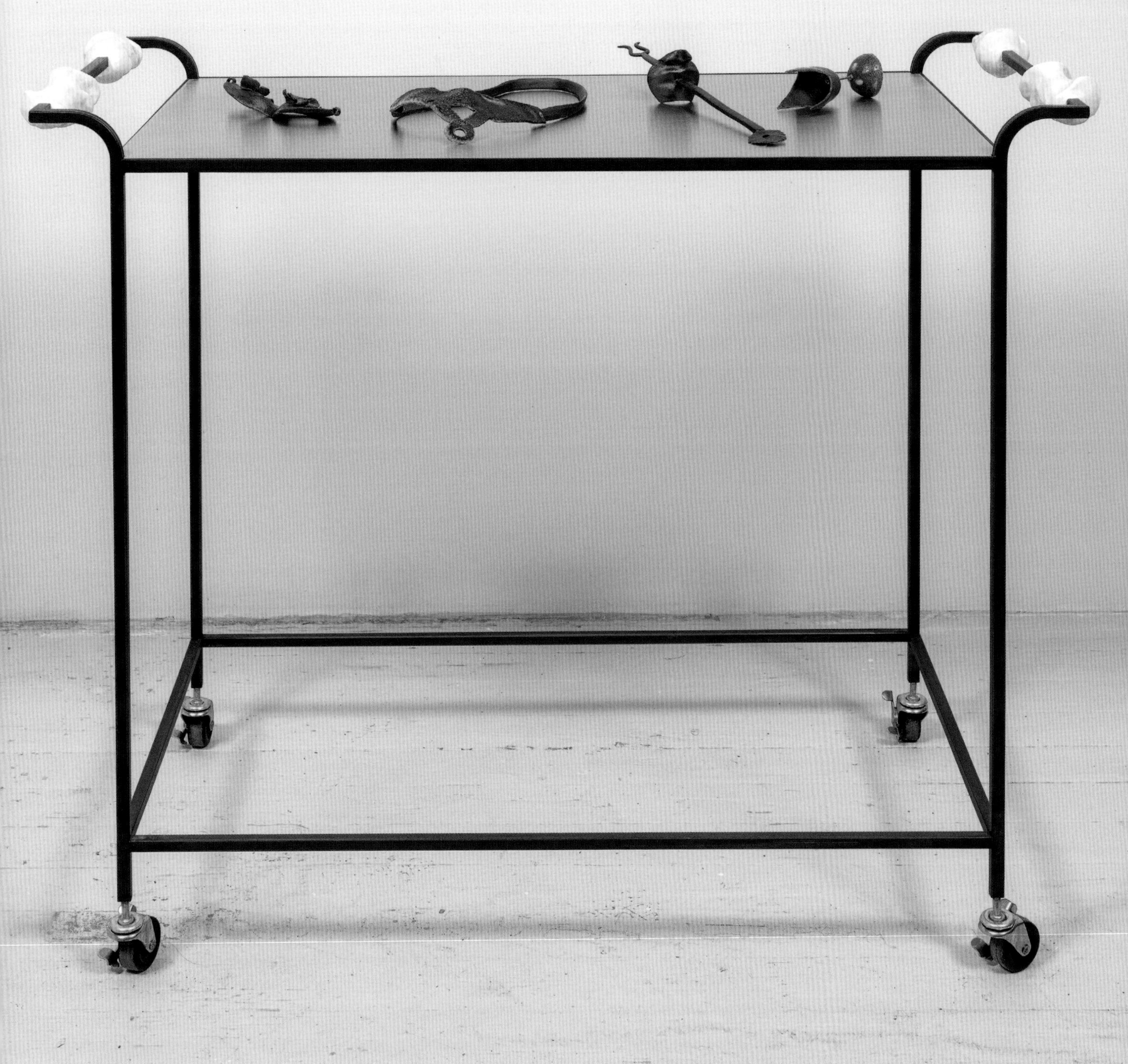

Operator I (with Blinder, Muter, Penetrator, Aborter), 2017. Ceramic, brass hardware, steel, wheels, 104 × 117 × 45.5 cm; 41 × 46¼ × 18 inches

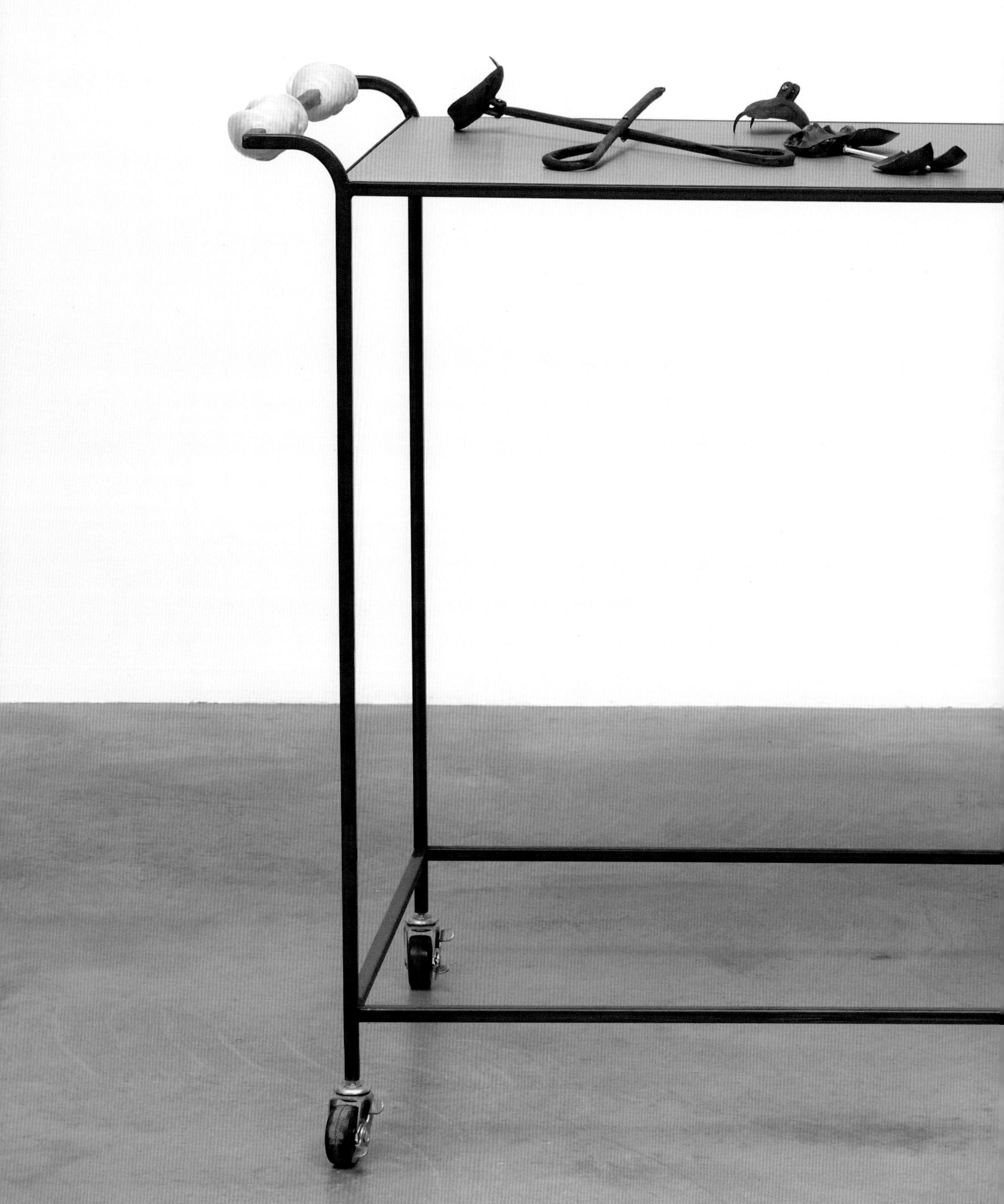

Operator II (with Opener, Destabilizer, Distancer, [R]Ejecter), Partially Dismantled, 2018. Ceramic, metal hardware, steel, wheels, 104 × 127 × 63.5 cm; 41 × 50 × 25 inches

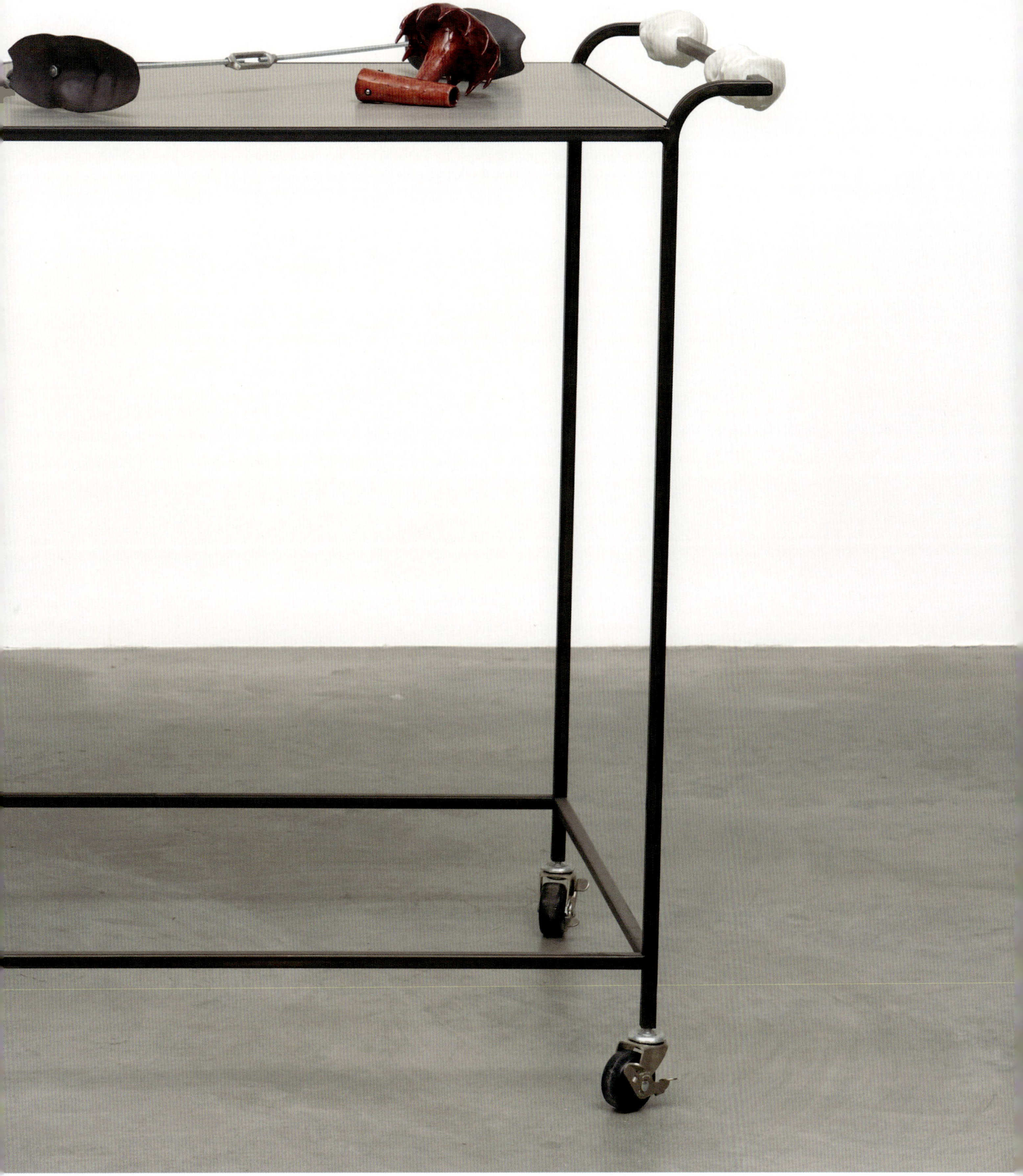

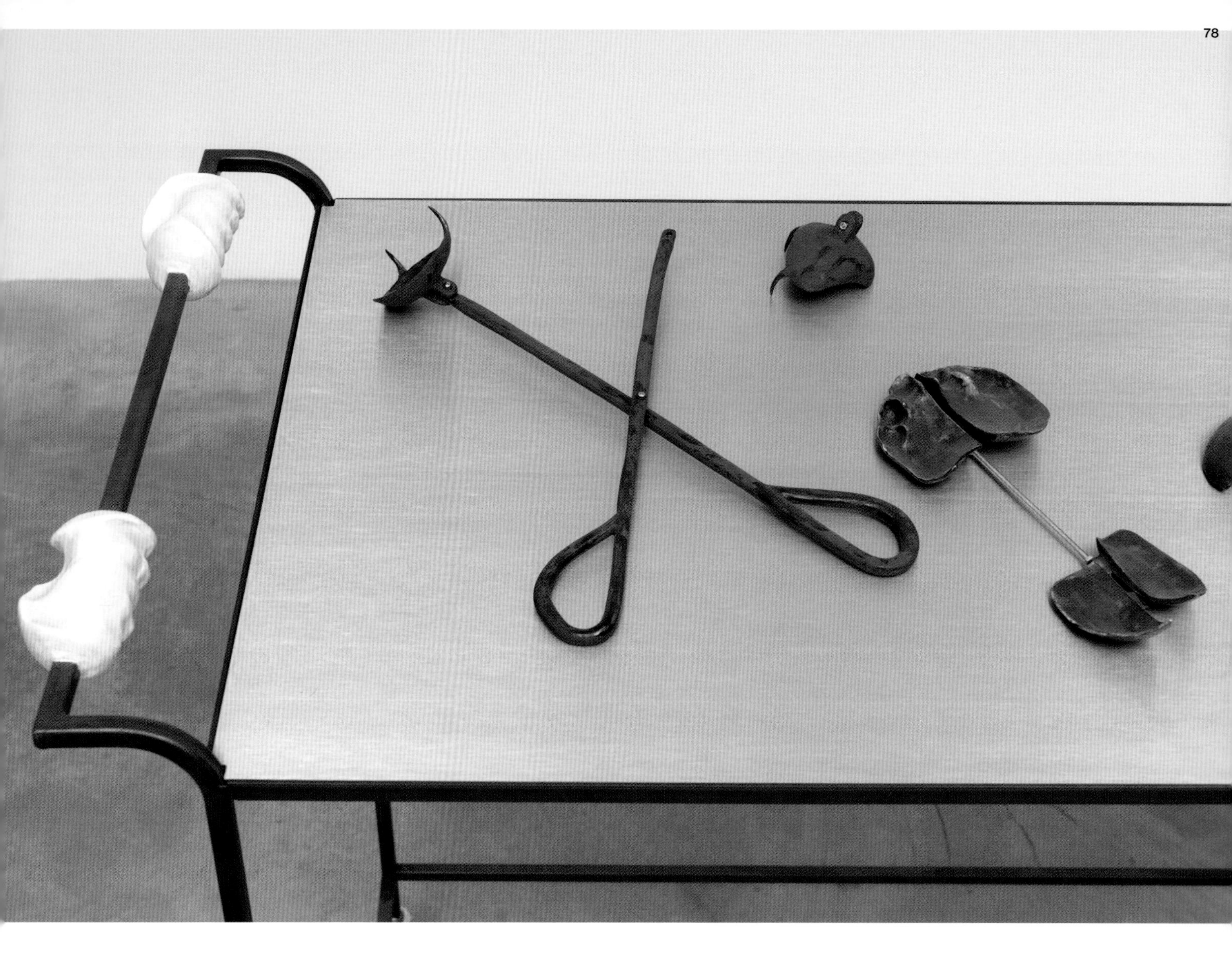

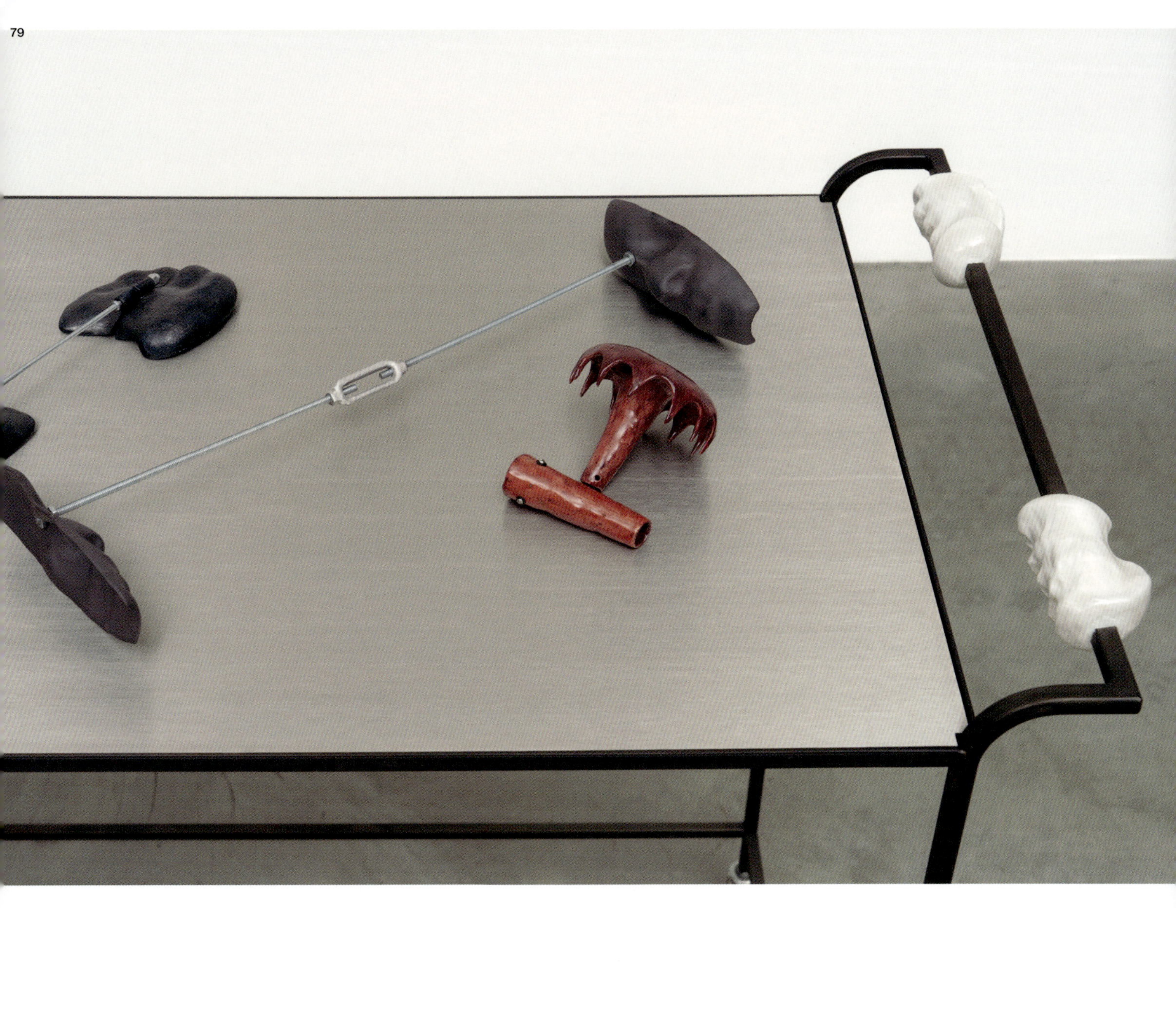

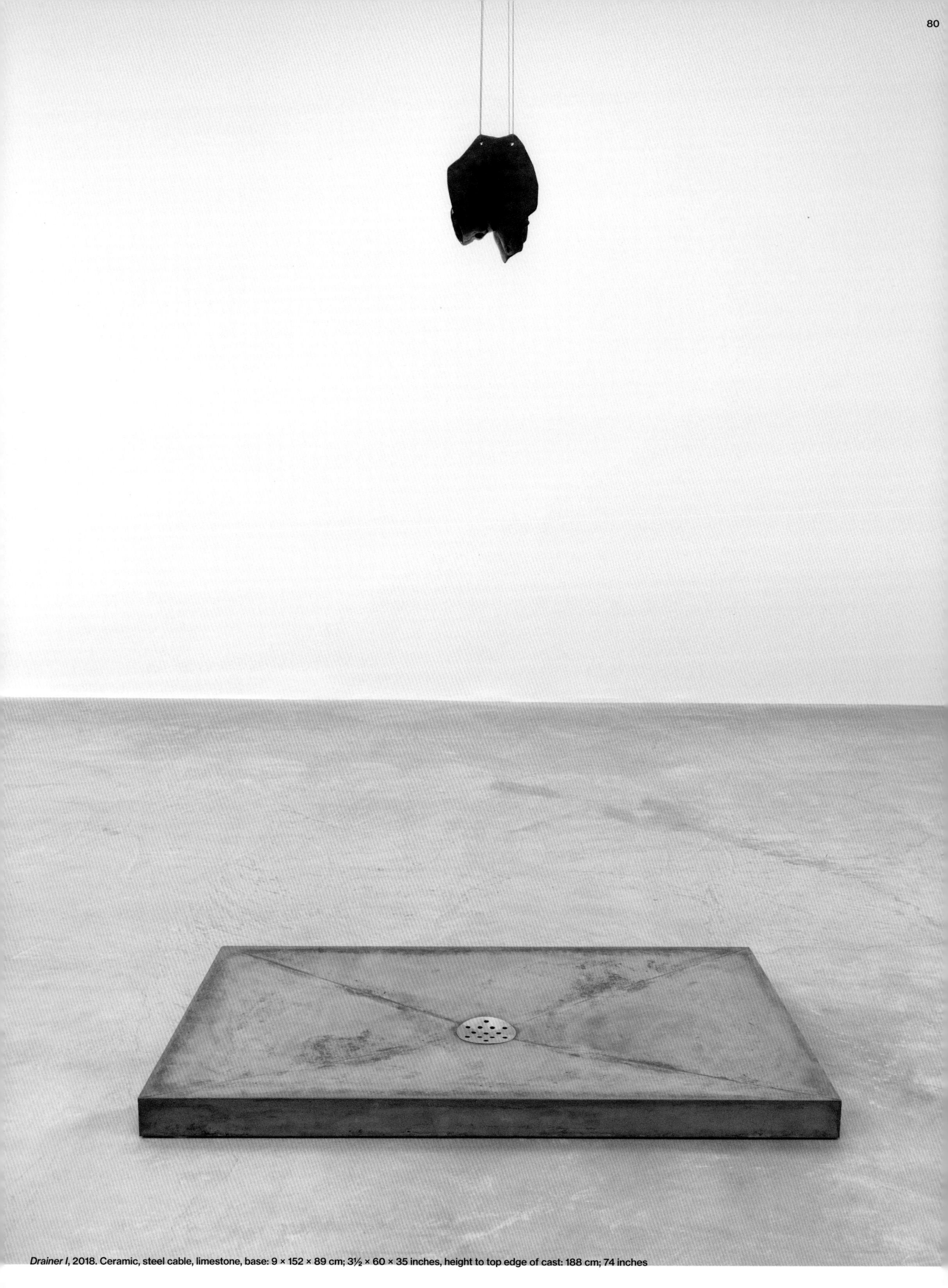

Drainer I, 2018. Ceramic, steel cable, limestone, base: 9 × 152 × 89 cm; 3½ × 60 × 35 inches, height to top edge of cast: 188 cm; 74 inches

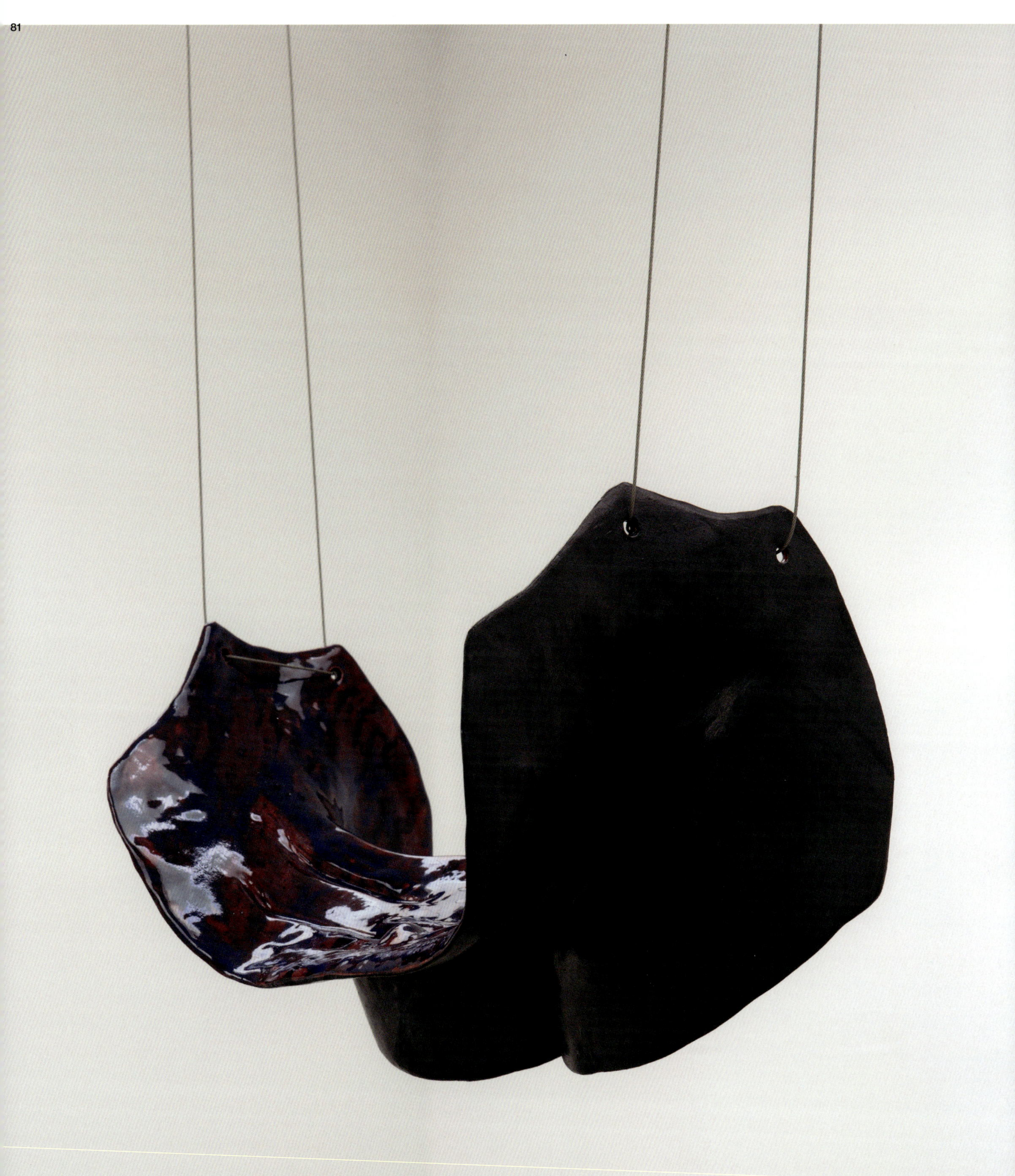

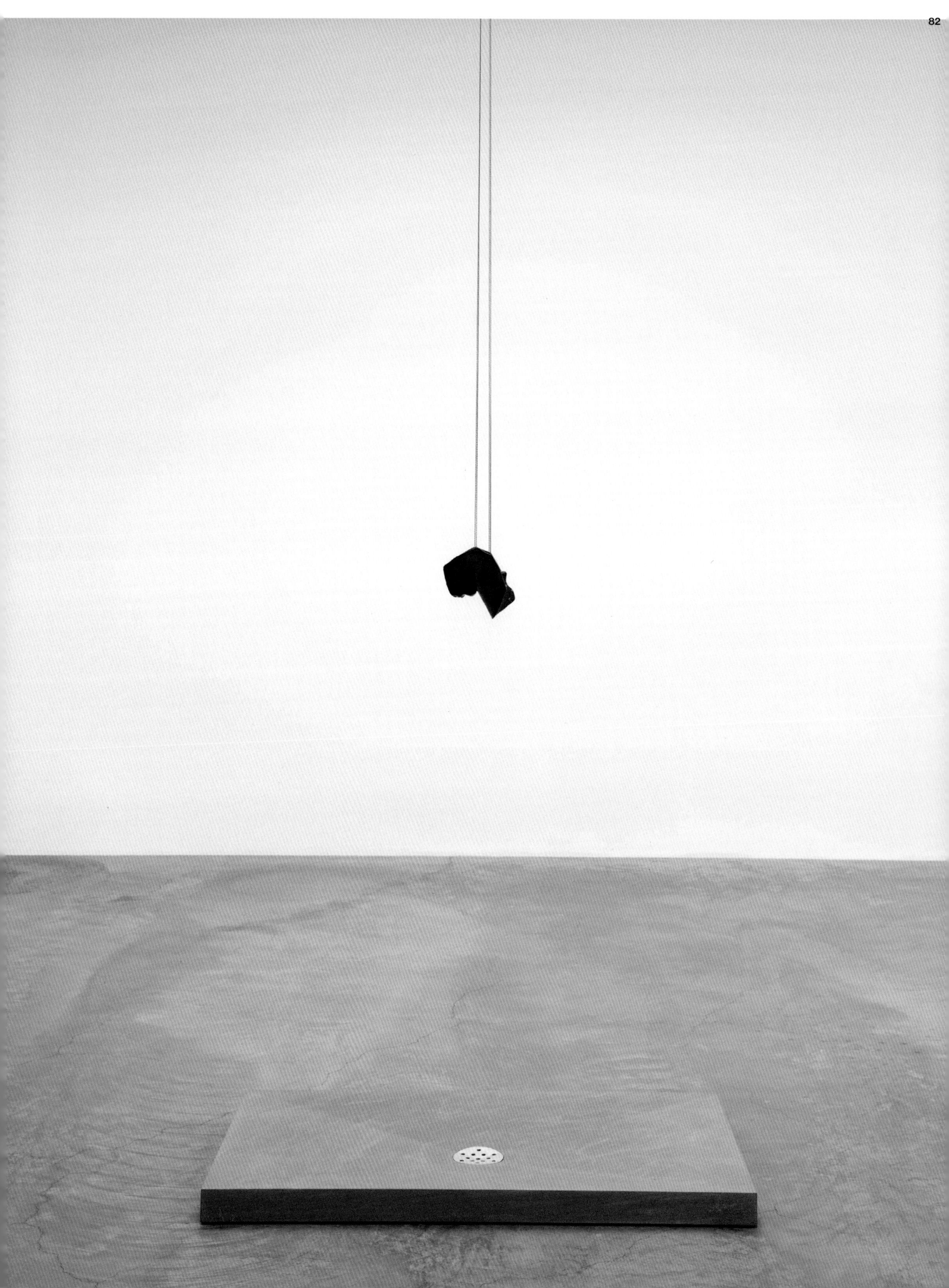

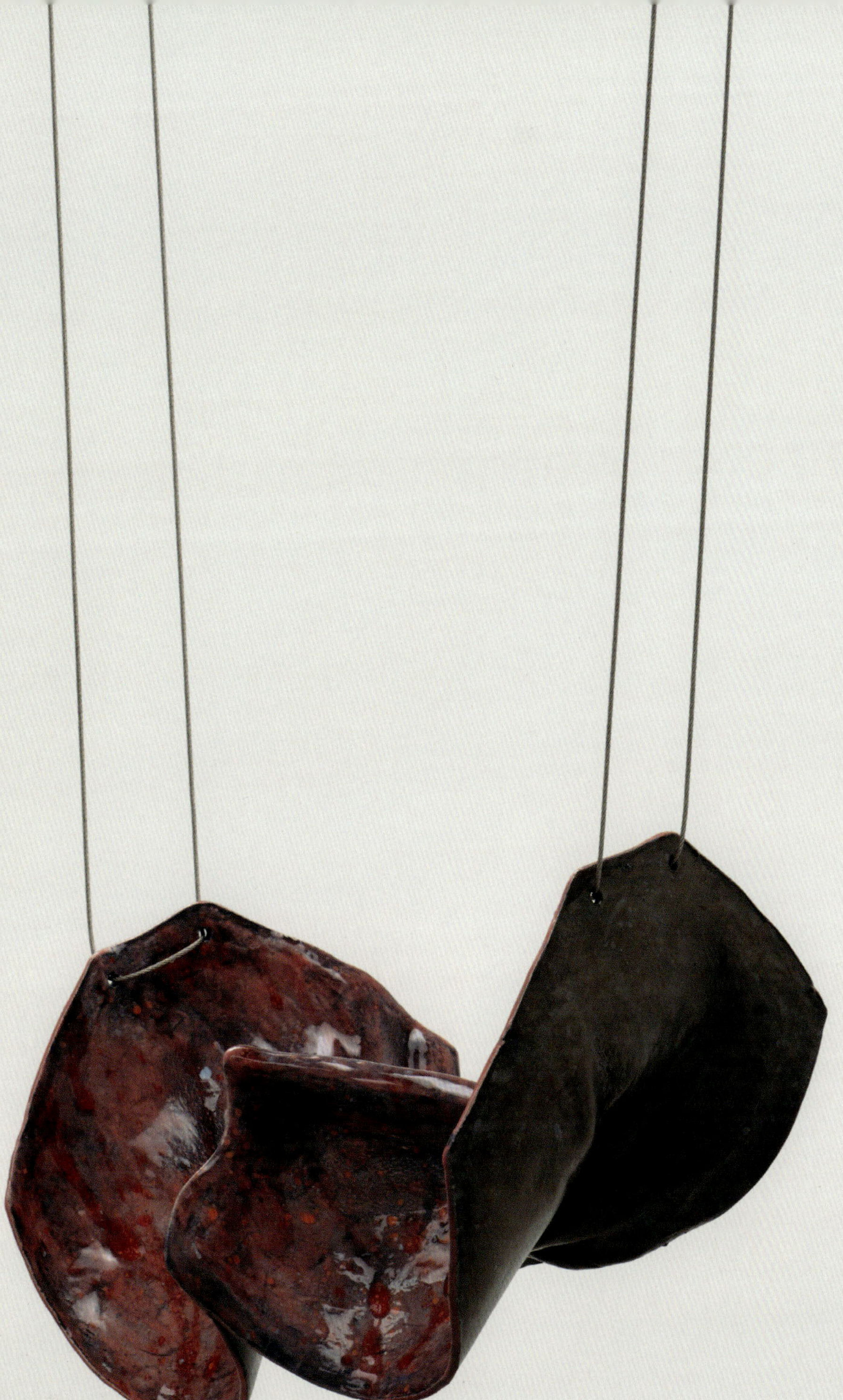

Drainer II, 2021. Ceramic, steel cable, limestone, base: 9 × 152 × 89 cm; 3½ × 60 × 35 inches, height to top edge of cast: 188 cm; 74 inches

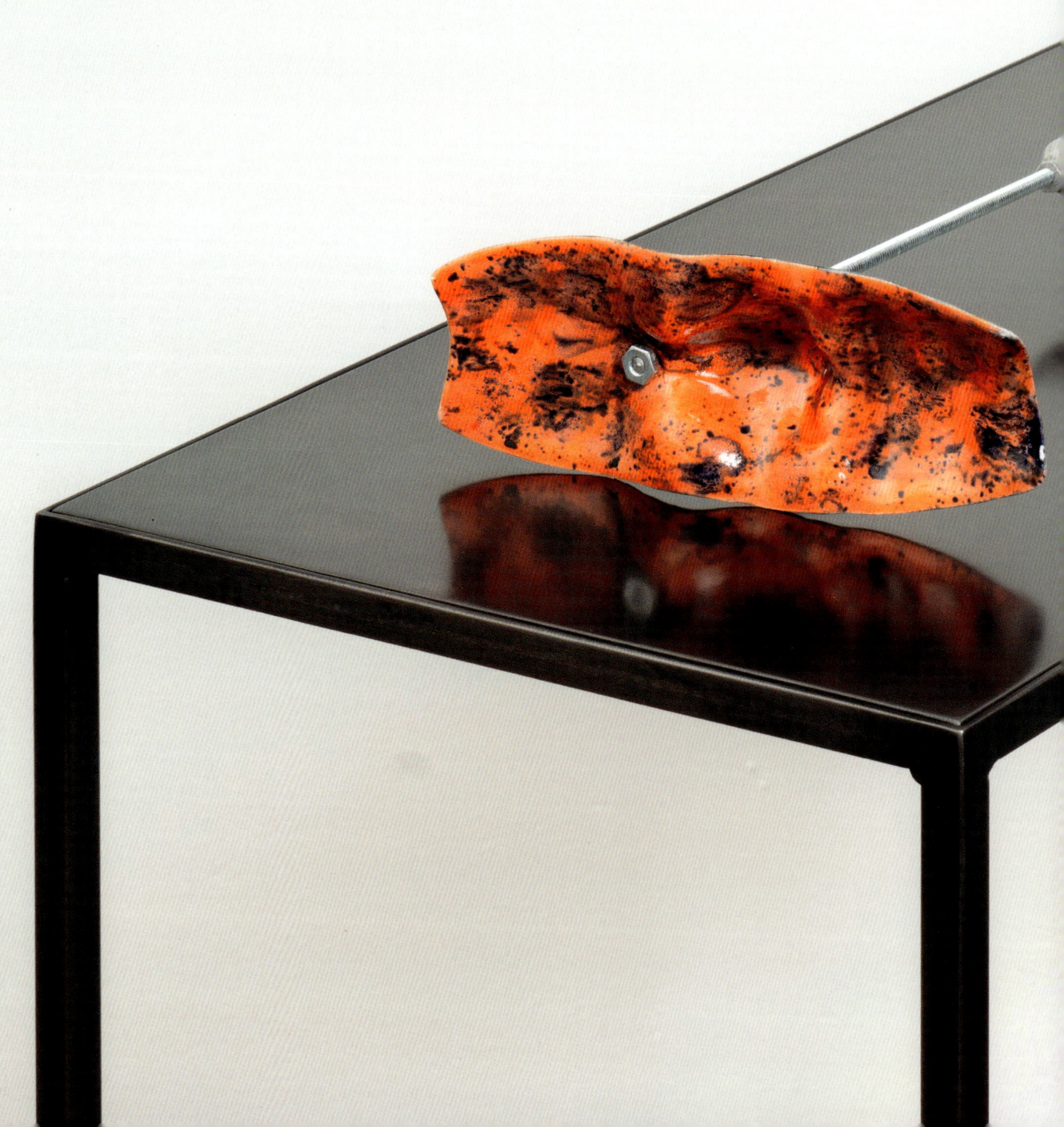

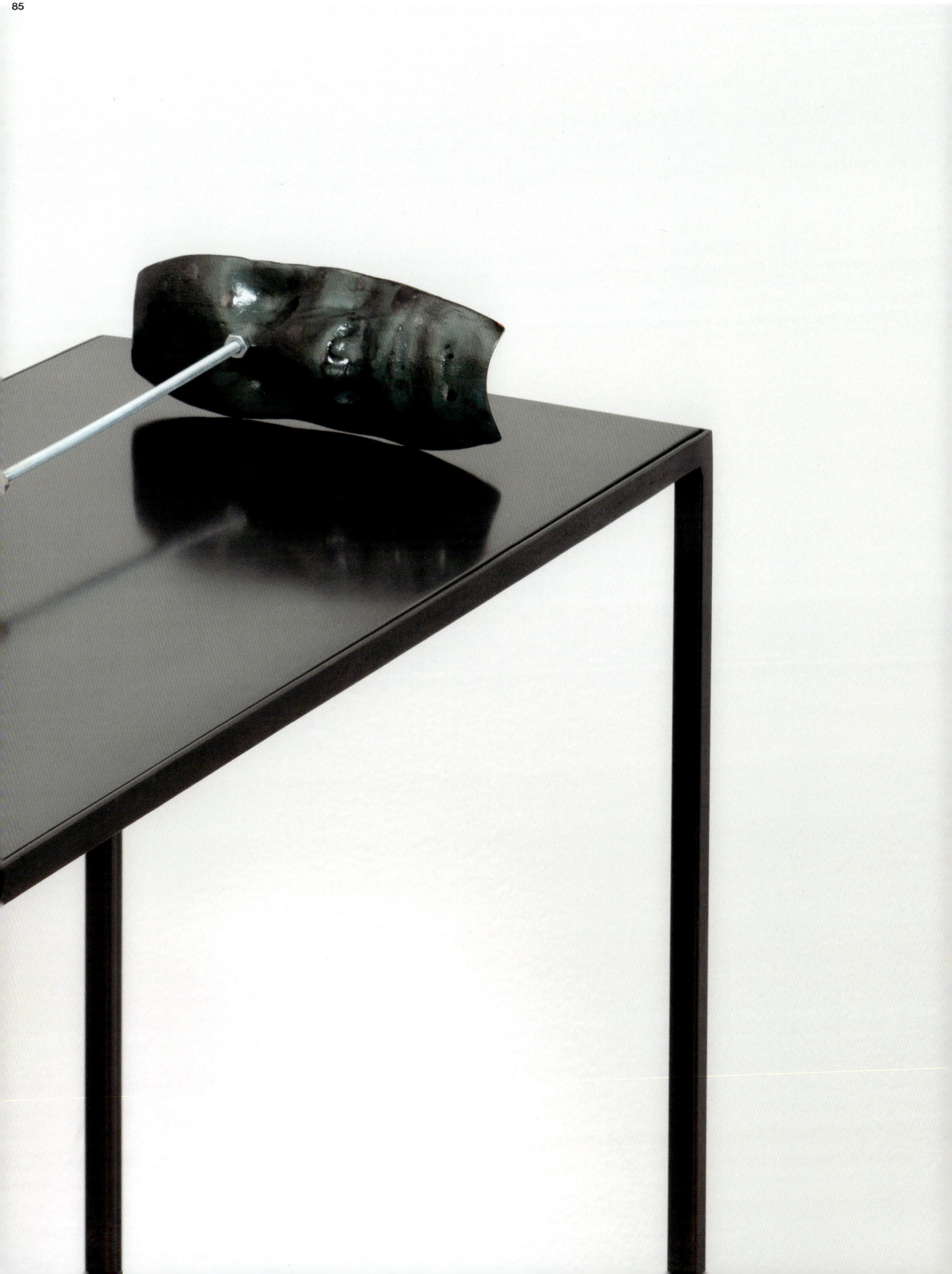

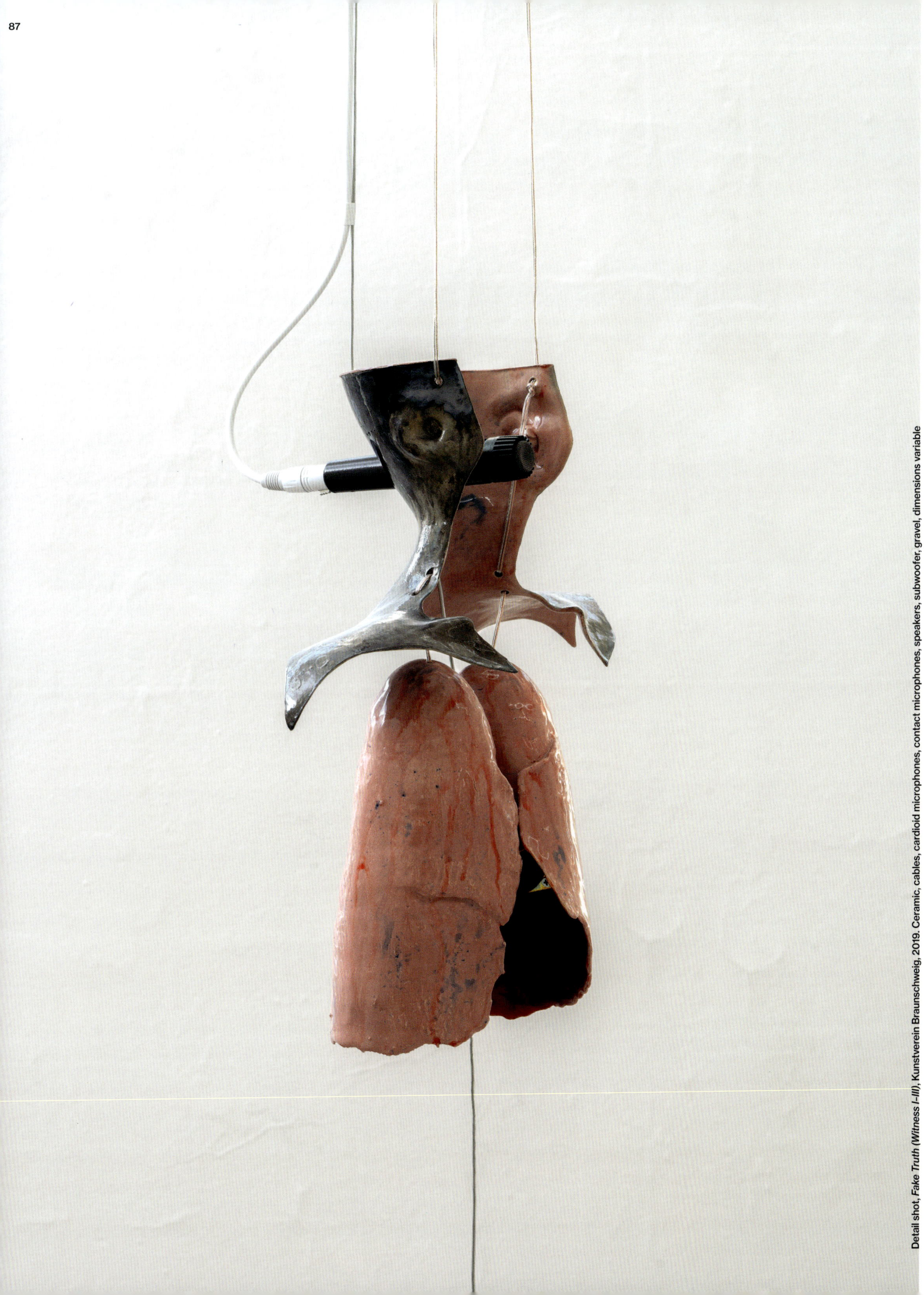

Detail shot, *Fake Truth (Witness I–III)*, Kunstverein Braunschweig, 2019. Ceramic, cables, cardioid microphones, contact microphones, speakers, subwoofer, gravel, dimensions variable

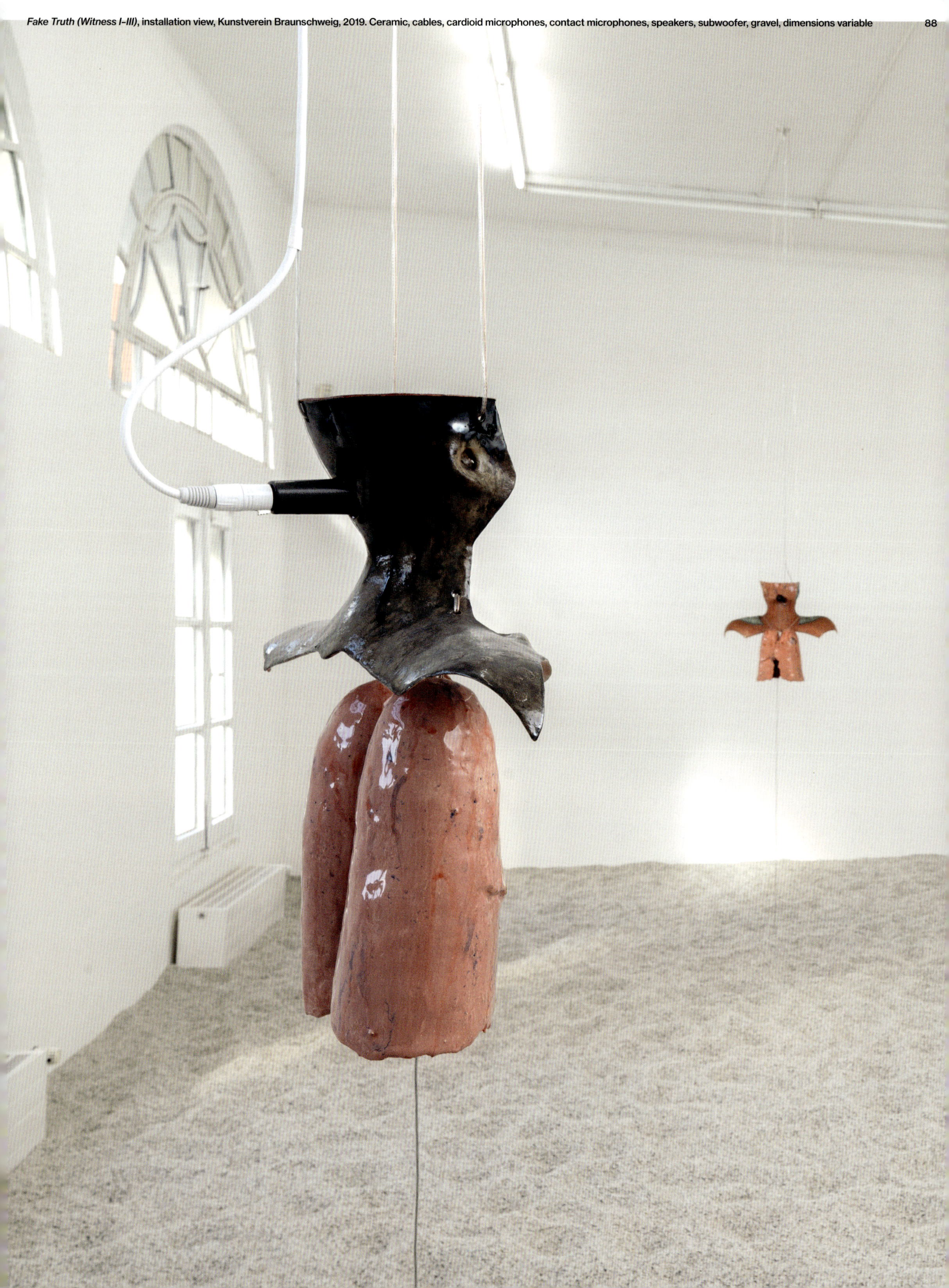

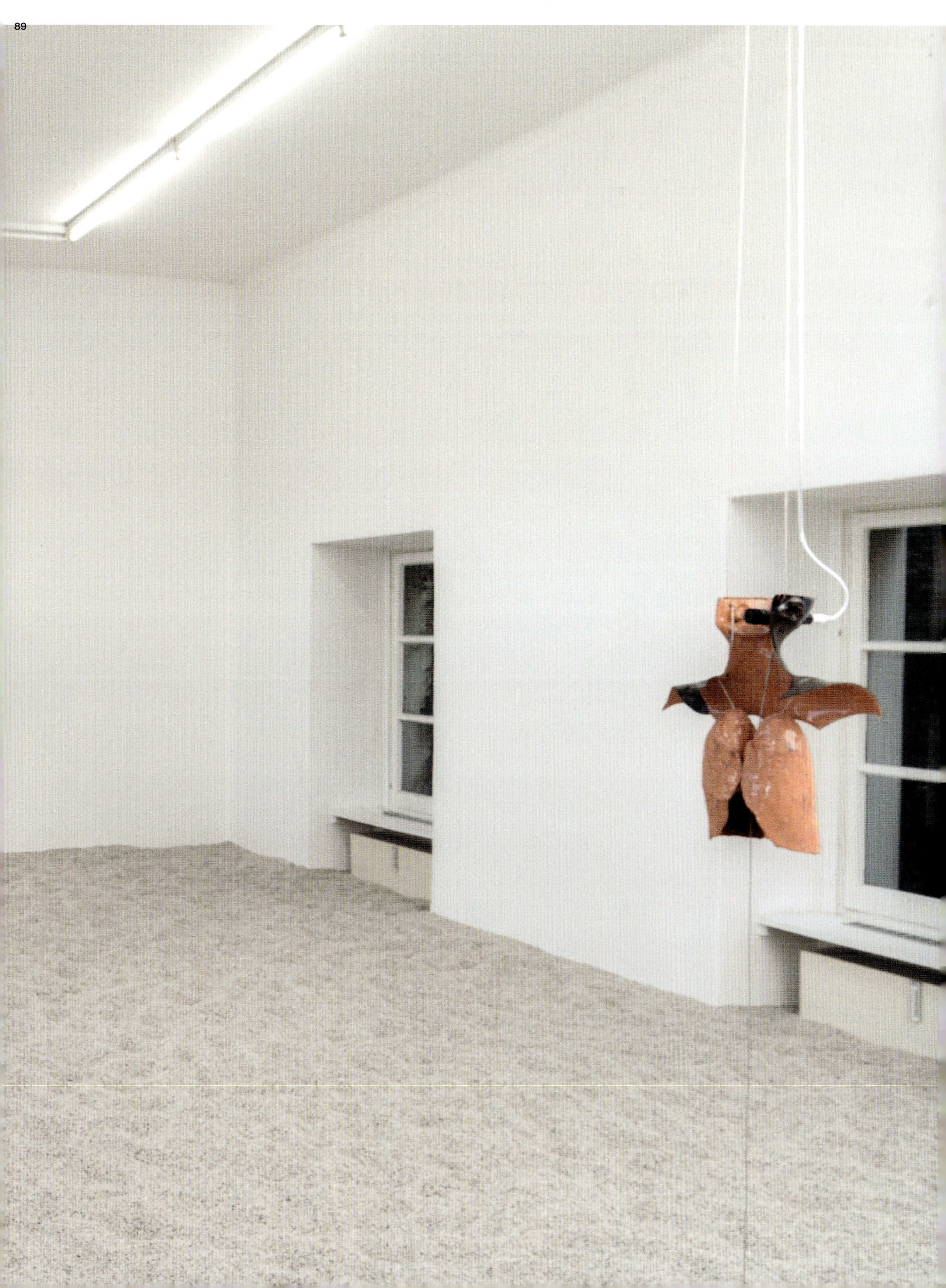

Mediator, 2020. Ceramic, stainless steel, granite, nylon hardware, 175 × 285 × 285 cm; 69 × 112¼ × 112¼ inches

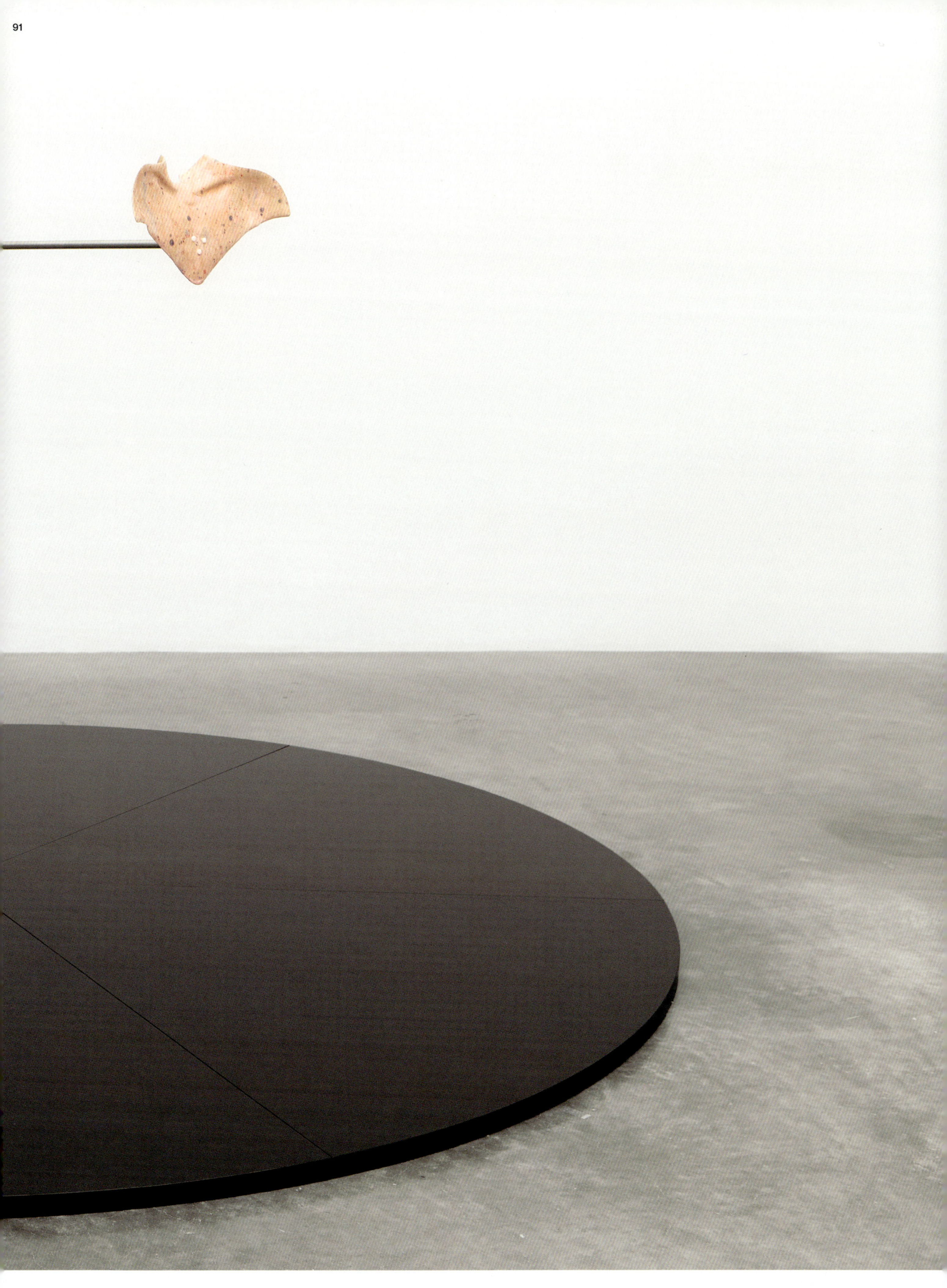

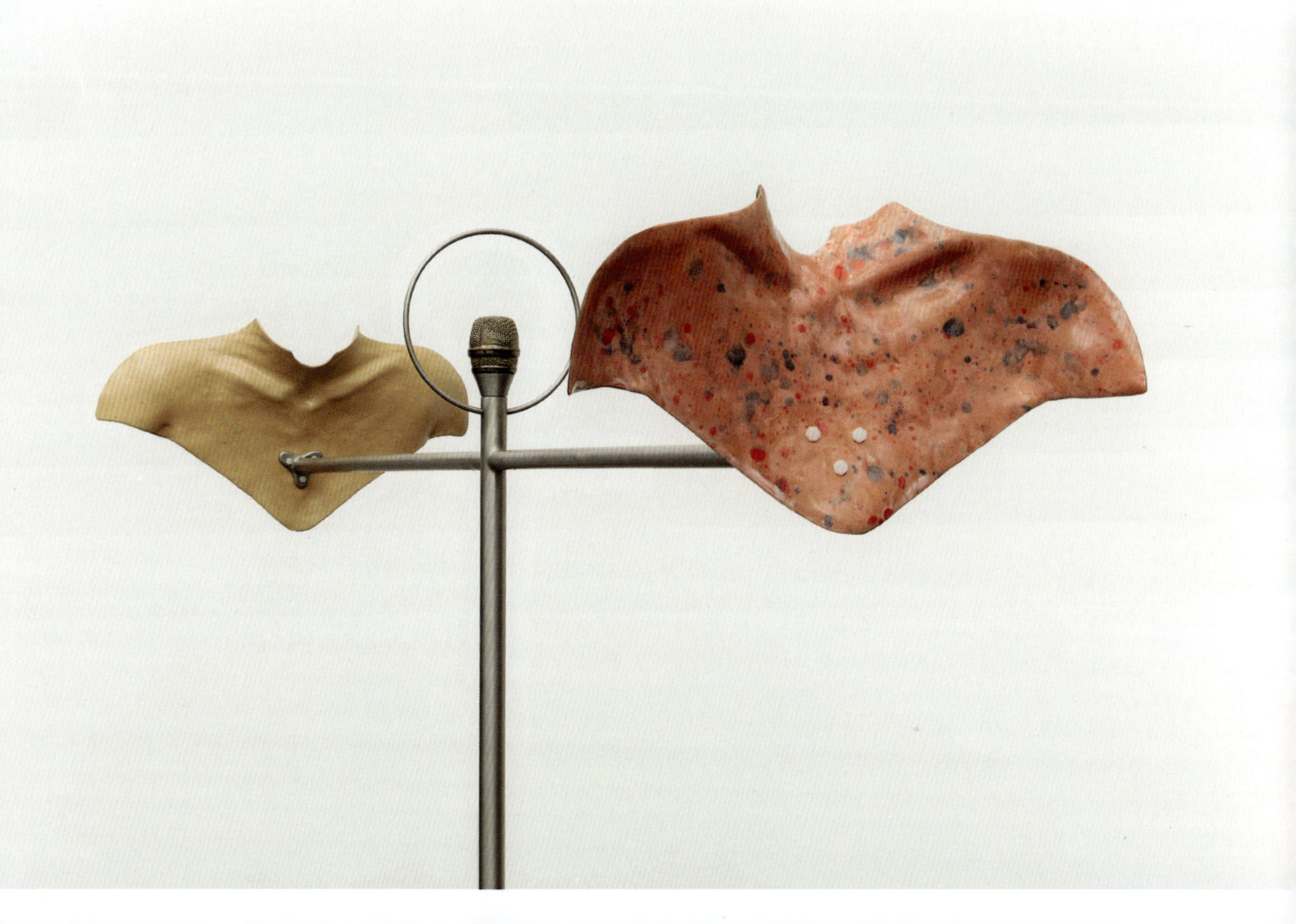

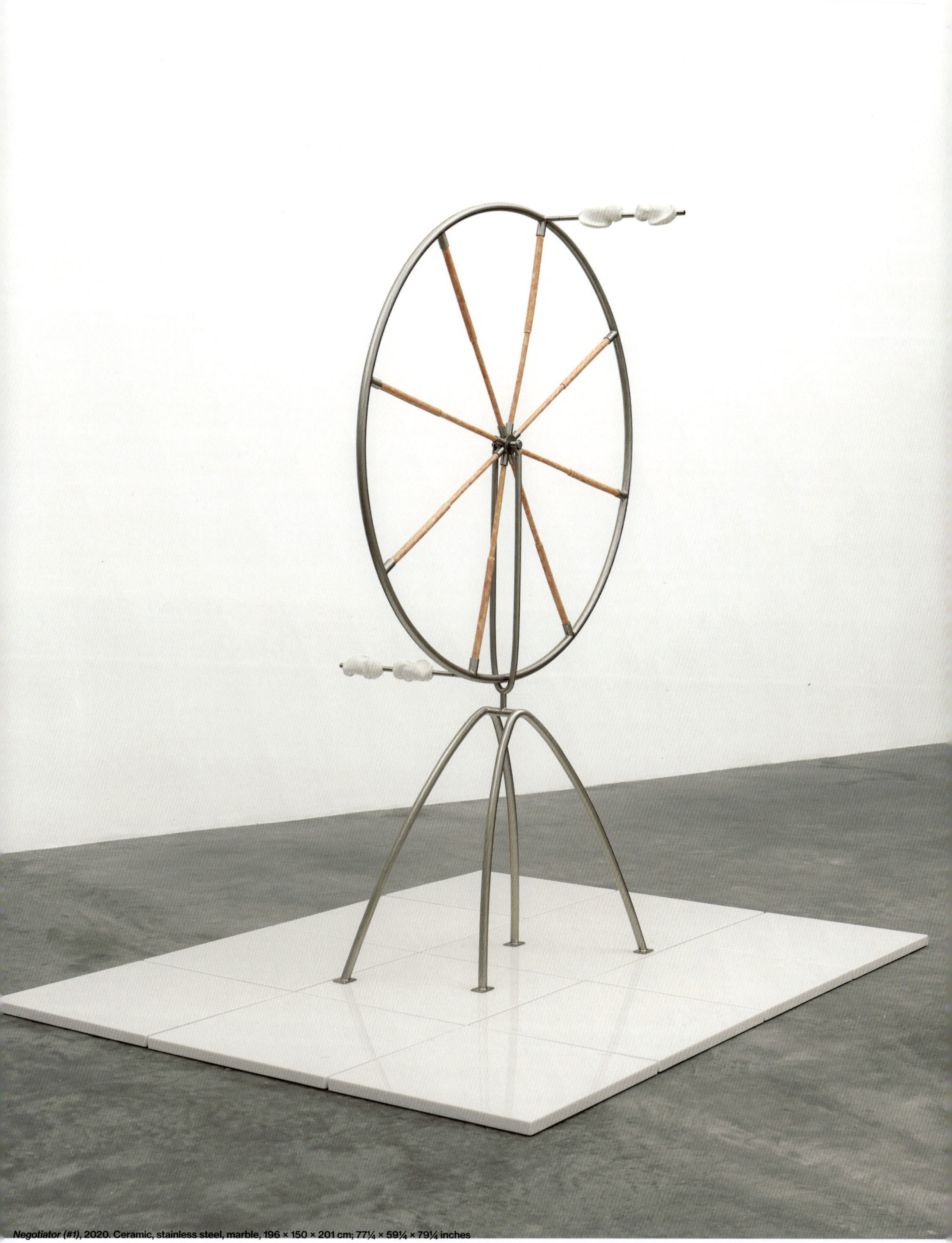

Negotiator (#1), 2020. Ceramic, stainless steel, marble, 196 × 150 × 201 cm; 77¼ × 59¼ × 79¼ inches

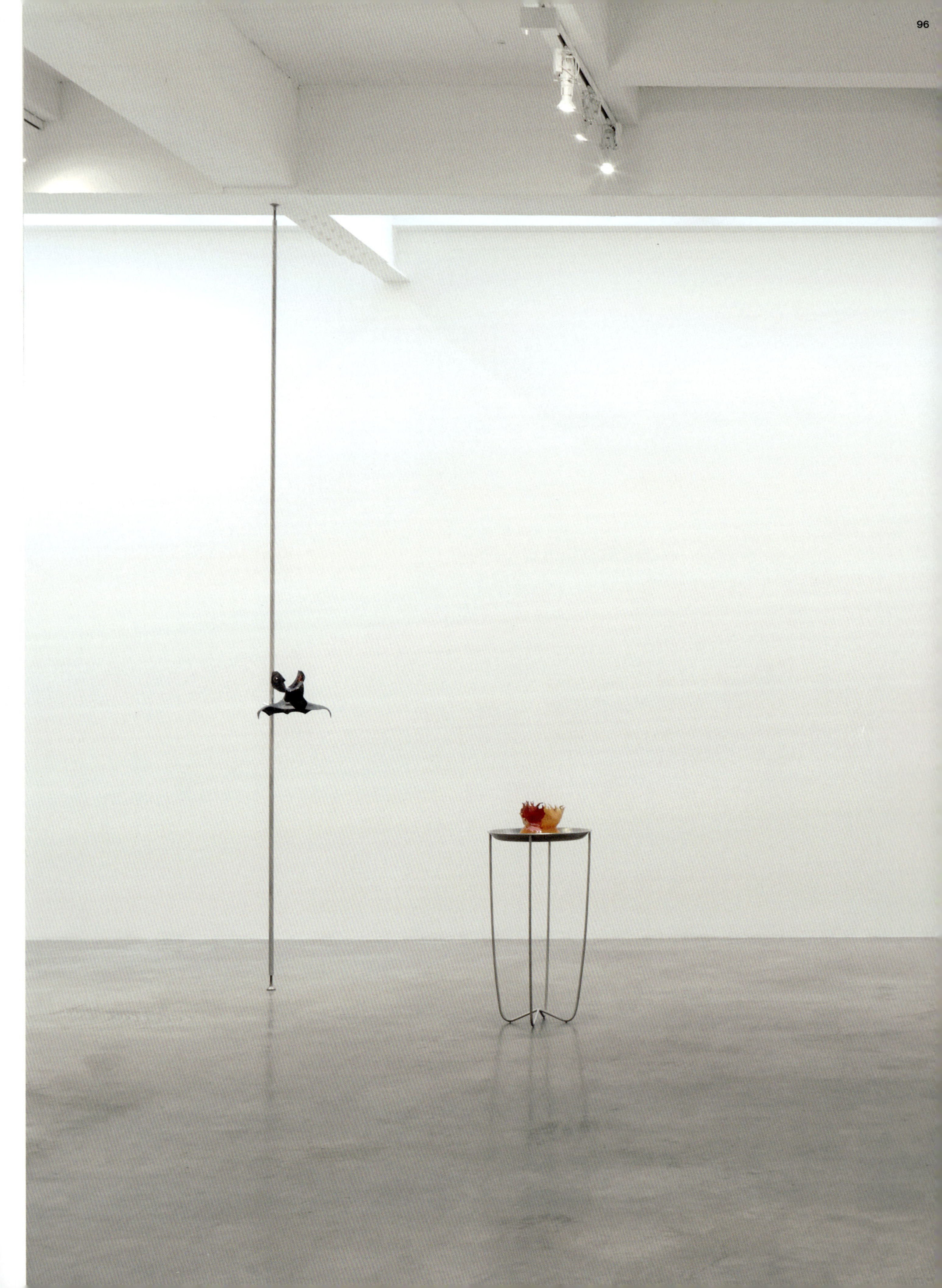

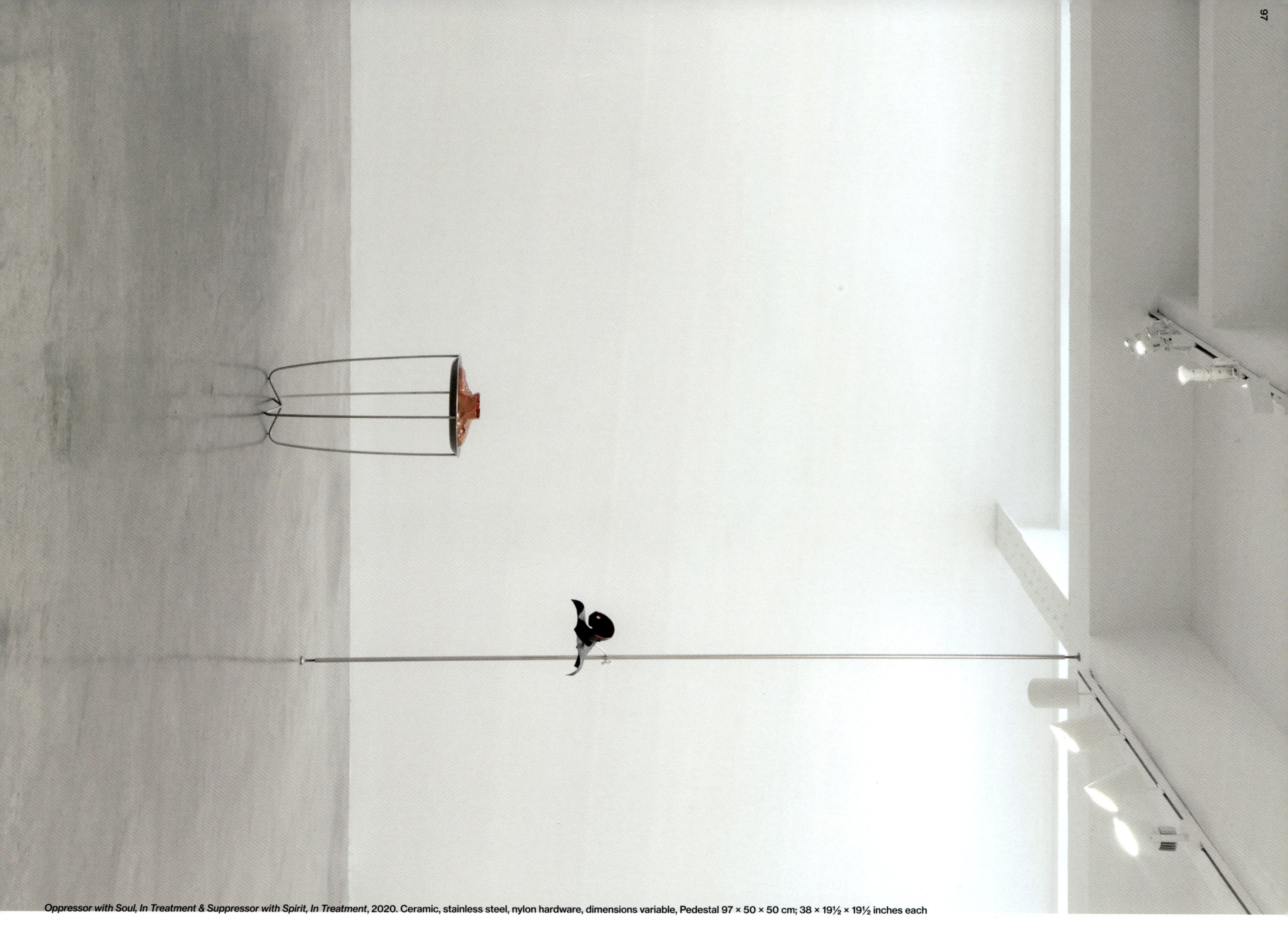

Oppressor with Soul, In Treatment & Suppressor with Spirit, In Treatment, 2020. Ceramic, stainless steel, nylon hardware, dimensions variable, Pedestal 97 × 50 × 50 cm; 38 × 19½ × 19½ inches each

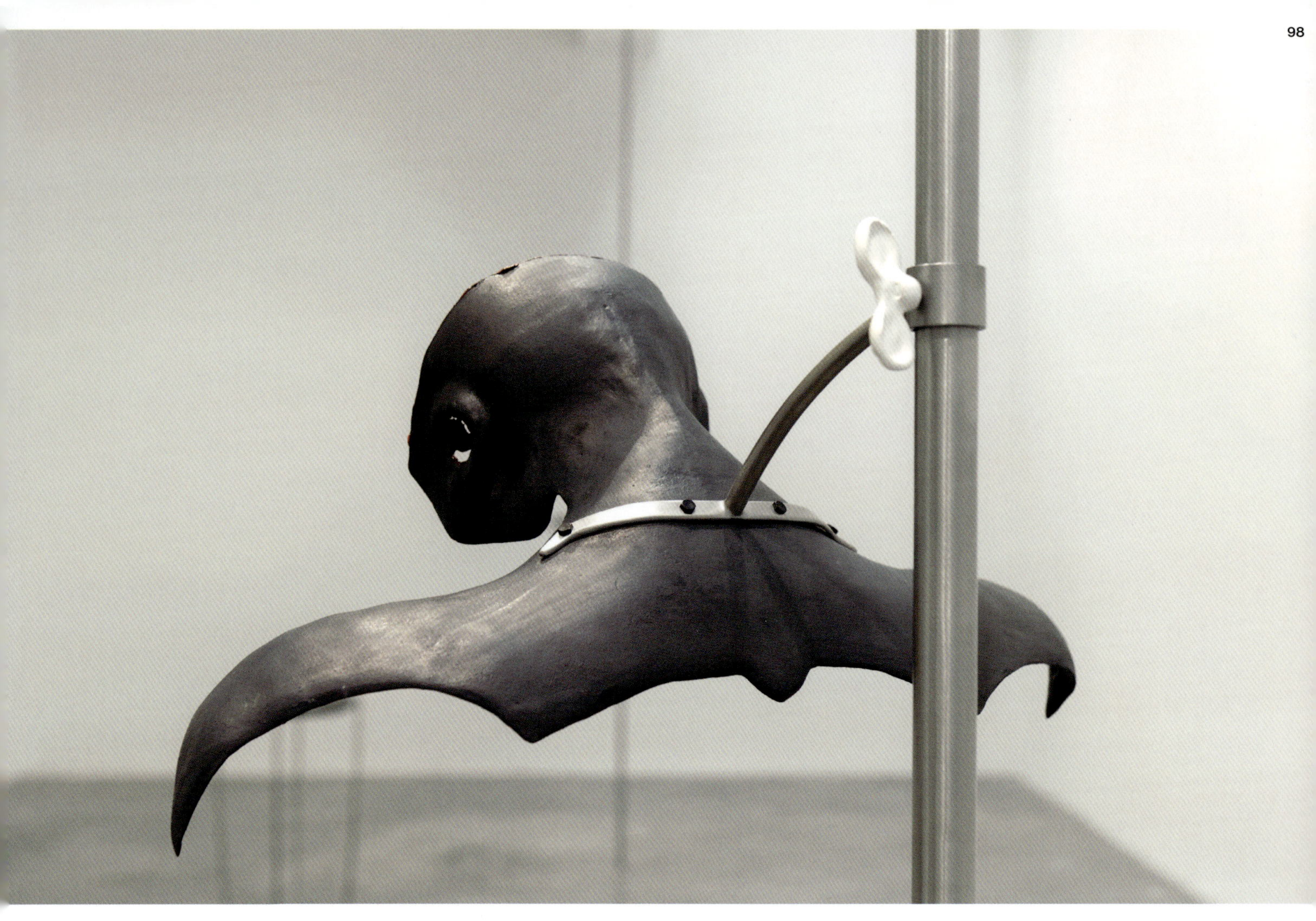

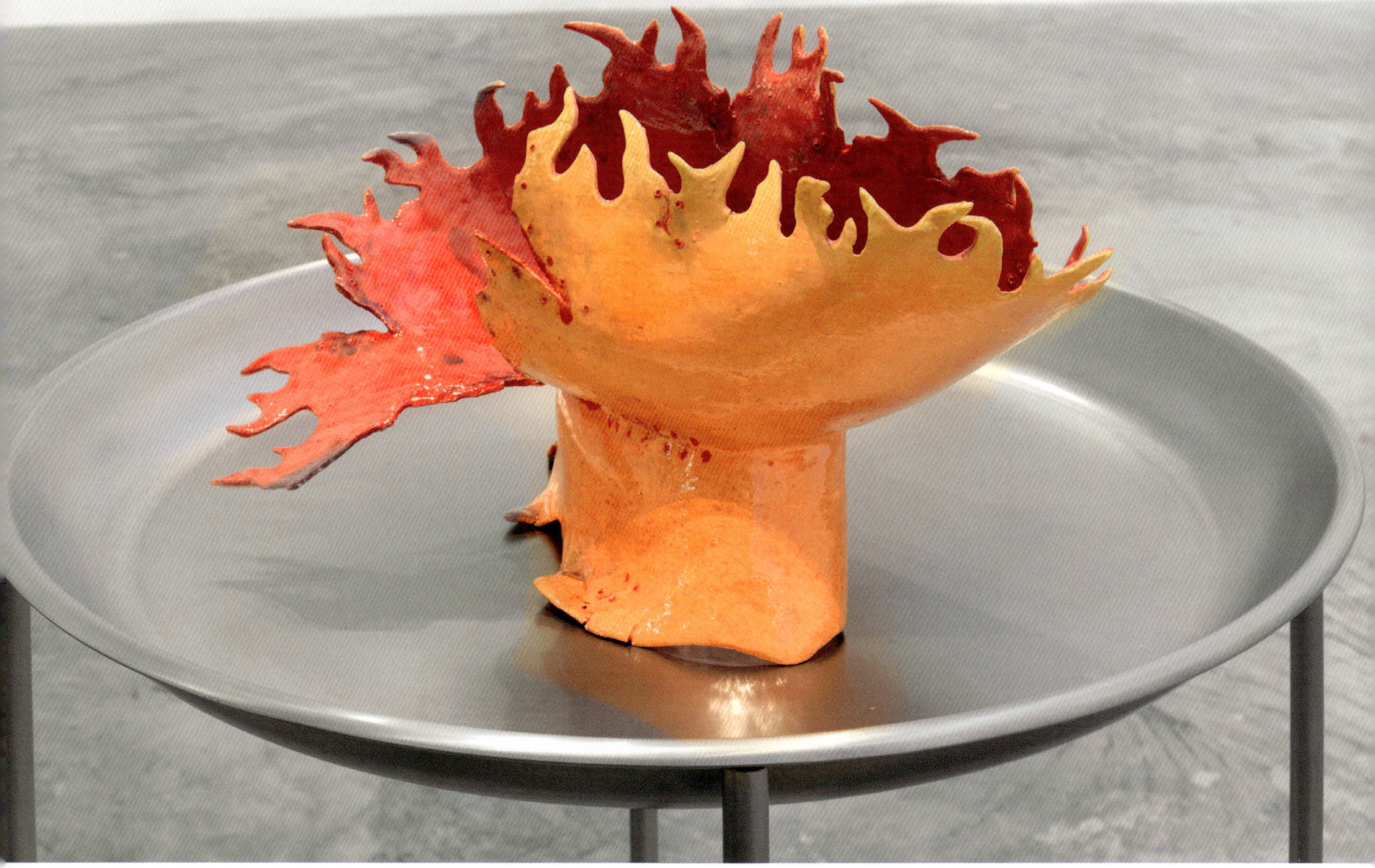

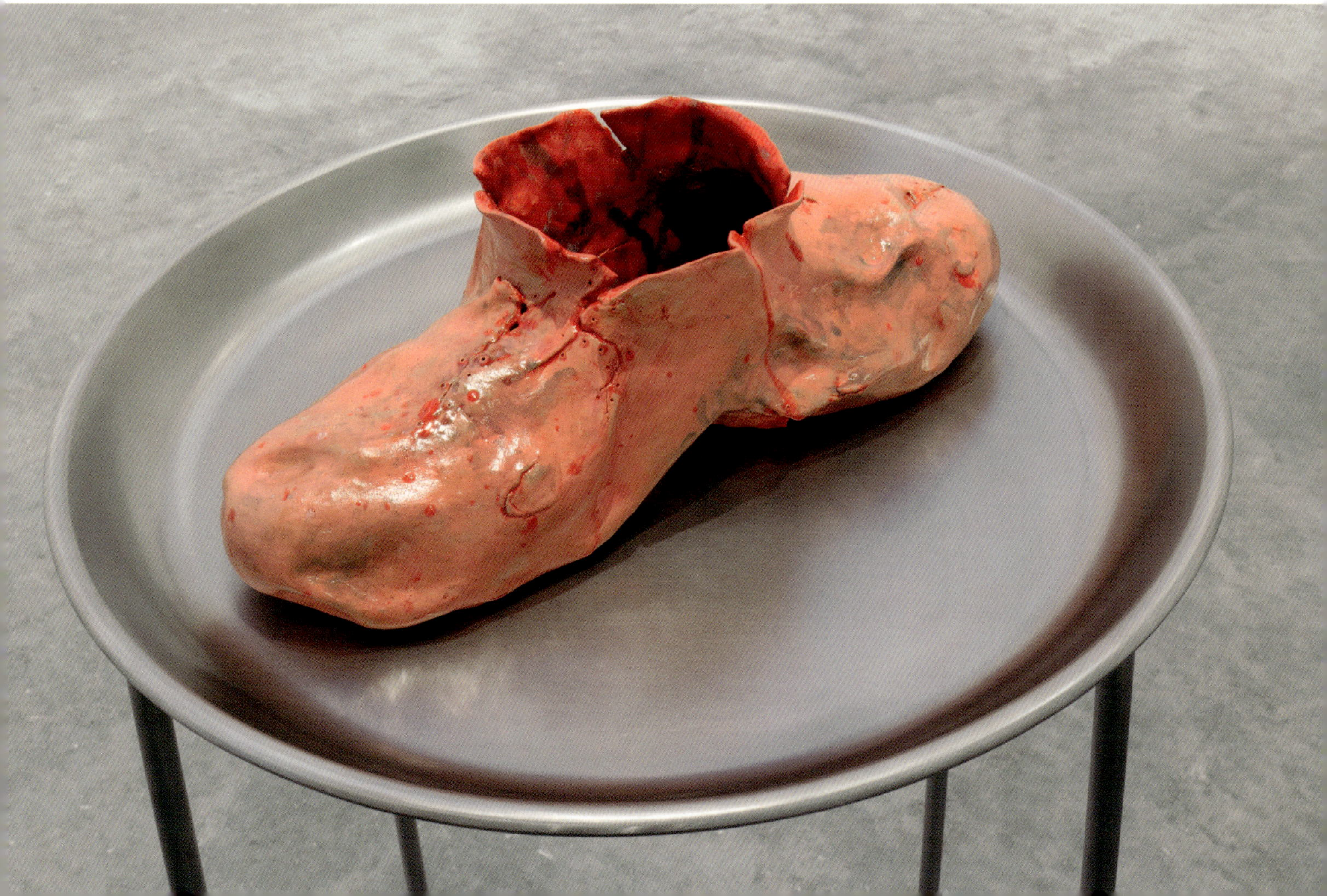

    Purifier I, 2021. Ceramic, stainless steel, Sculpture 11 × 58 × 16 cm; 4⅛ × 22⅛ × 6¼ inches, Pedestal 94 × 71 × 28 cm; 37 × 28 × 11 inches

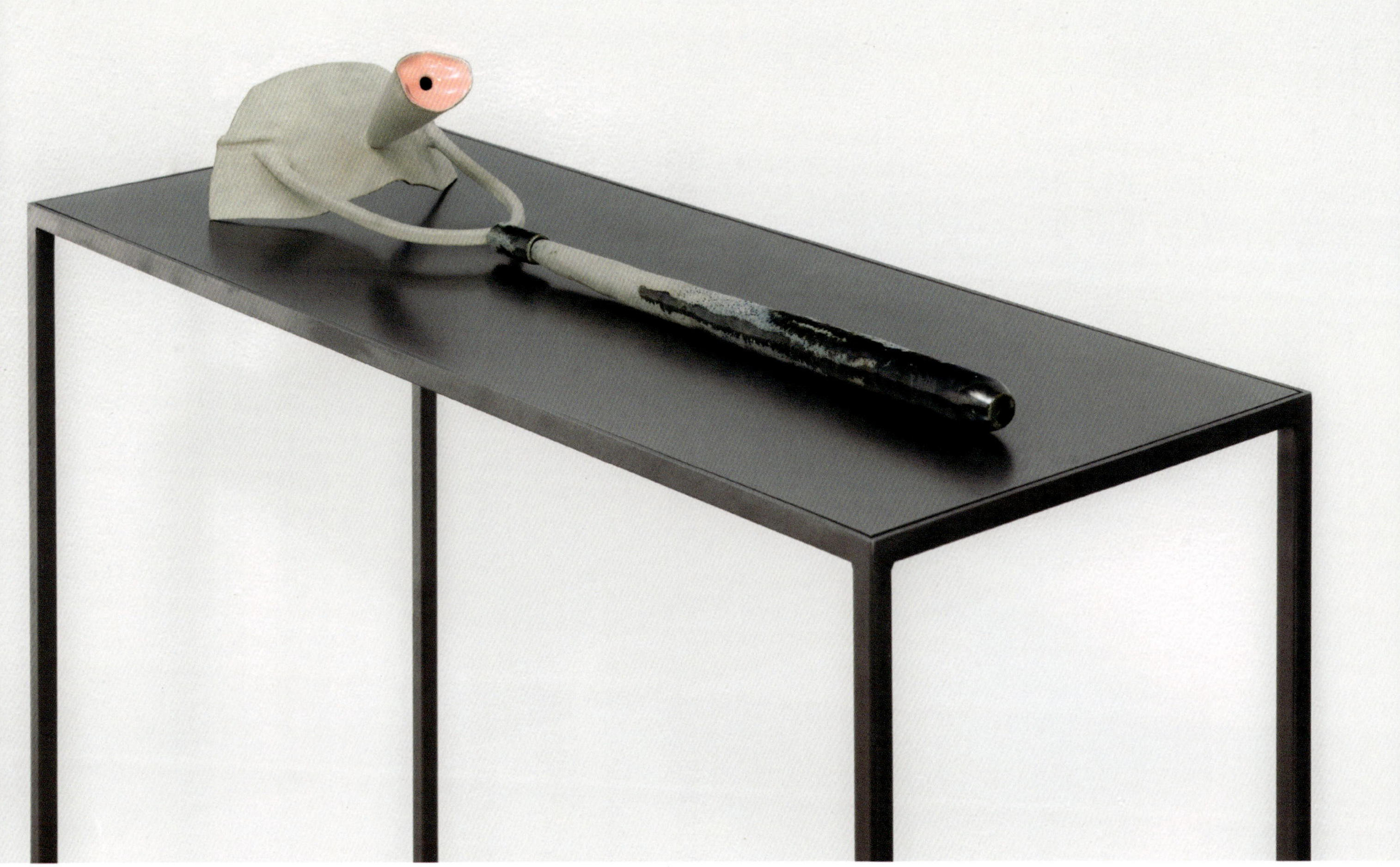

Purifier II, 2021. Ceramic, stainless steel, Sculpture 13 × 63 × 17 cm; 5 × 24⅛ × 6⅛ inches, Pedestal 94 × 71 × 28 cm; 37 × 28 × 11 inches

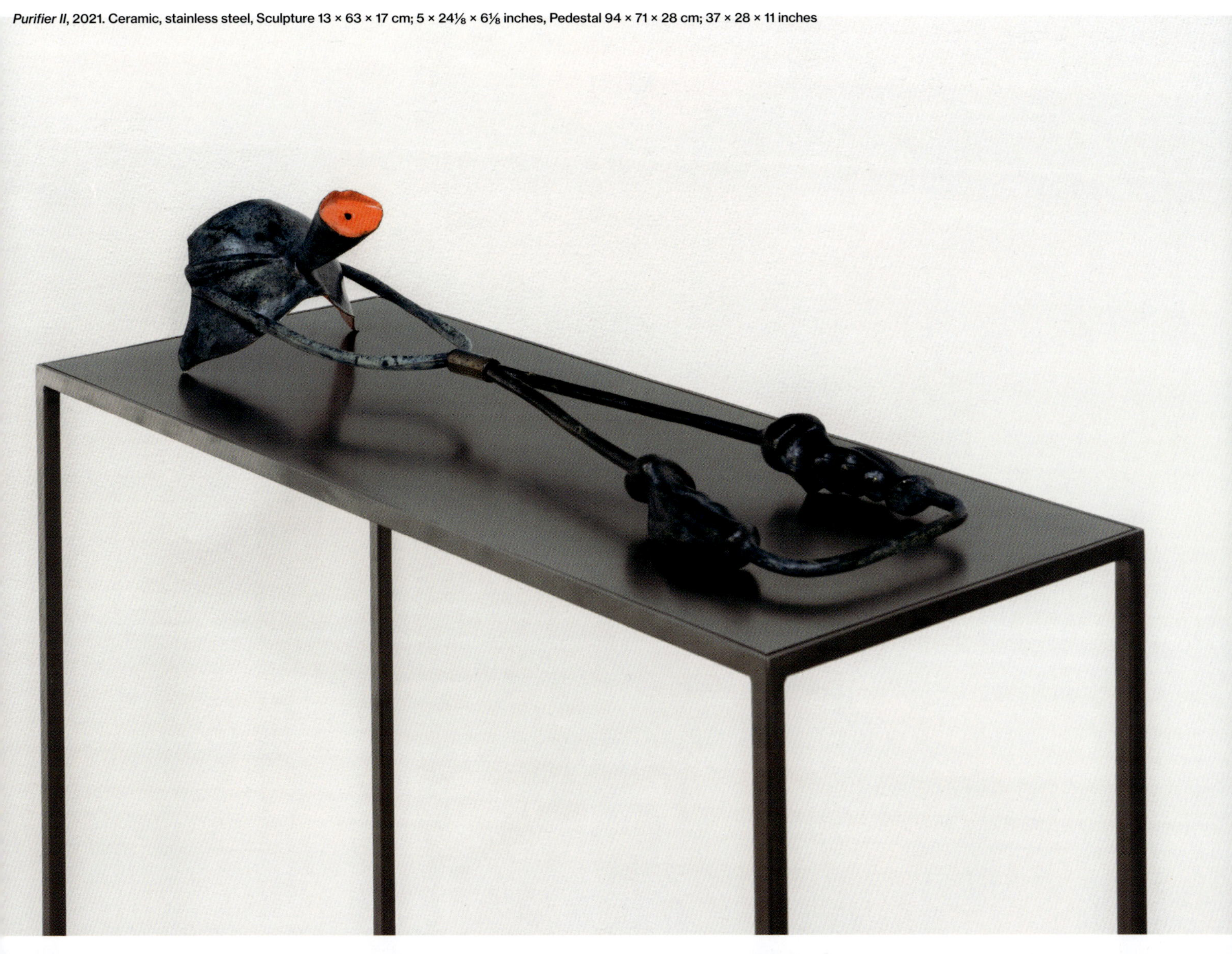

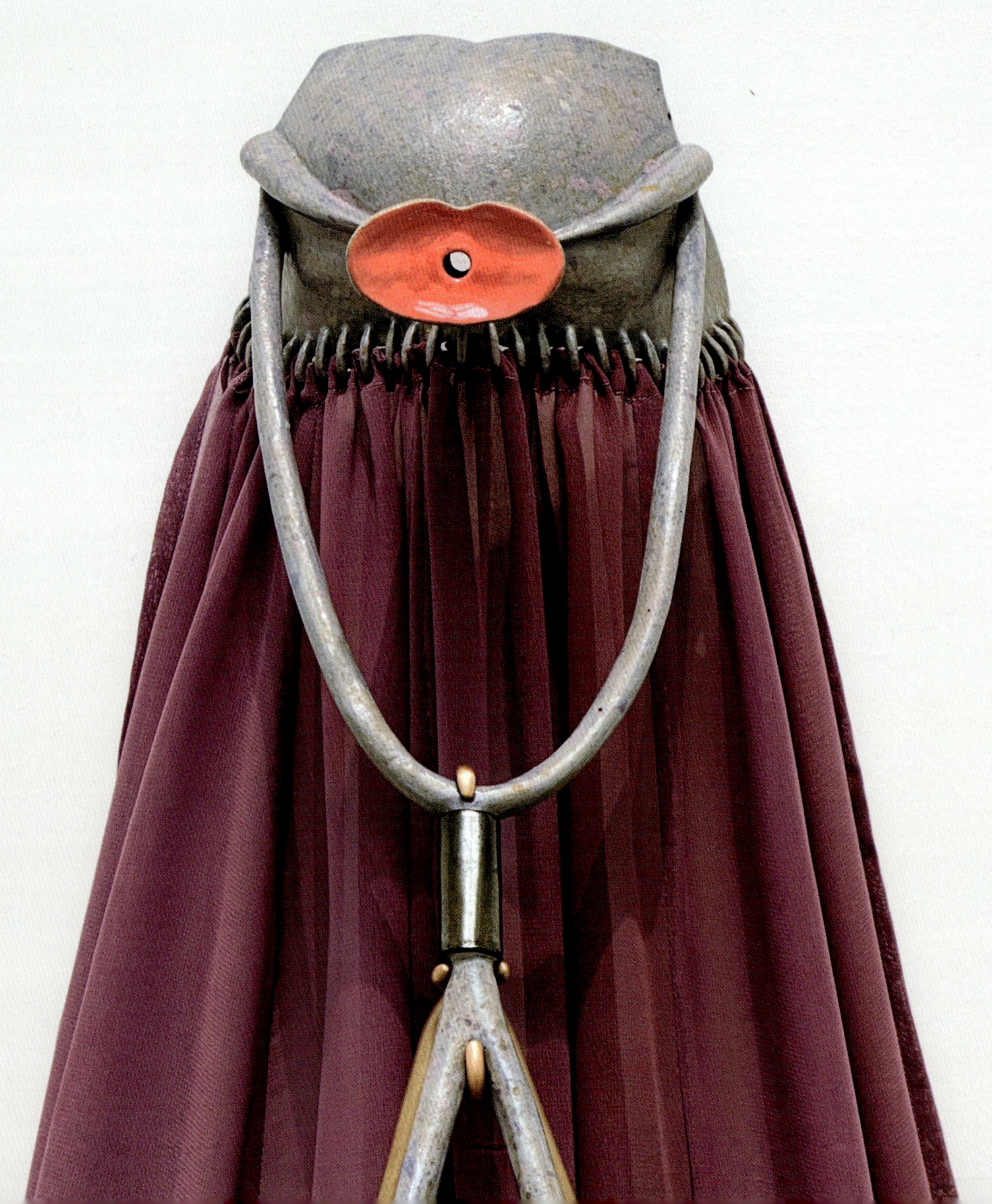

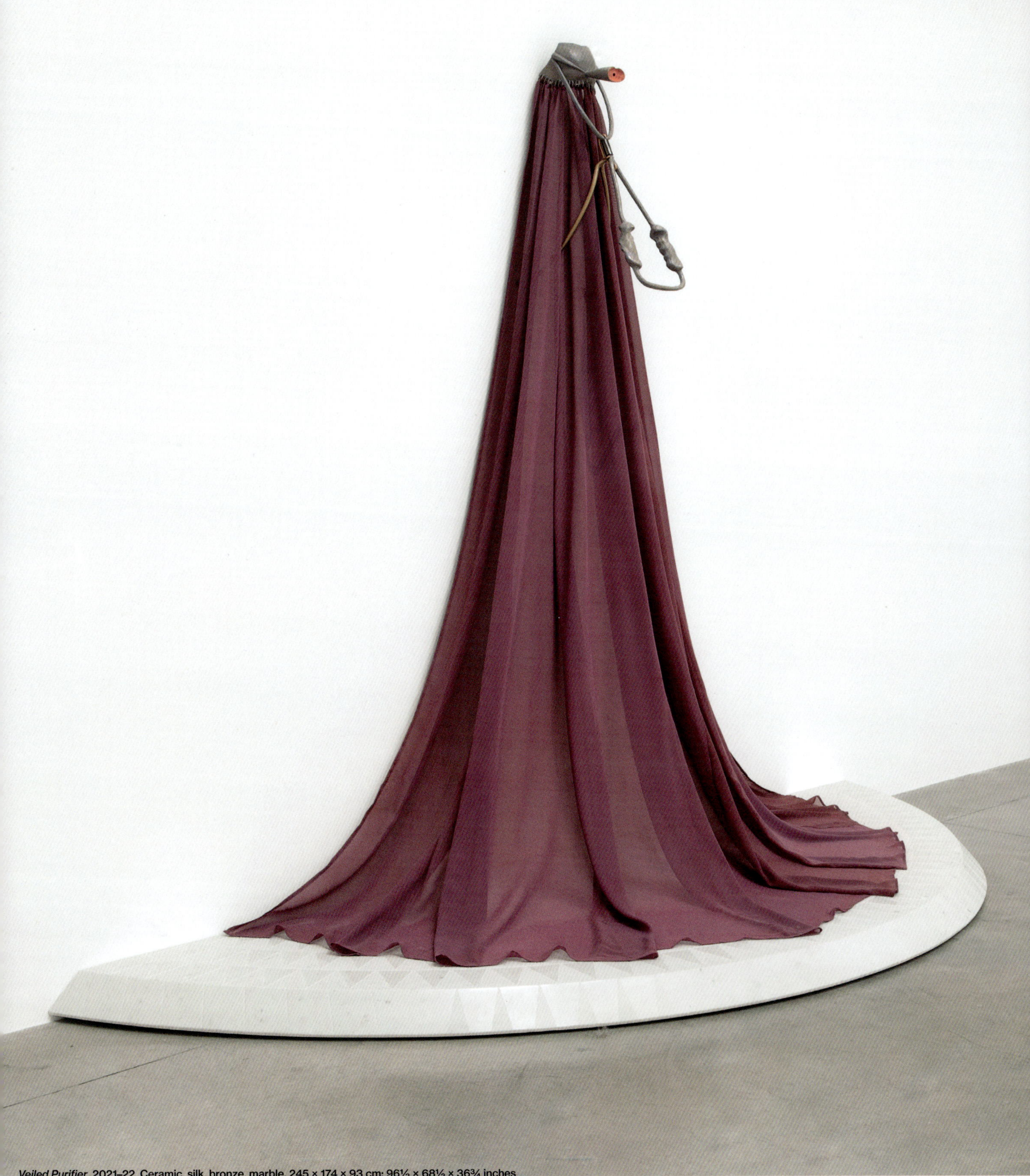

Veiled Purifier, 2021–22. Ceramic, silk, bronze, marble, 245 × 174 × 93 cm; 96½ × 68½ × 36¾ inches

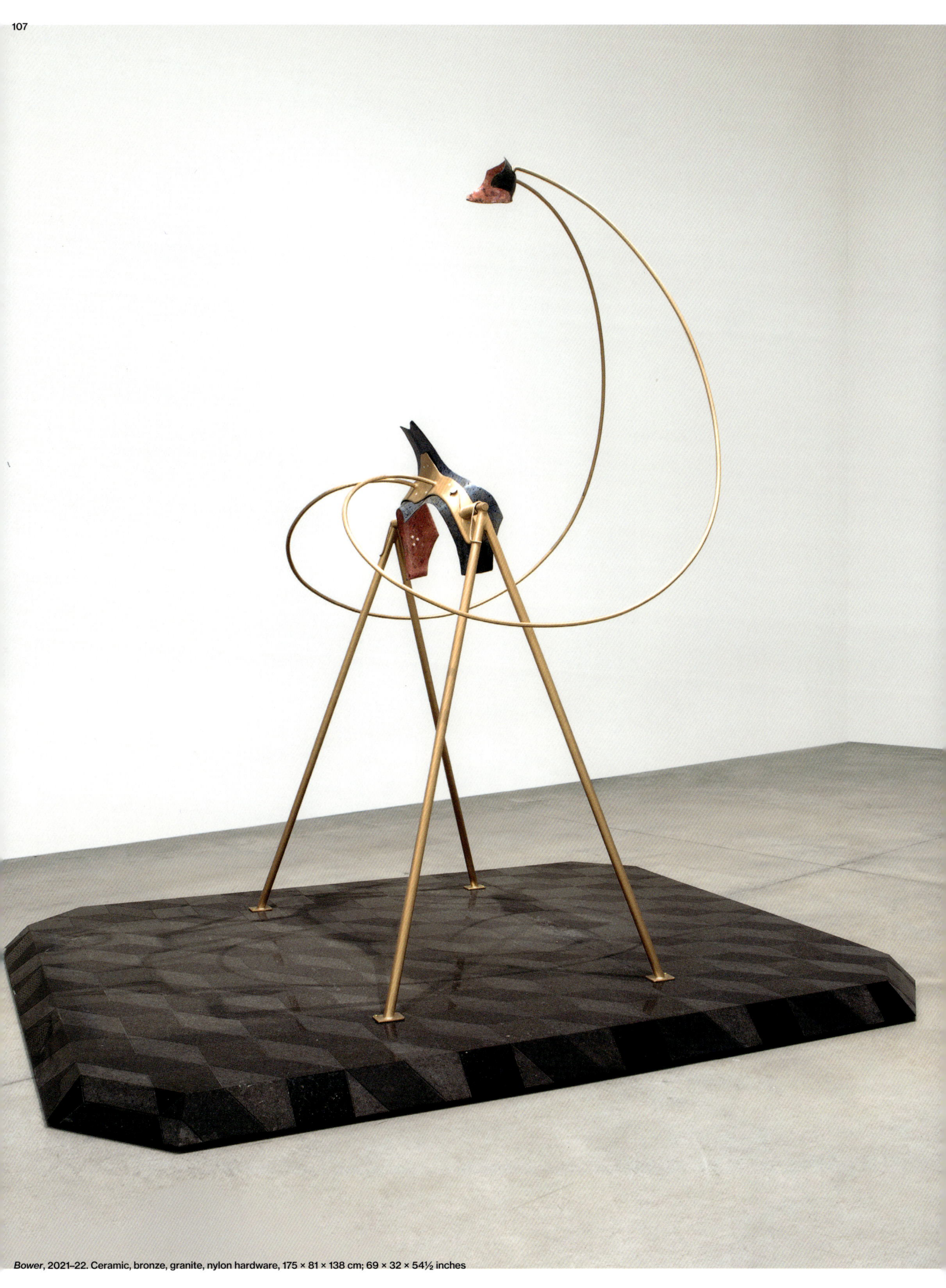

Bower, 2021–22. Ceramic, bronze, granite, nylon hardware, 175 × 81 × 138 cm; 69 × 32 × 54½ inches

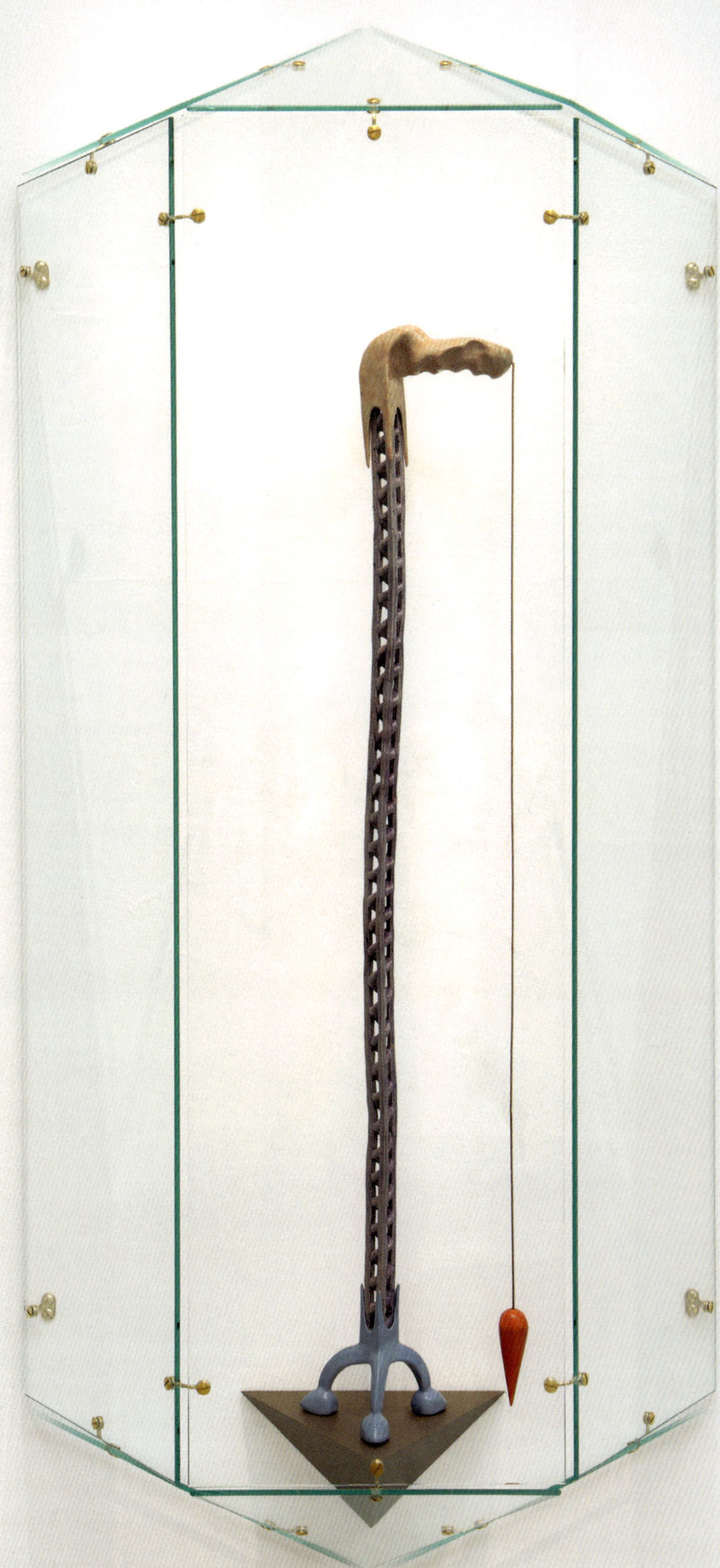

Stabilizer, 2021–22. Ceramic, bronze, brass cable, glass case, 136 × 61 × 27 cm; 53½ × 24 × 10½ inches

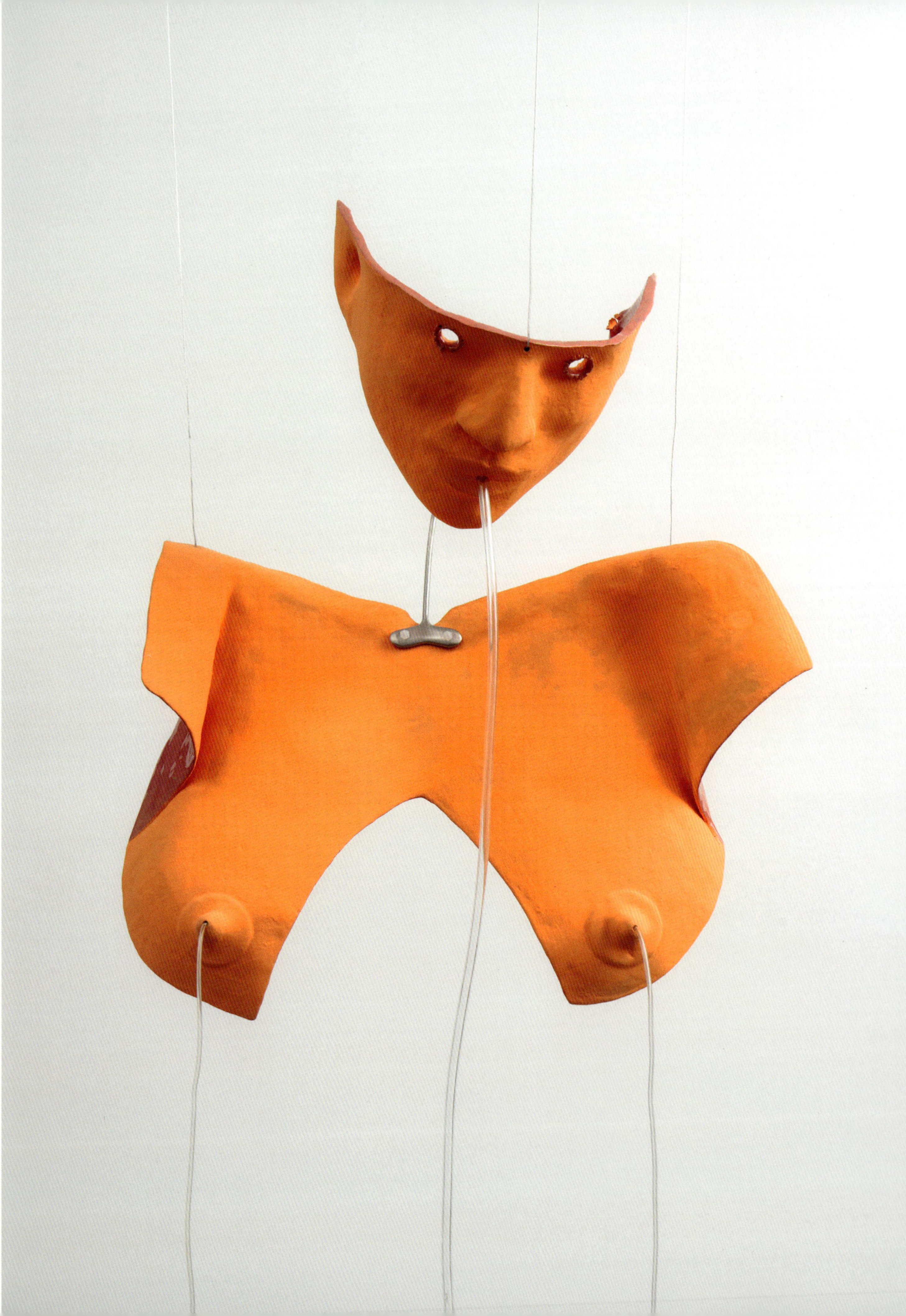

Nourisher, 2022. Ceramic, medical PVC tubes, stainless steel, steel cable, 177 × 81 × 61 cm; 69½ × 32 × 24 inches

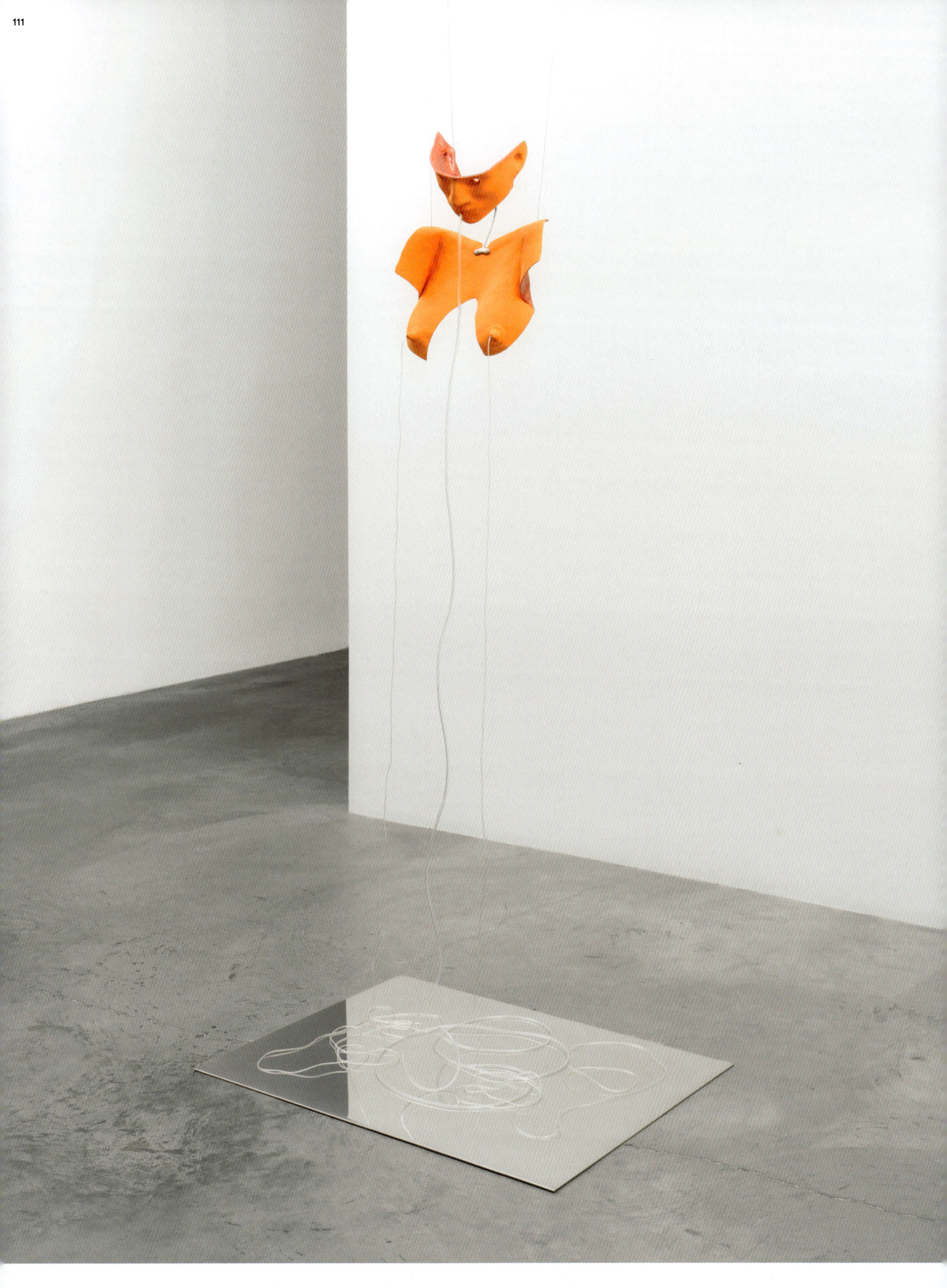

	Attachment I, 2022. Ceramic, stainless steel, 118 × 27 × 13 cm; 46½ × 10½ × 5¼ inches

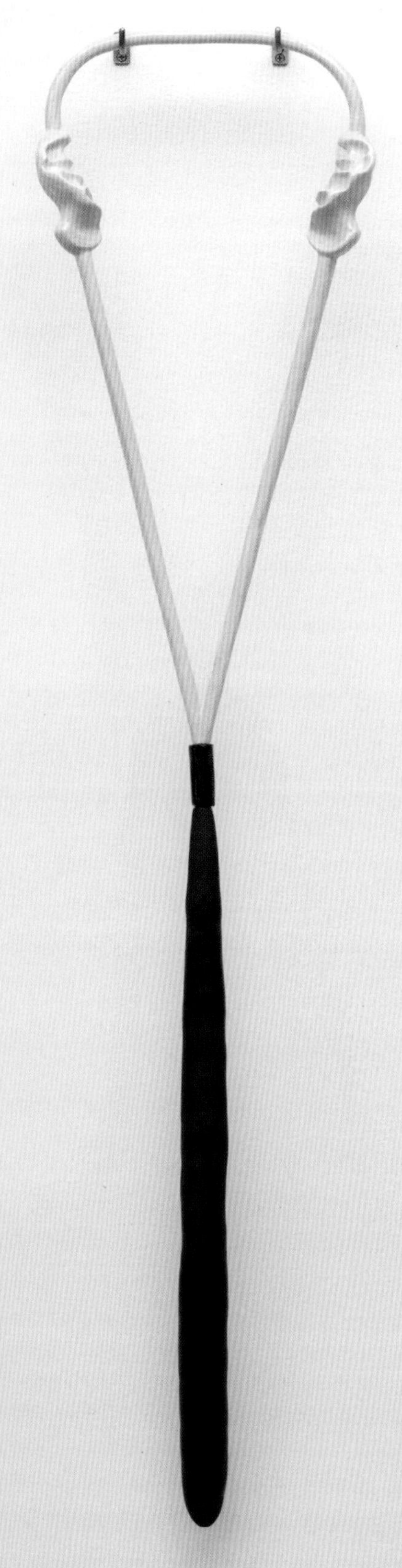

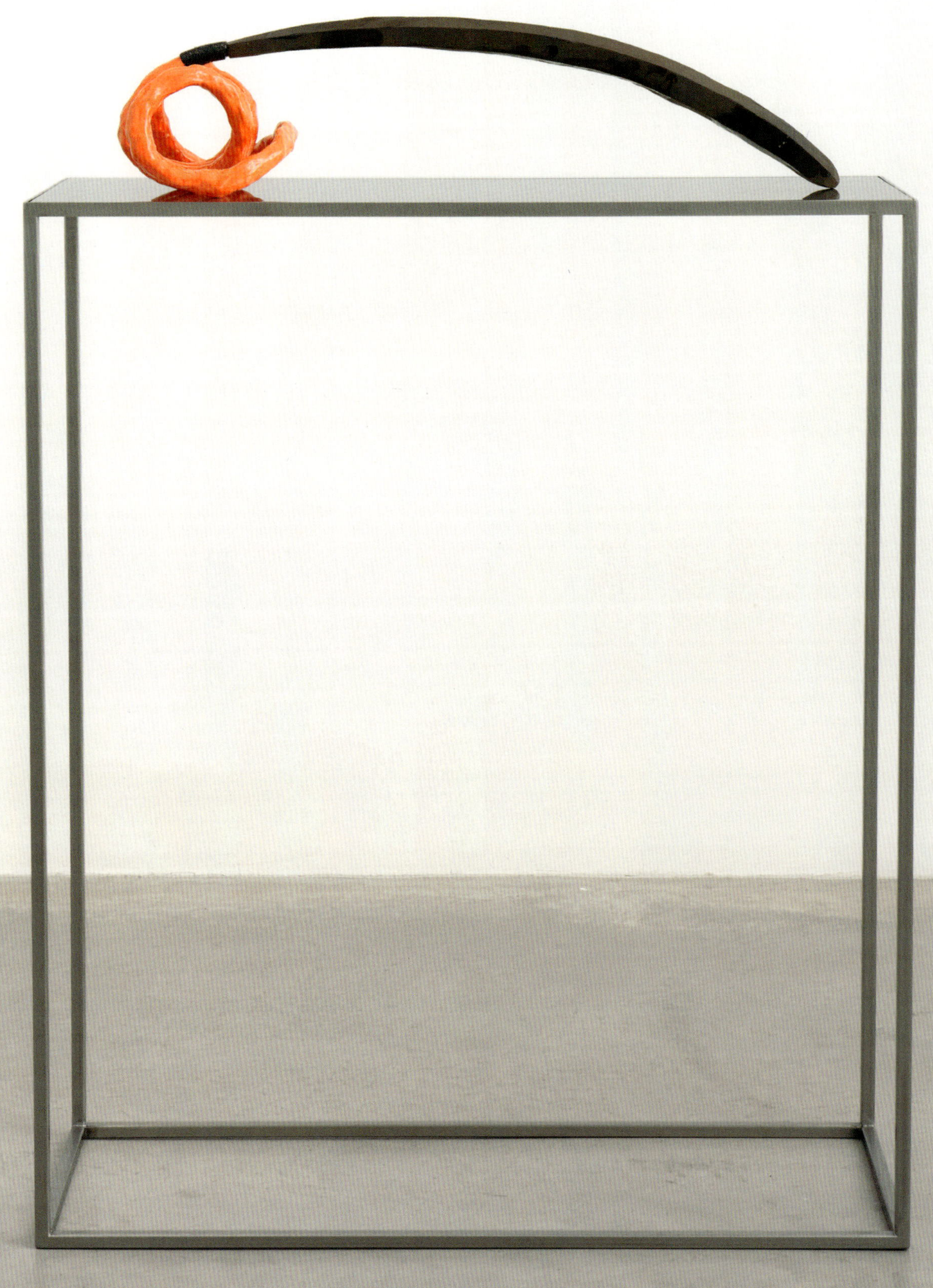

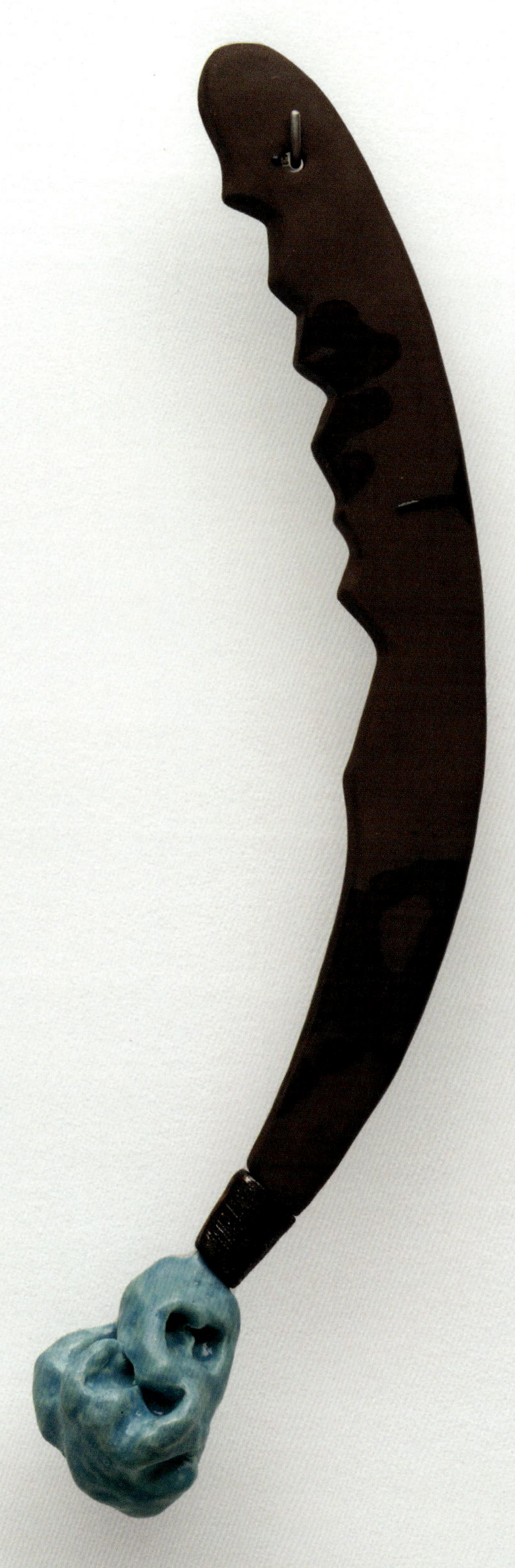

Attachment III, 2022. Ceramic, stainless steel, 65 × 20 × 13 cm; 25½ × 8 × 5 inches

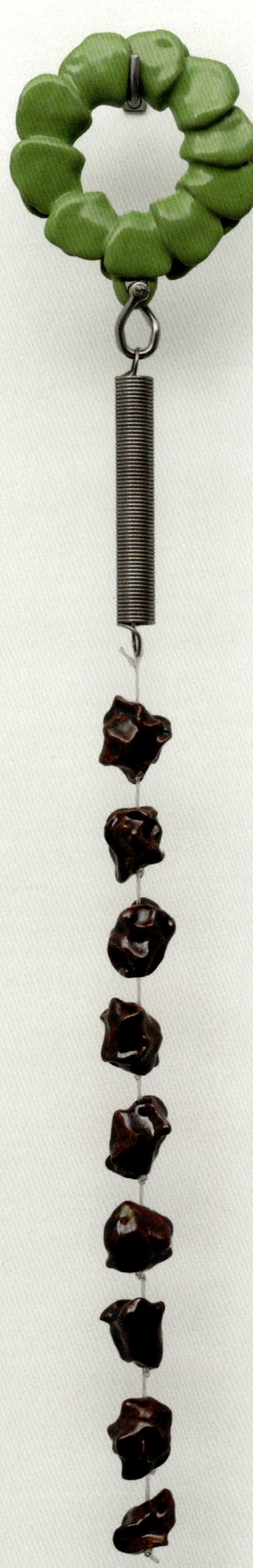

Attachment IV, Flexible, 2022. Ceramic, medical PVC tubes, stainless steel hardware, 78 × 13 × 9 cm; 30¾ × 5 × 3½ inches

Attachment V, Flexible with Quick Release, 2022. Ceramic, medical PVC tubes, stainless steel hardware, wire rope, 86 × 34 × 13 cm; 33¾ × 13½ × 5 inches

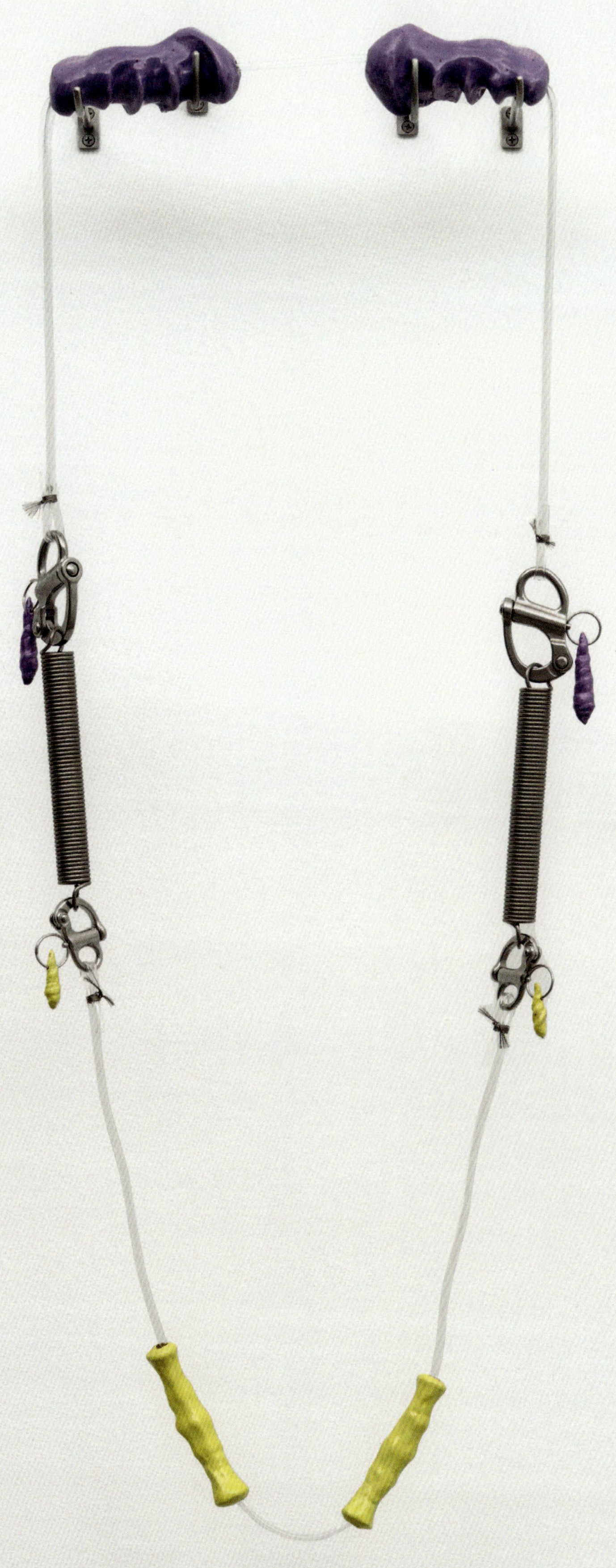

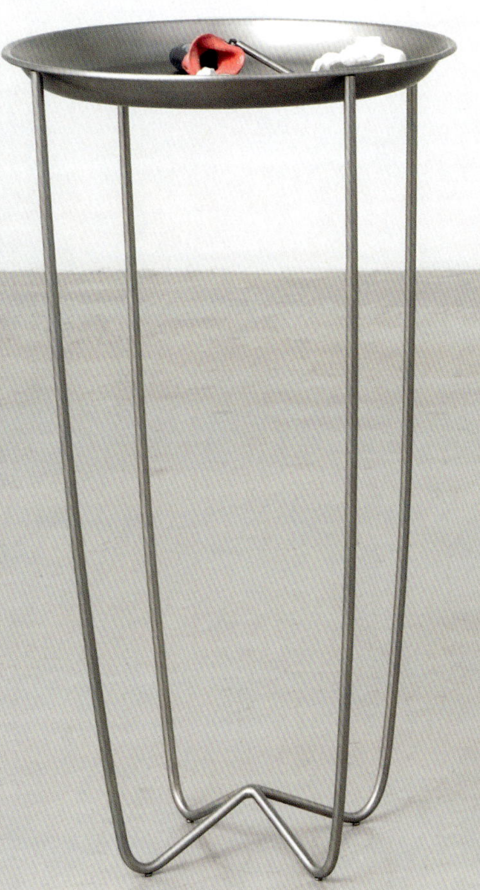

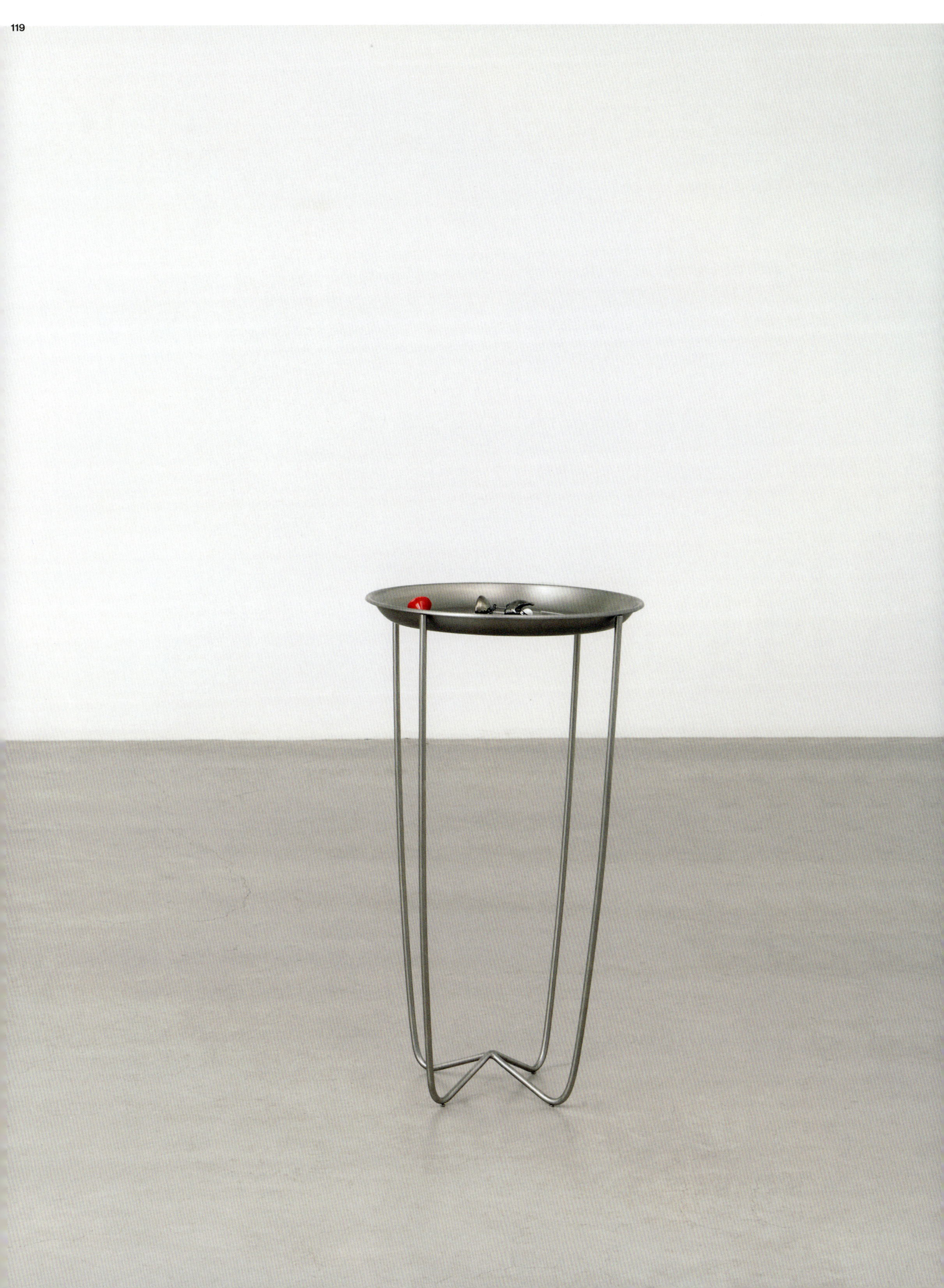

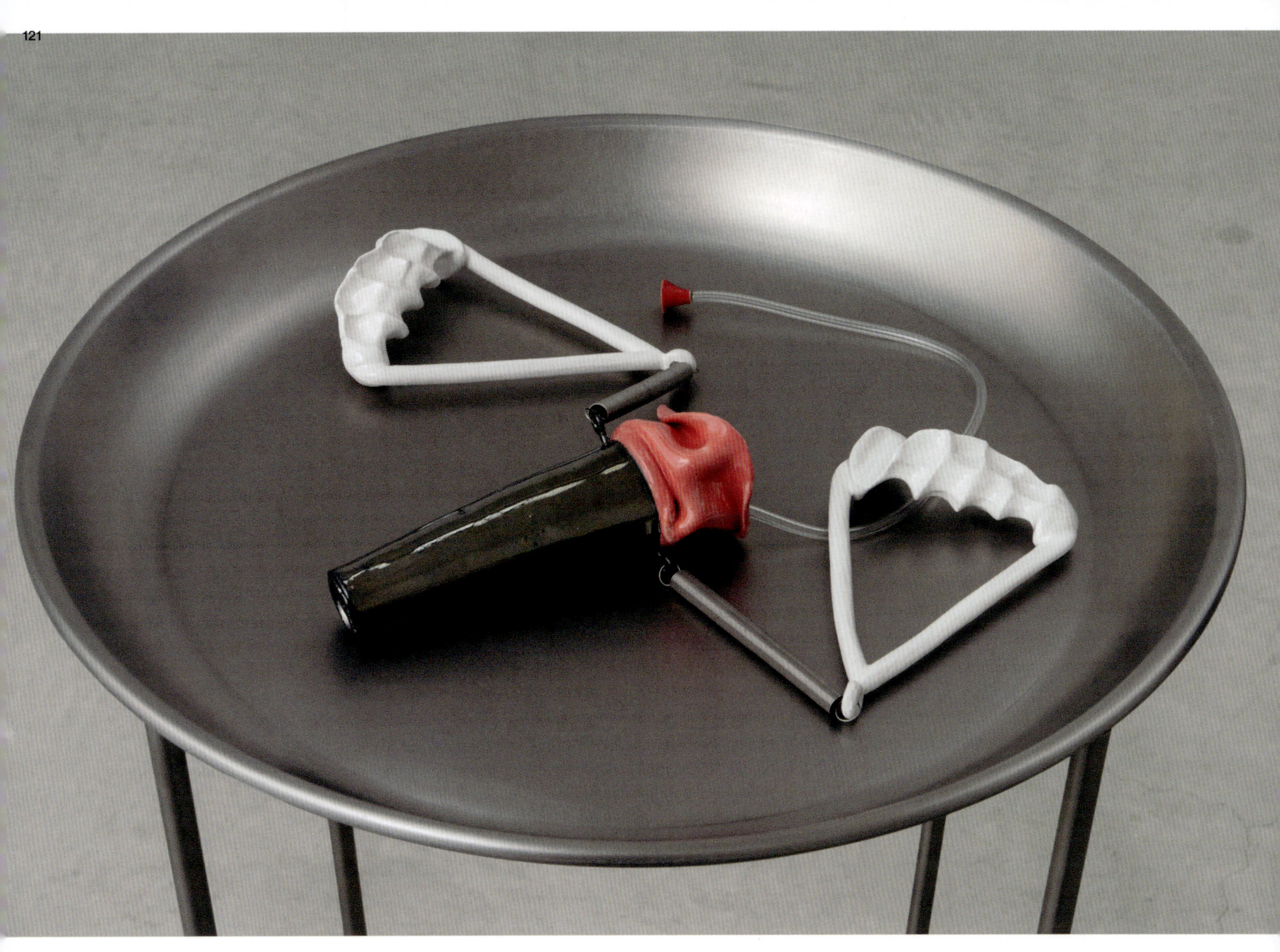

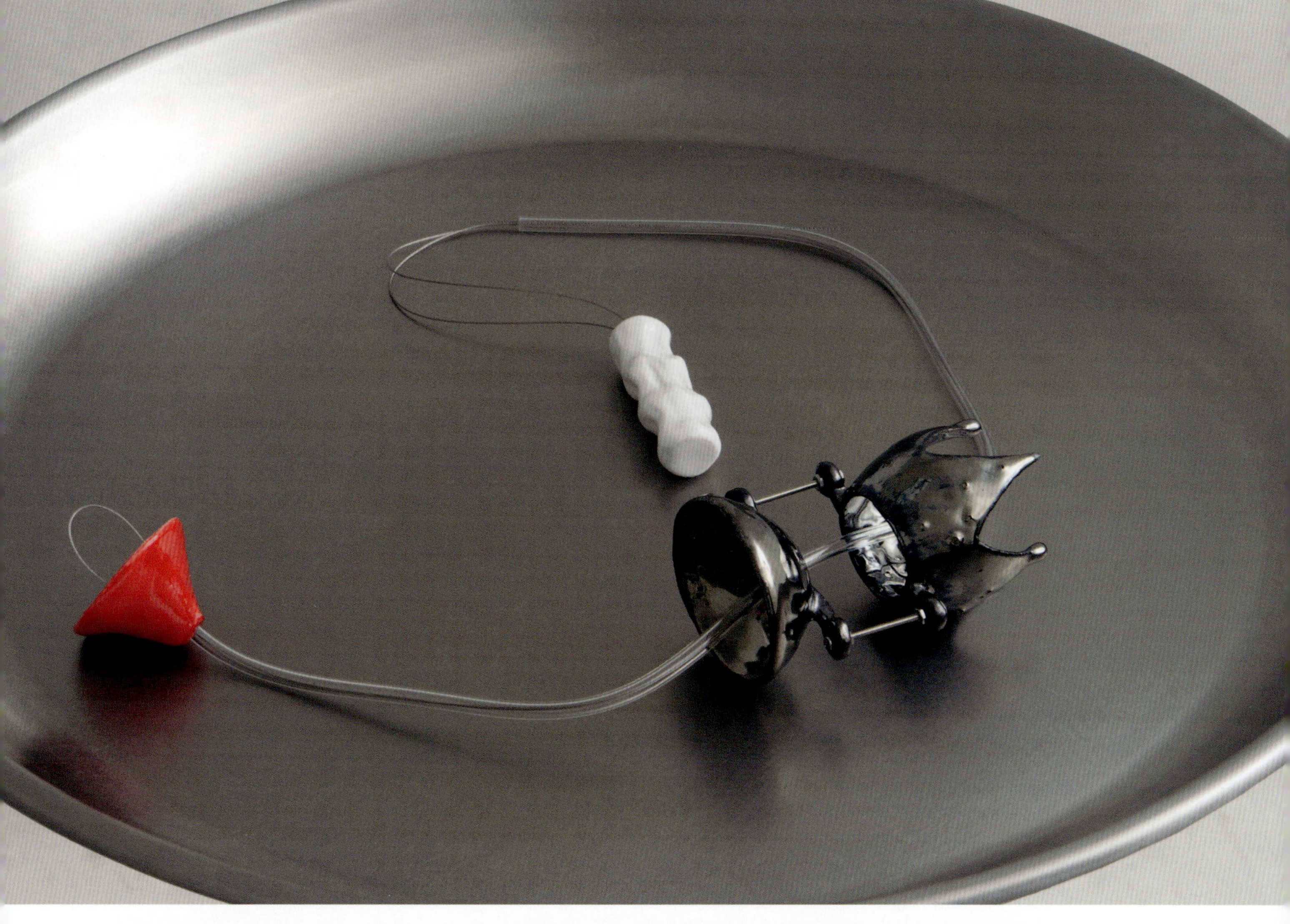

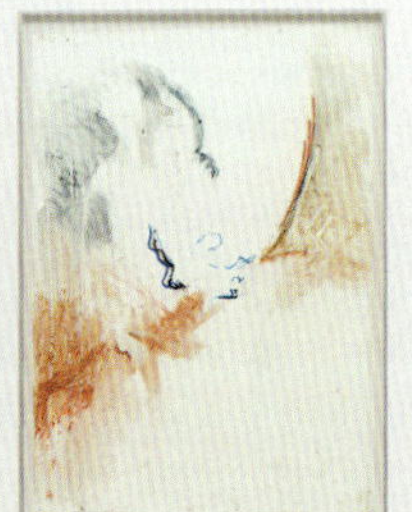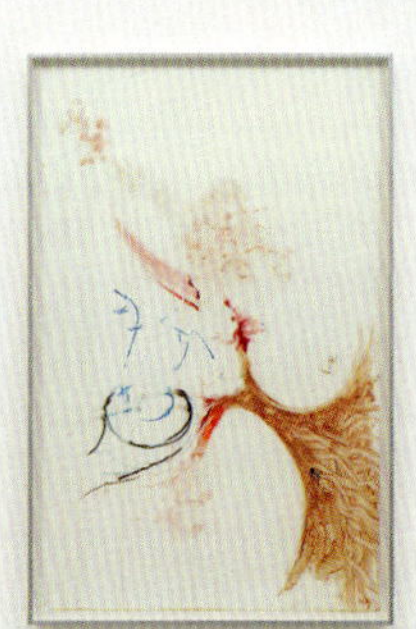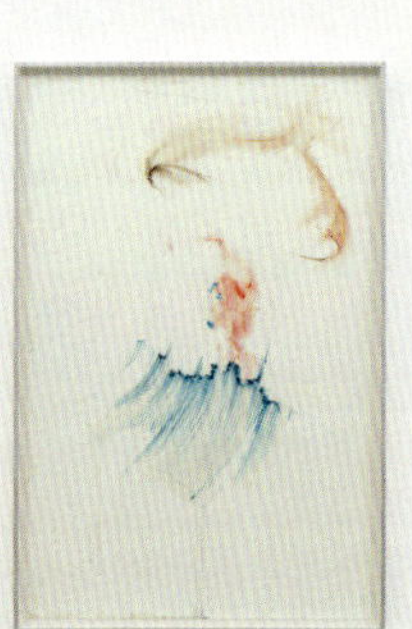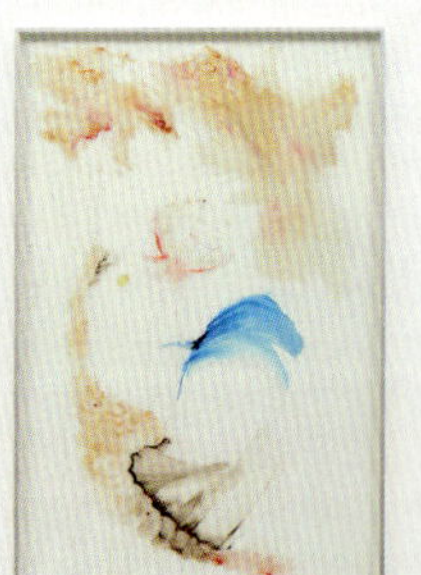

Me, Ourself & You, installation view, Matthew Marks Gallery, New York, 2022 © Julia Phillips, courtesy of Matthew Marks Gallery

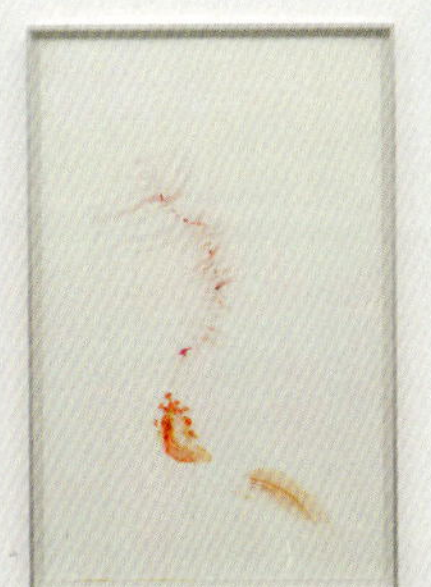 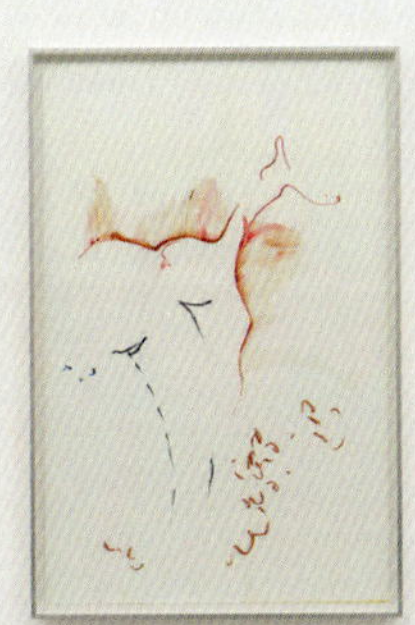 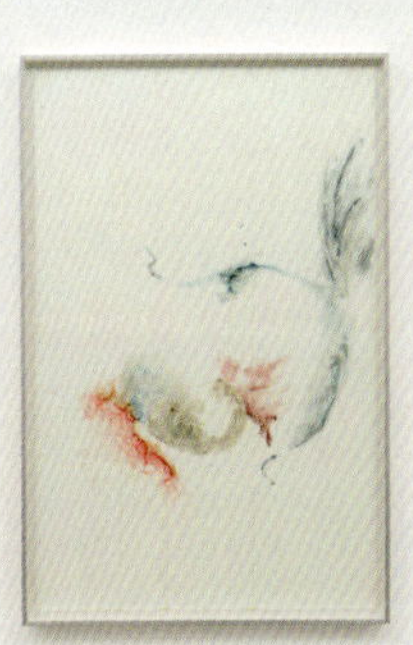 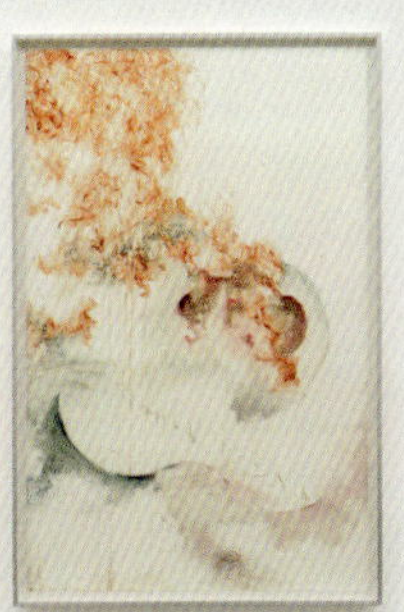

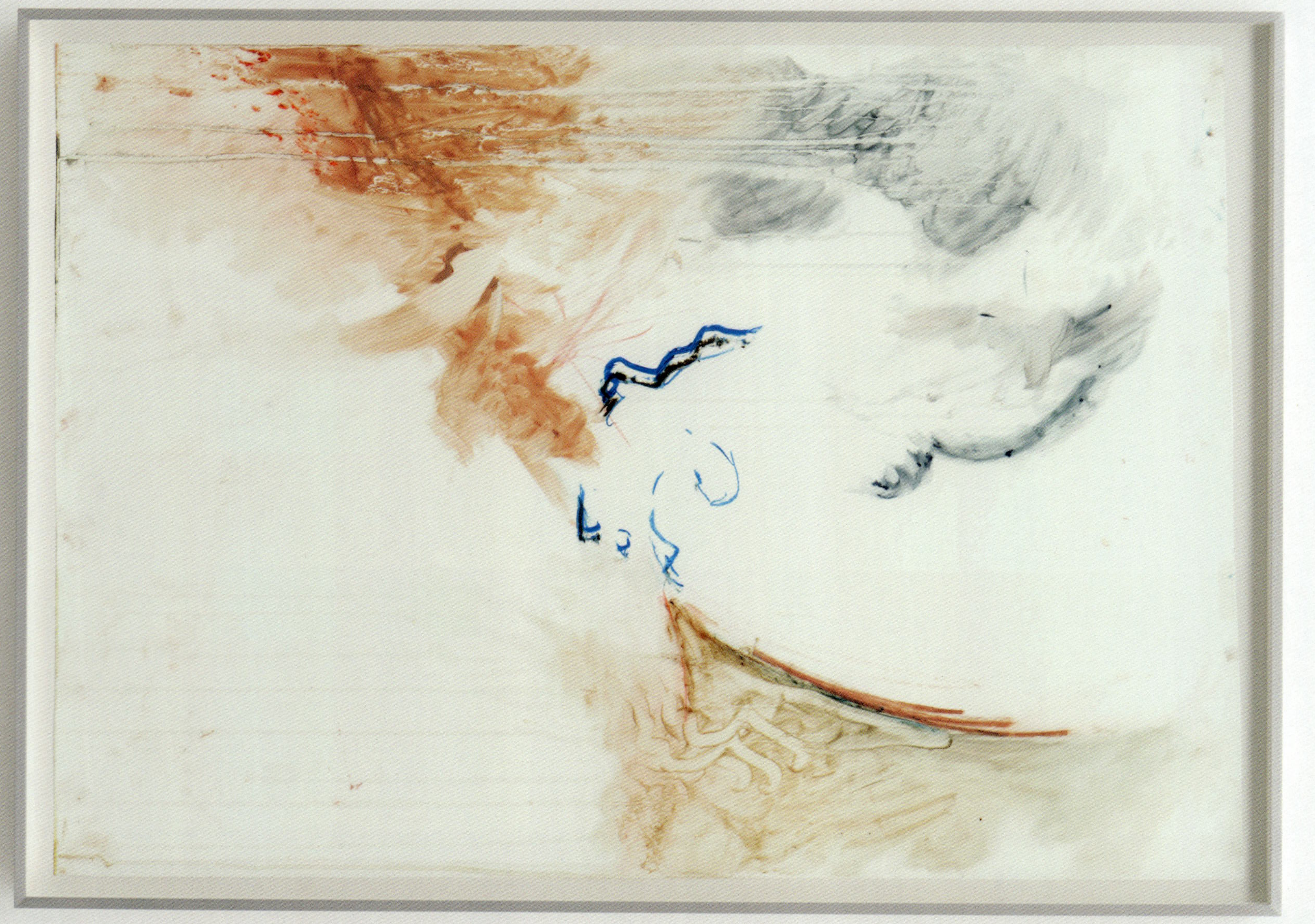

Conception Drawing I (Within Between?), 2020–21. Oil pastel and vegetable oil on Dura-Lar in artist's frame, 97 × 68 cm; 38 × 26⅞ inches

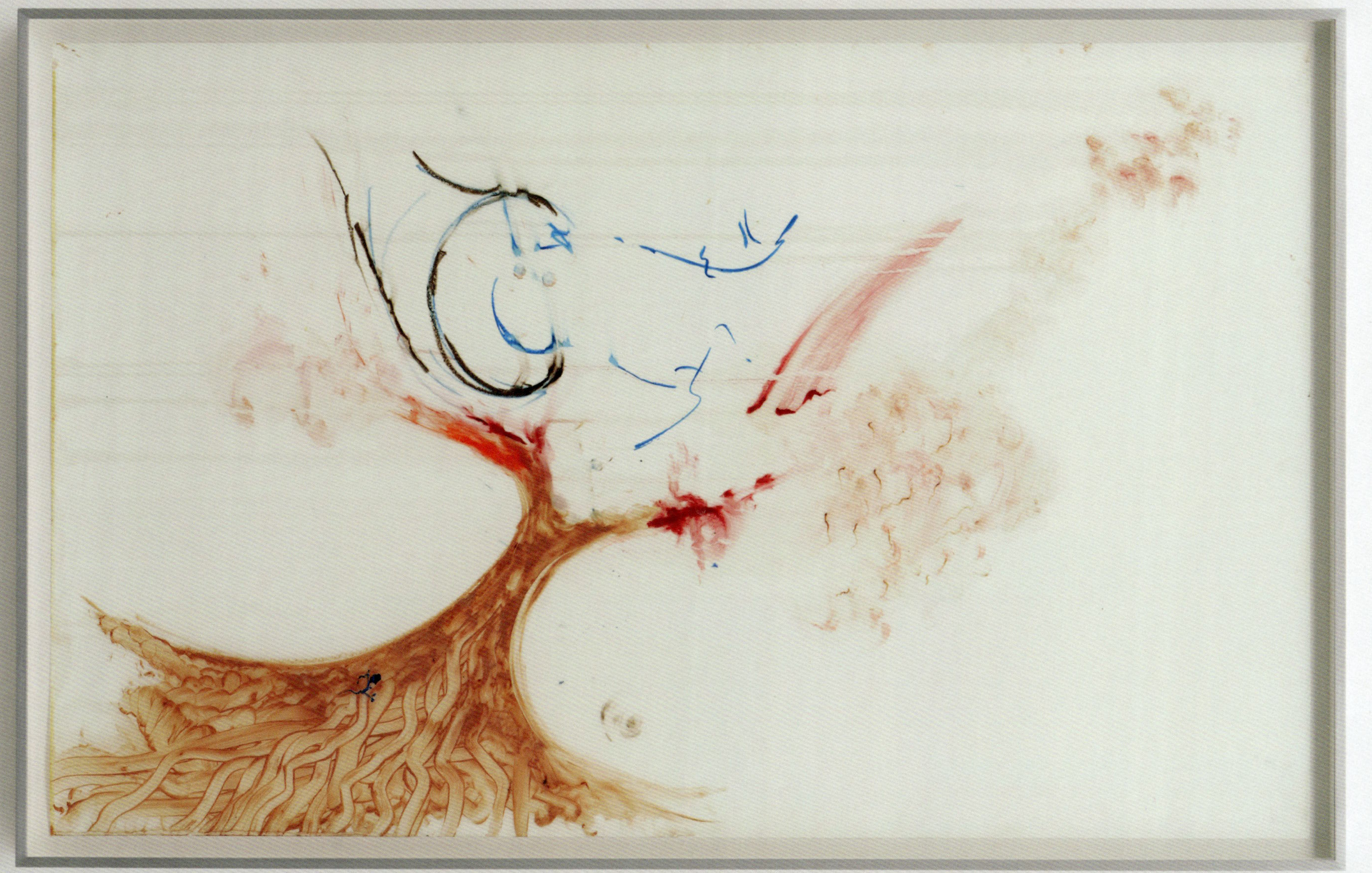

Conception Drawing II (Tissue?), 2020–21. Oil pastel and vegetable oil on Dura-Lar in artist's frame, 106 × 68 cm; 42 × 27 inches

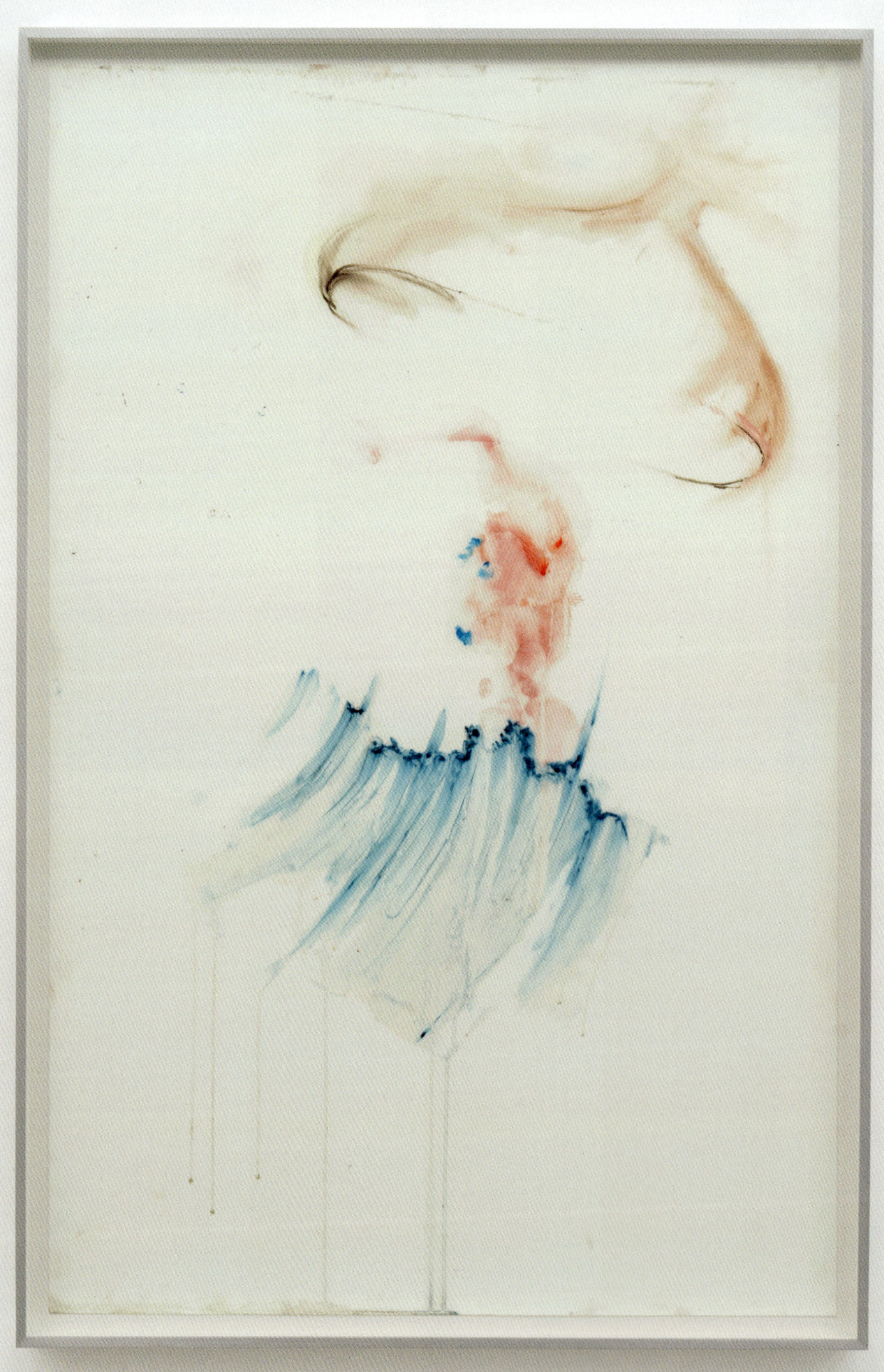

Conception Drawing III (Tube Suck / Float?), 2020–21. Oil pastel and vegetable oil on Dura-Lar in artist's frame, 106 × 68 cm; 42 × 27 inches

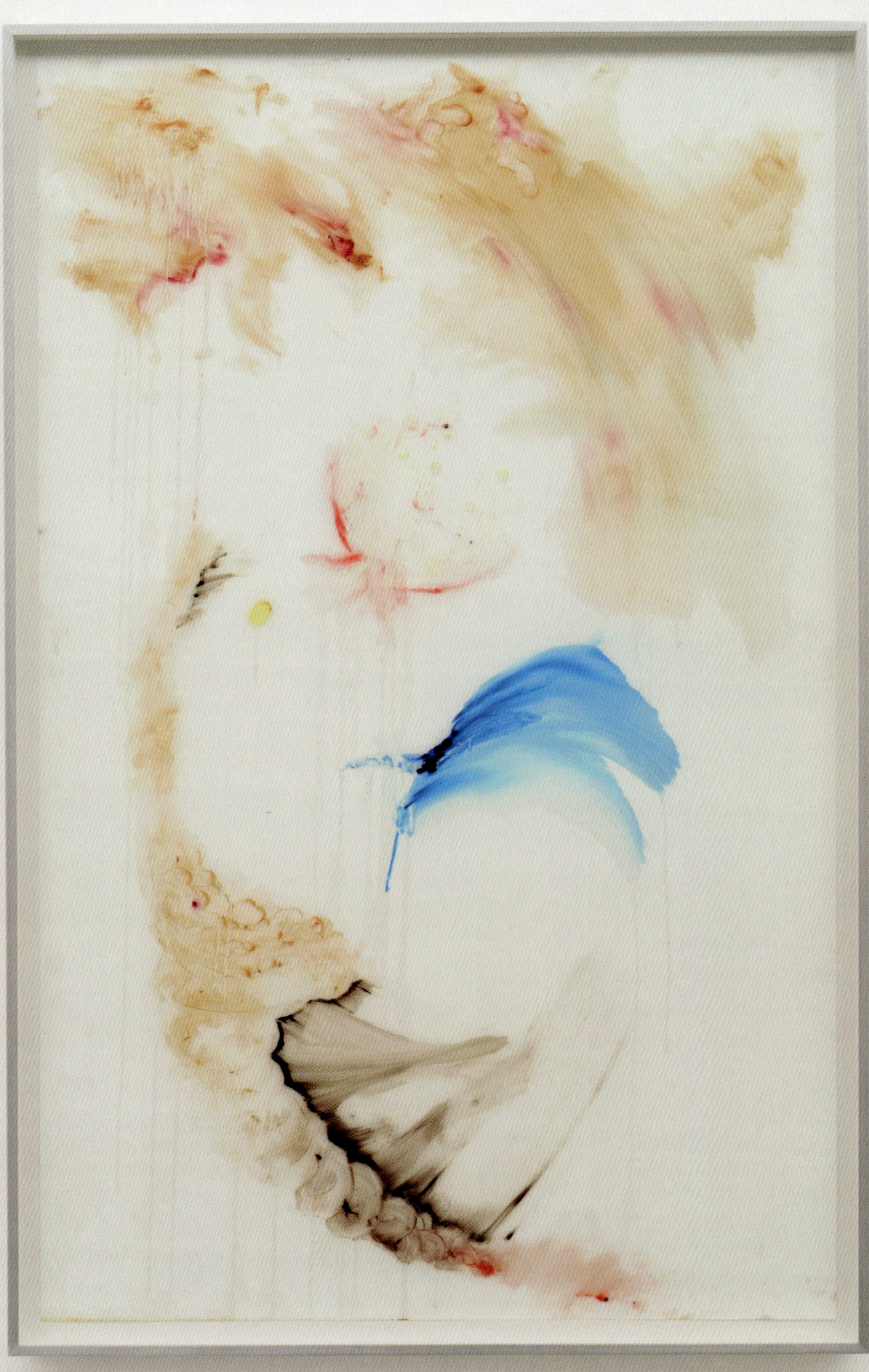

Conception Drawing IV (Ovulation / Eisprung?), 2020–21. Oil pastel and vegetable oil on Dura-Lar in artist's frame, 106 × 68 cm; 42 × 27 inches

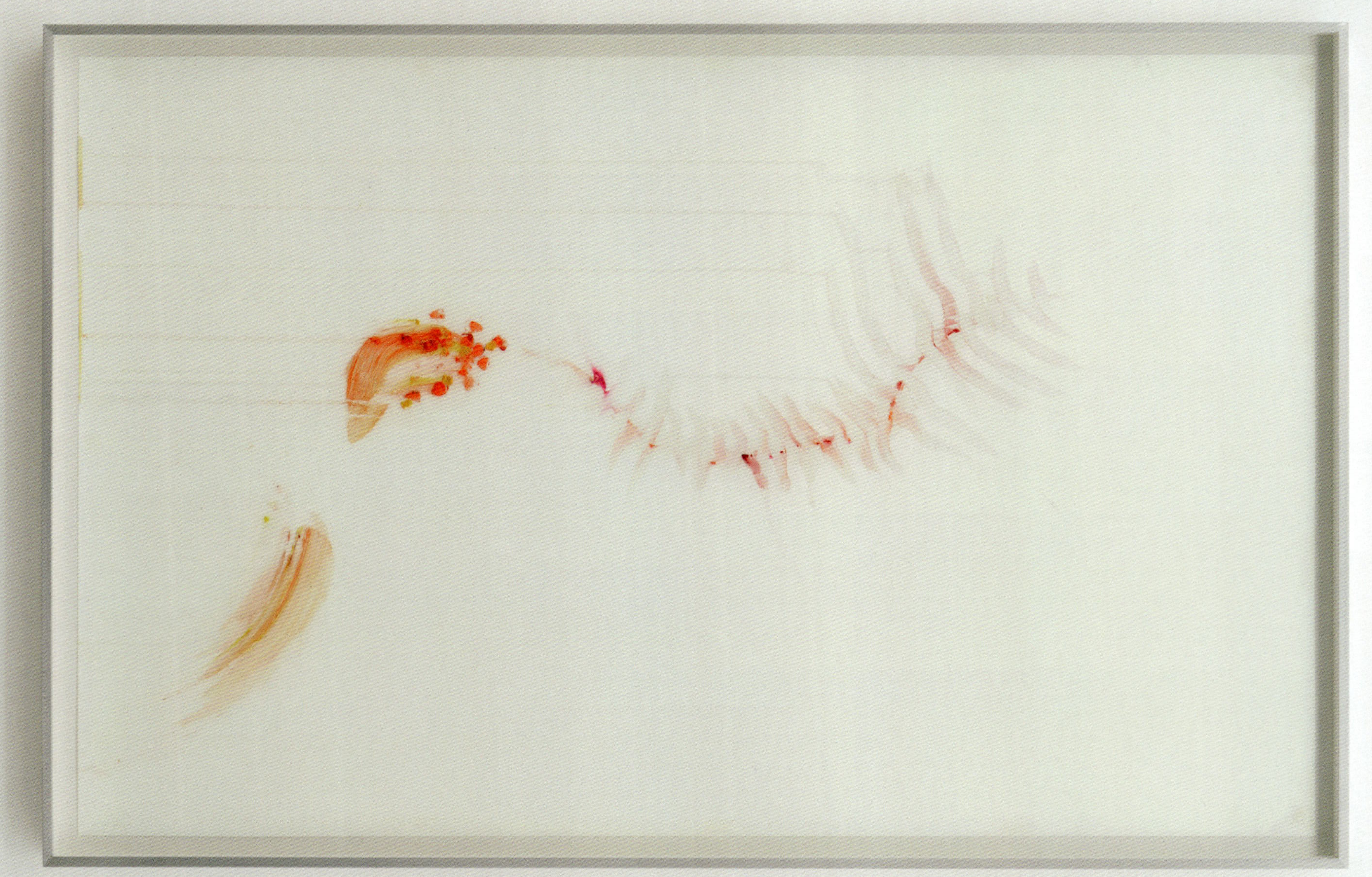

Conception Drawing V (Any Egg for a Big Flush?), 2020–21. Oil pastel and vegetable oil on Dura-Lar in artist's frame, 106 × 68 cm; 42 × 27 inches

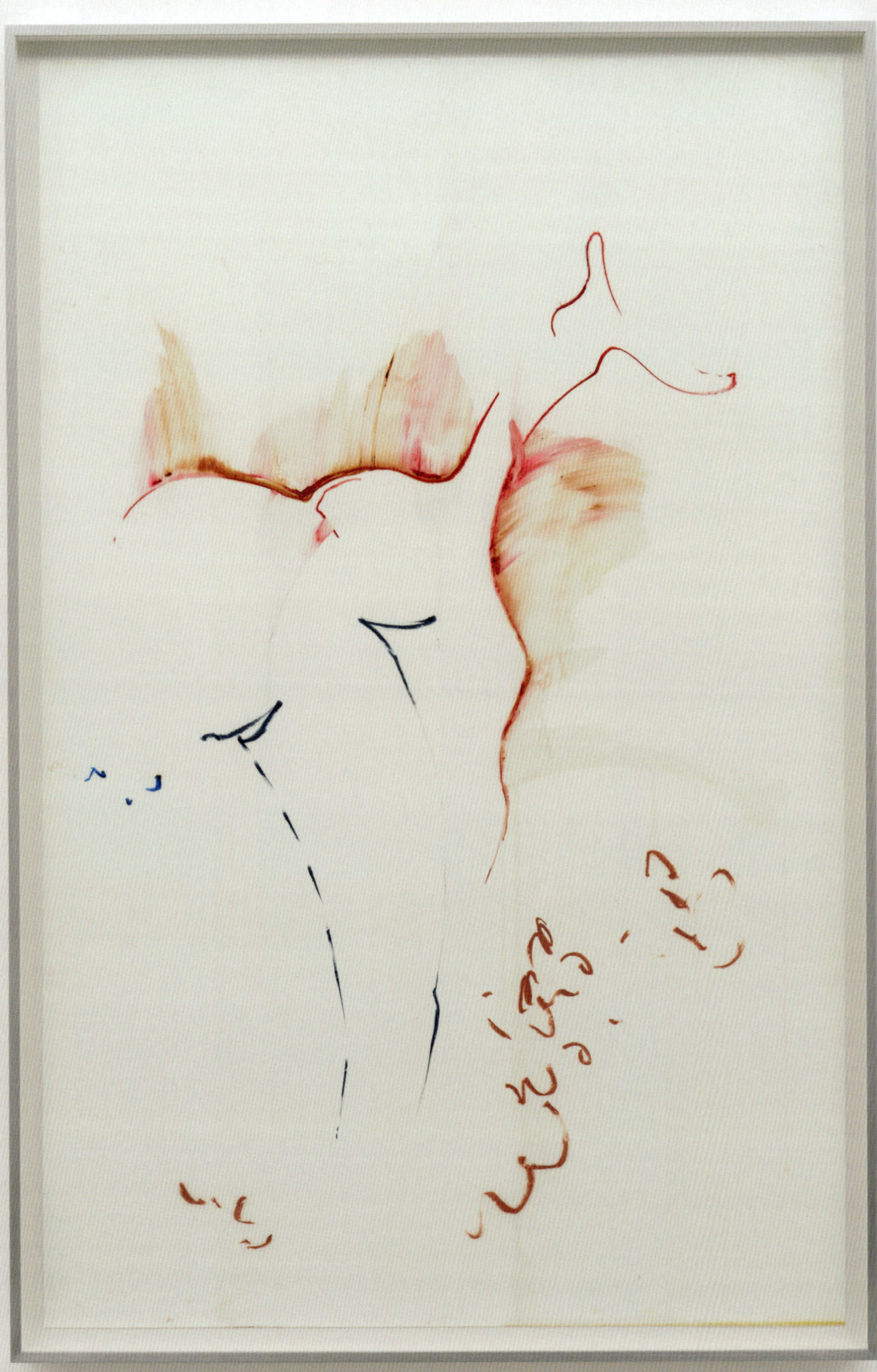

Conception Drawing VI (Soft Tubes?), 2020–21. Oil pastel and vegetable oil on Dura-Lar in artist's frame, 106 × 68 cm; 42 × 27 inches

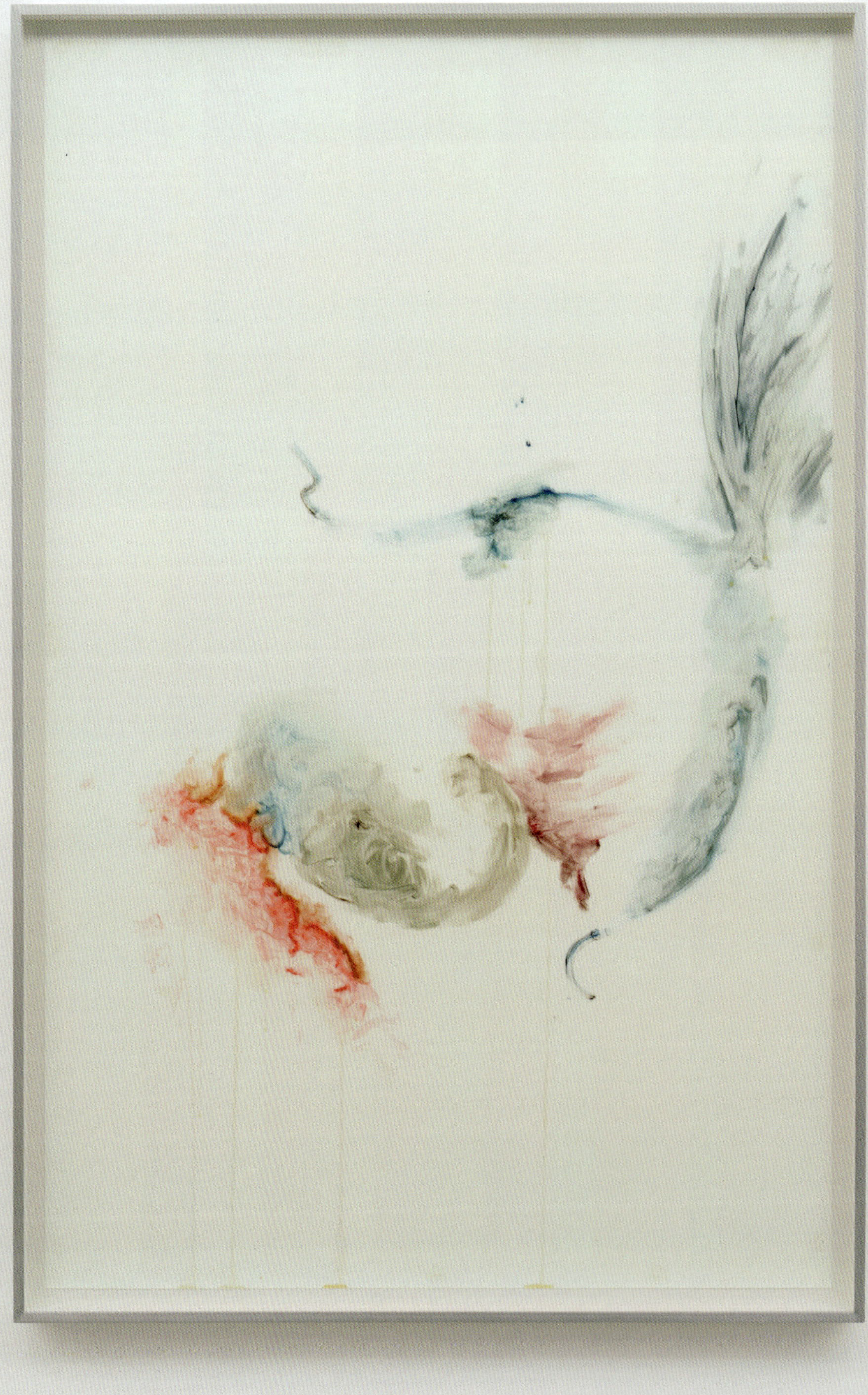

Conception Drawing VII (Implantation?), 2020–21. Oil pastel and vegetable oil on Dura-Lar in artist's frame, 106 × 68 cm; 42 × 27 inches

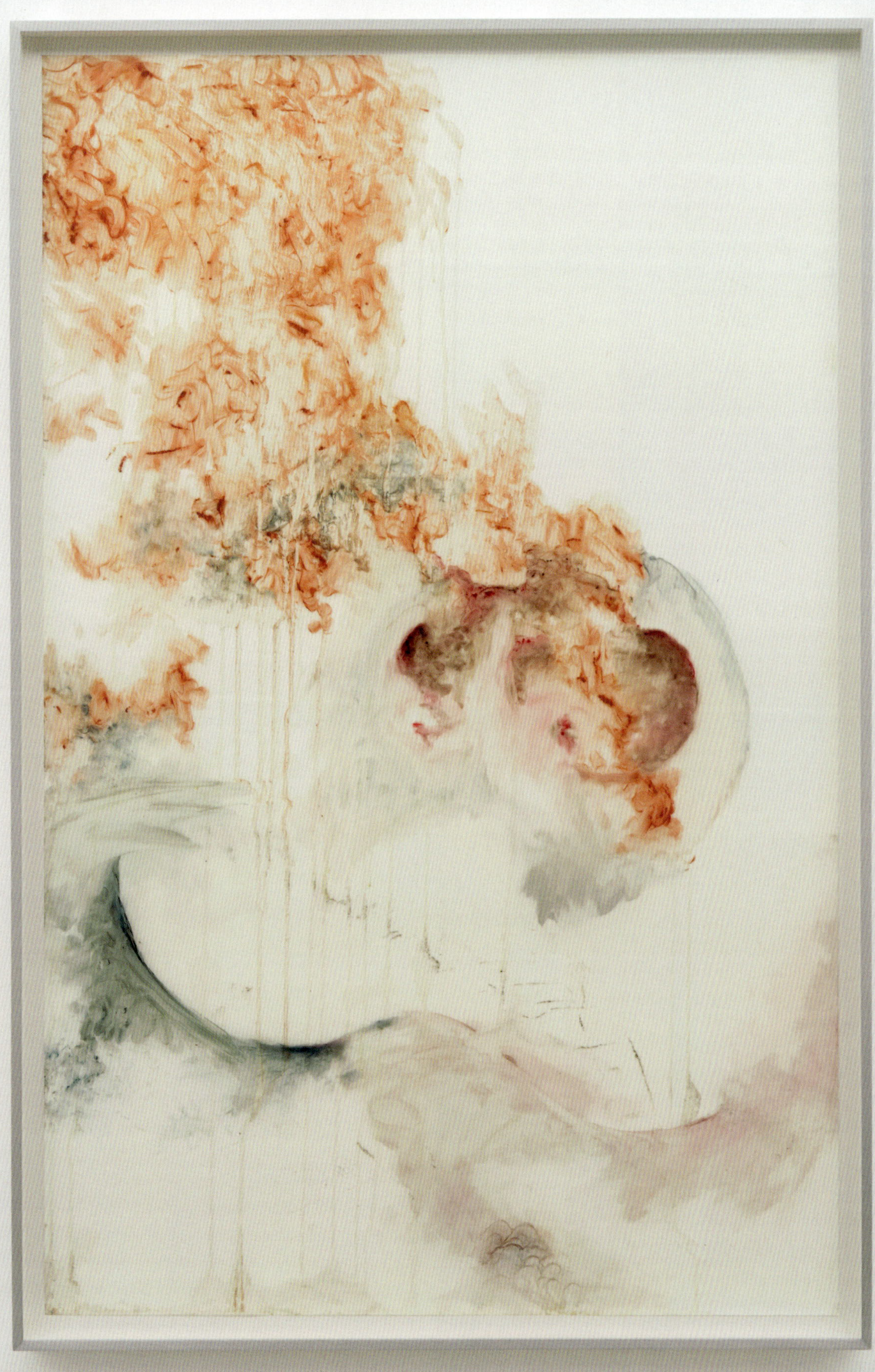

Conception Drawing VIII (Cell Accumulation / Embryo?), 2020–21. Oil pastel and vegetable oil on Dura-Lar in artist's frame, 106 × 68 cm; 42 × 27 inches

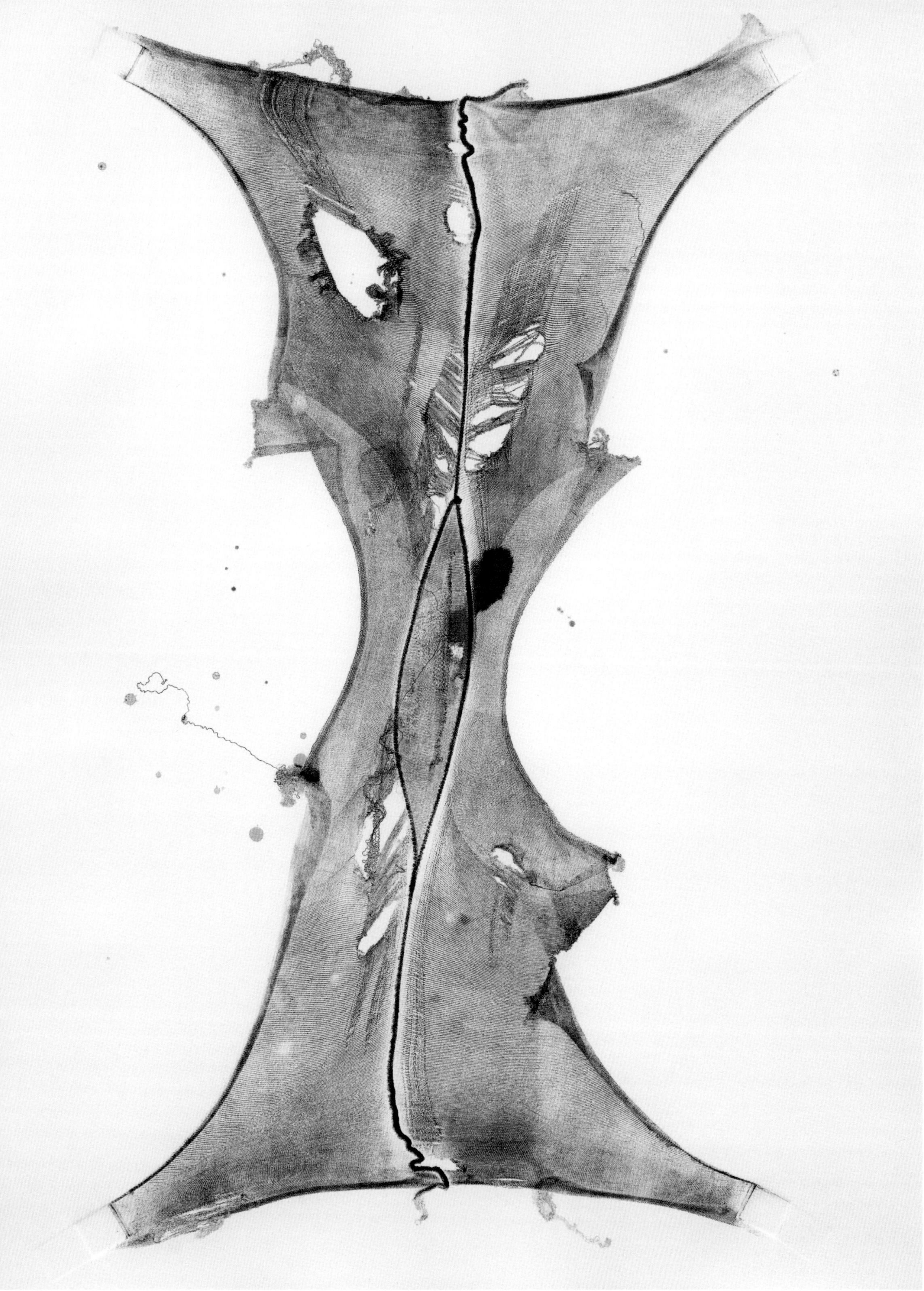

Expanded X, Treated Twice, 2018. Four collagraphs with blind embossing in artist's frames, 80 × 61 cm; 31¾ × 24⅛ inches each

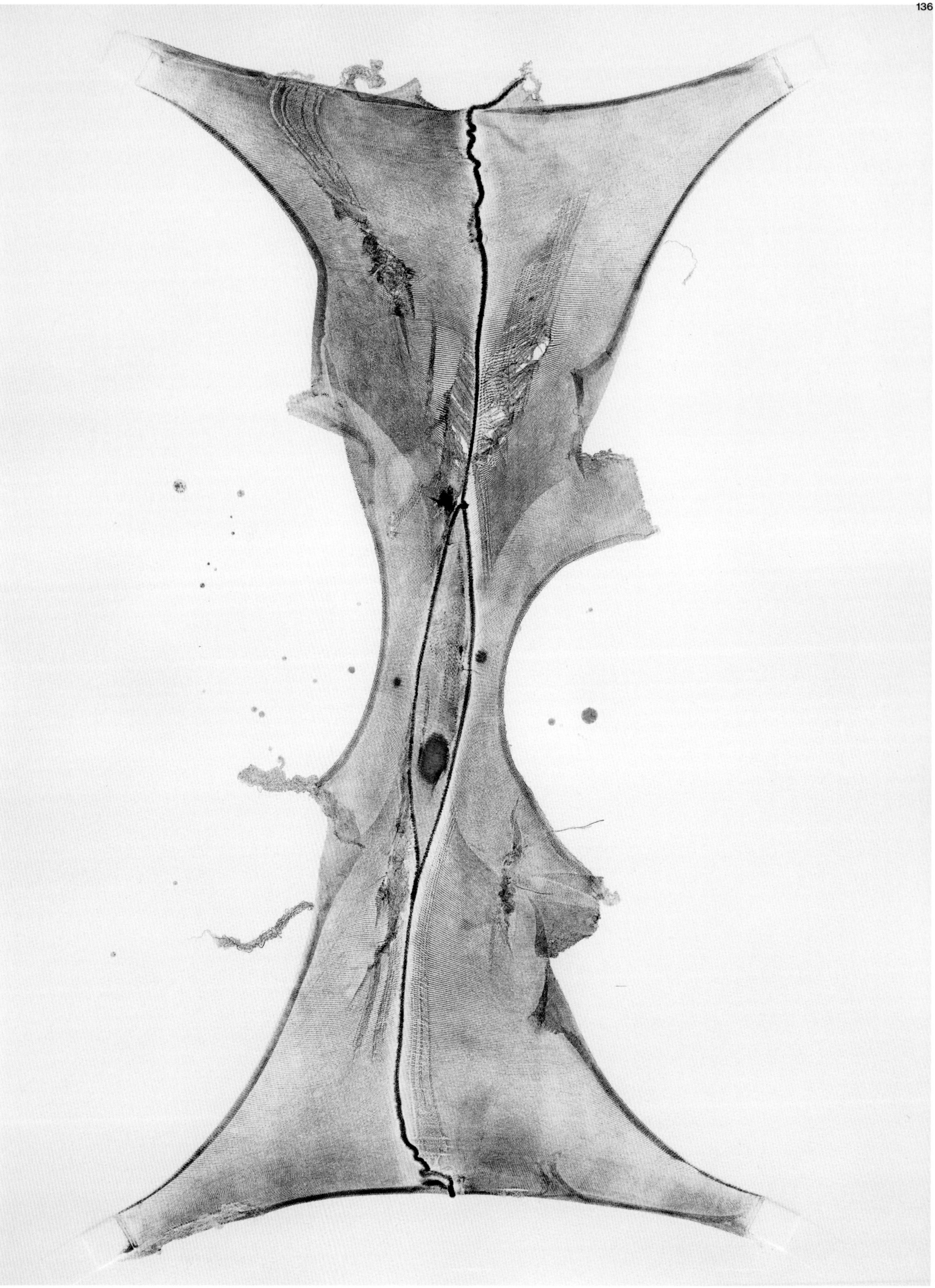

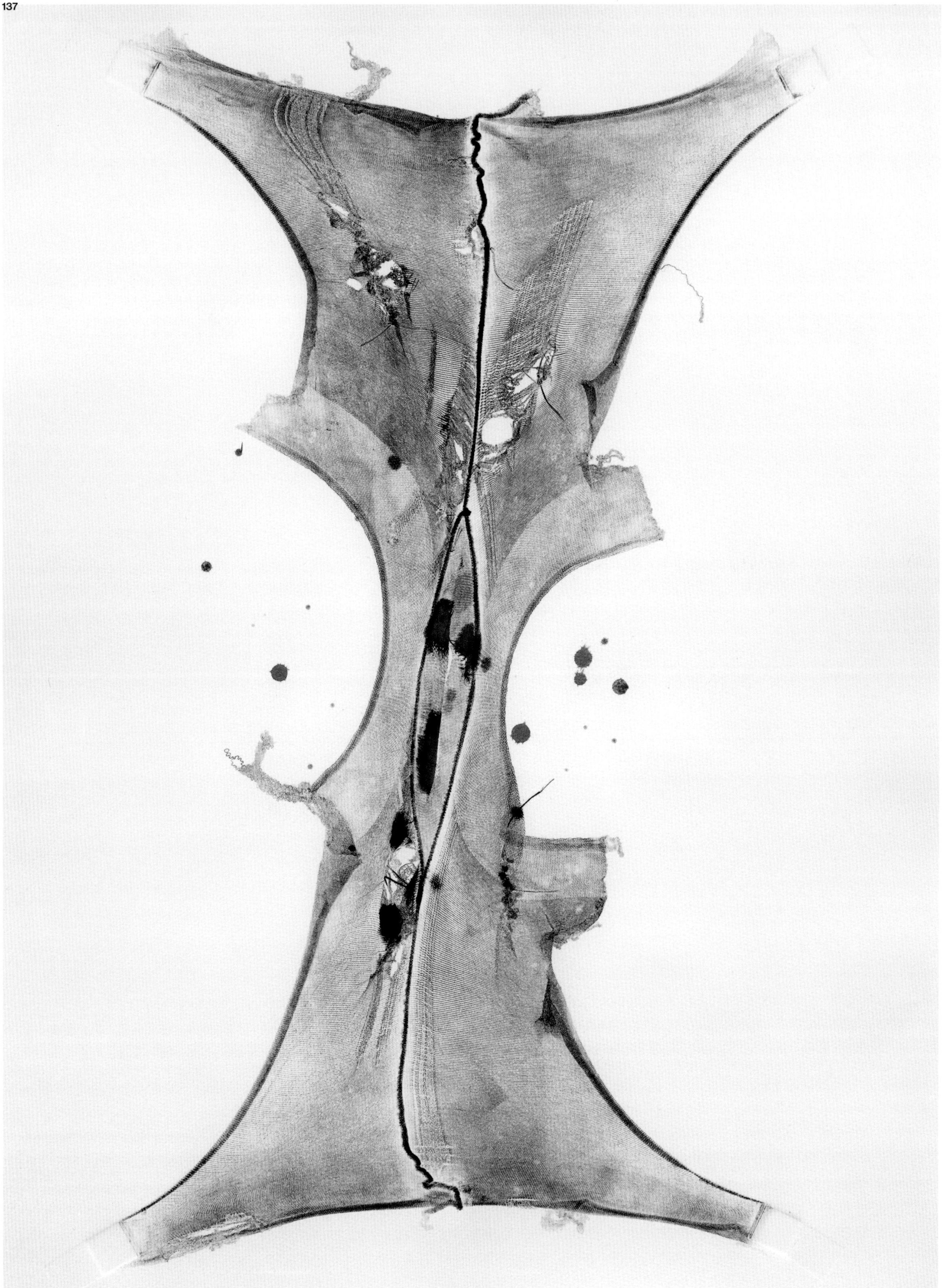

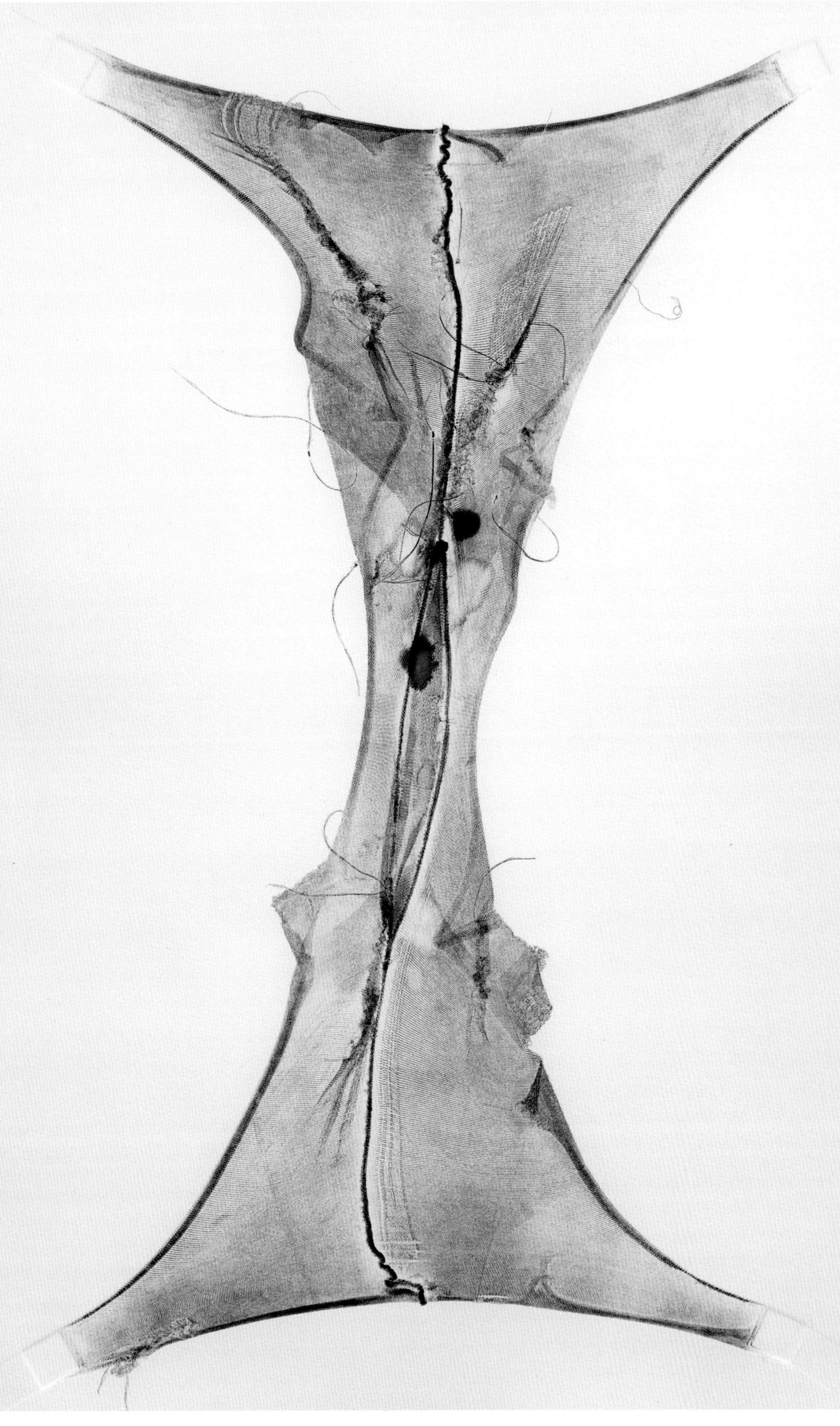

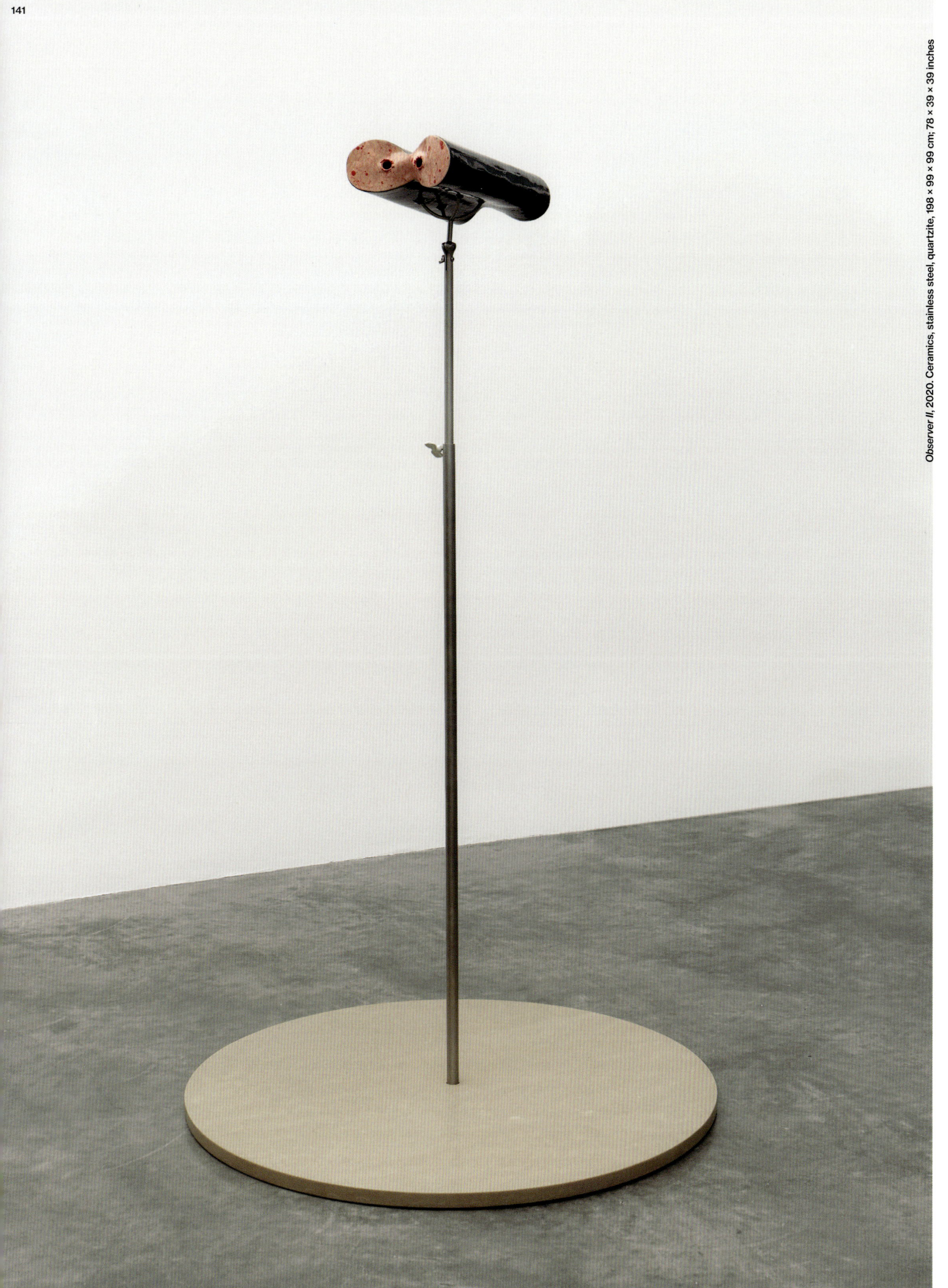

Observer II, 2020. Ceramics, stainless steel, quartzite, 198 × 99 × 99 cm; 78 × 39 × 39 inches

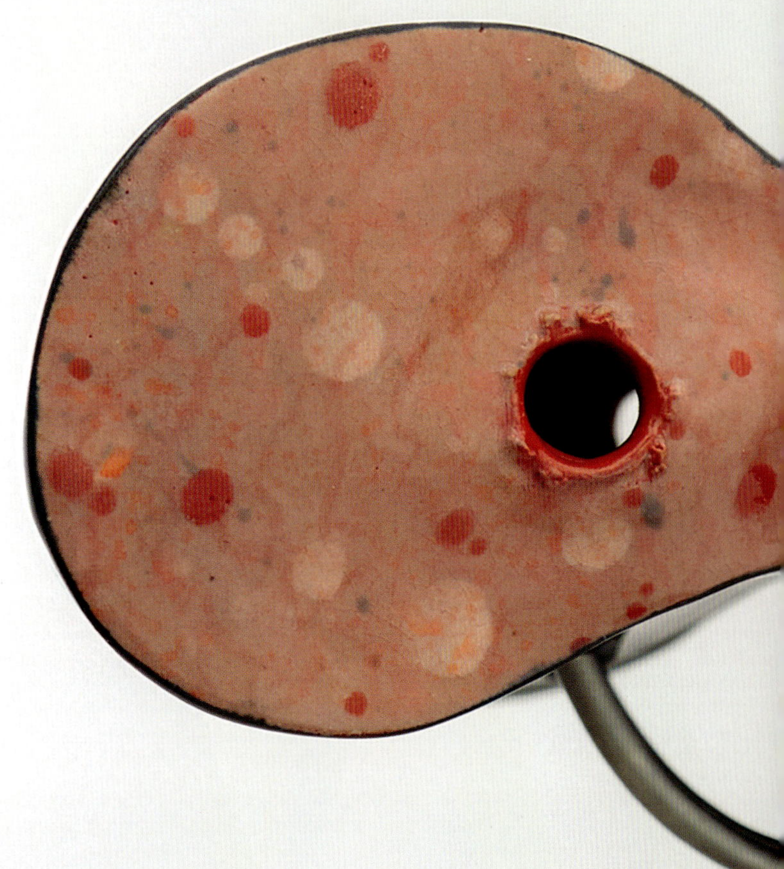

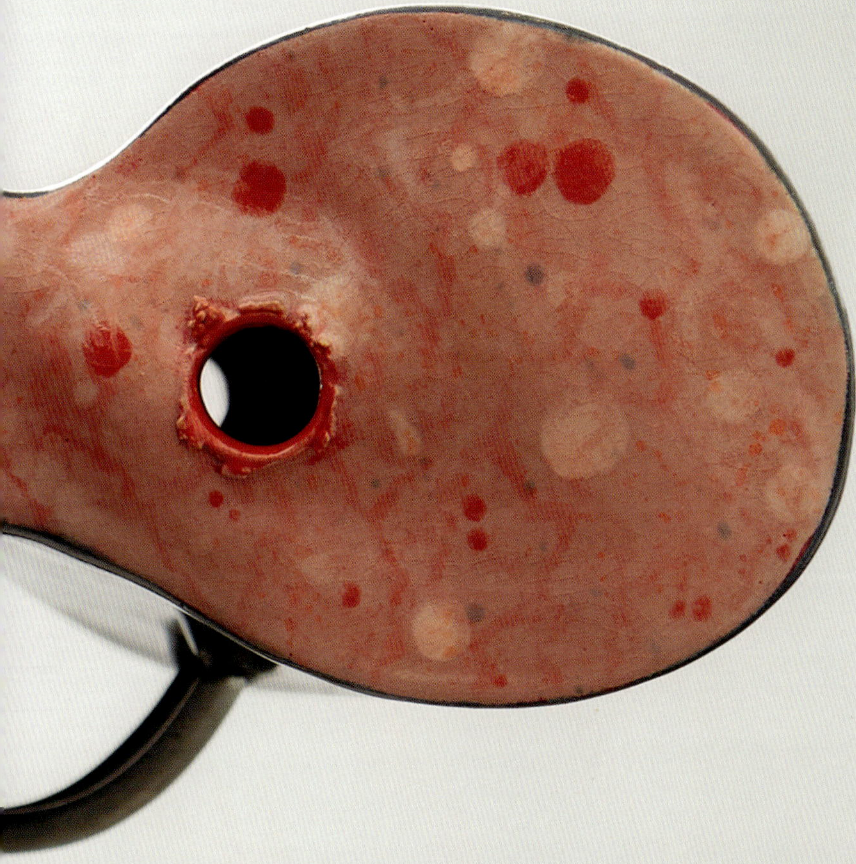

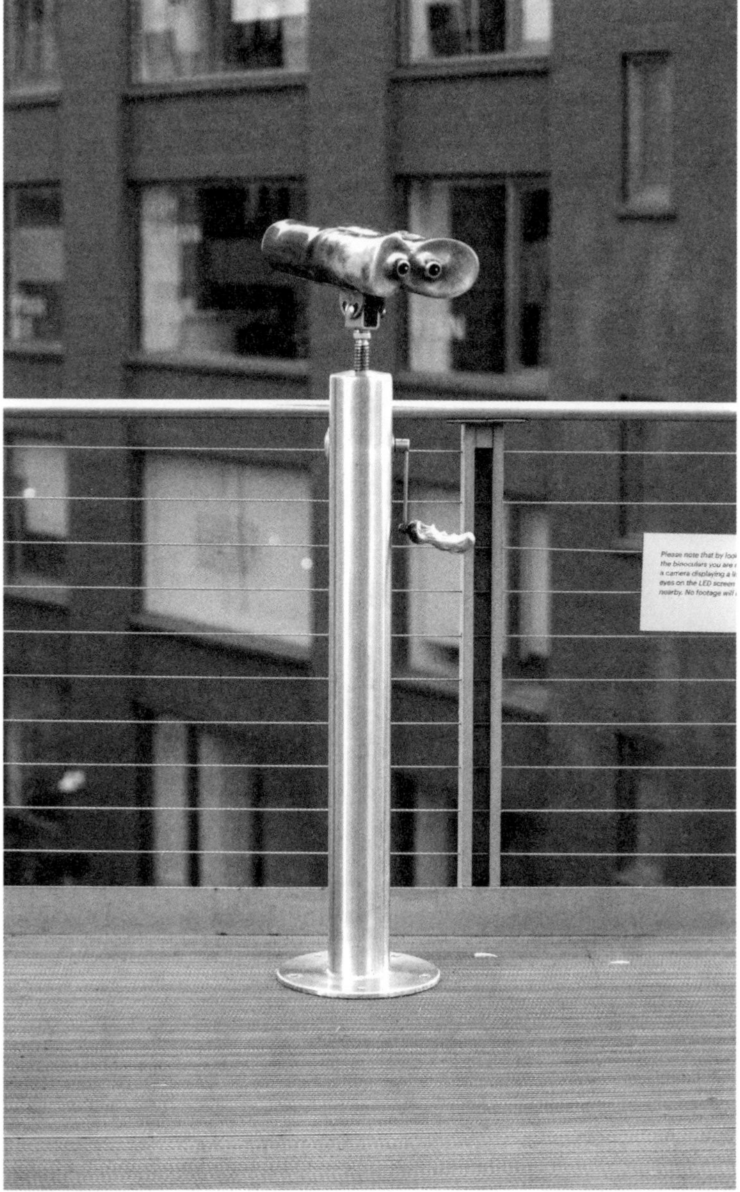

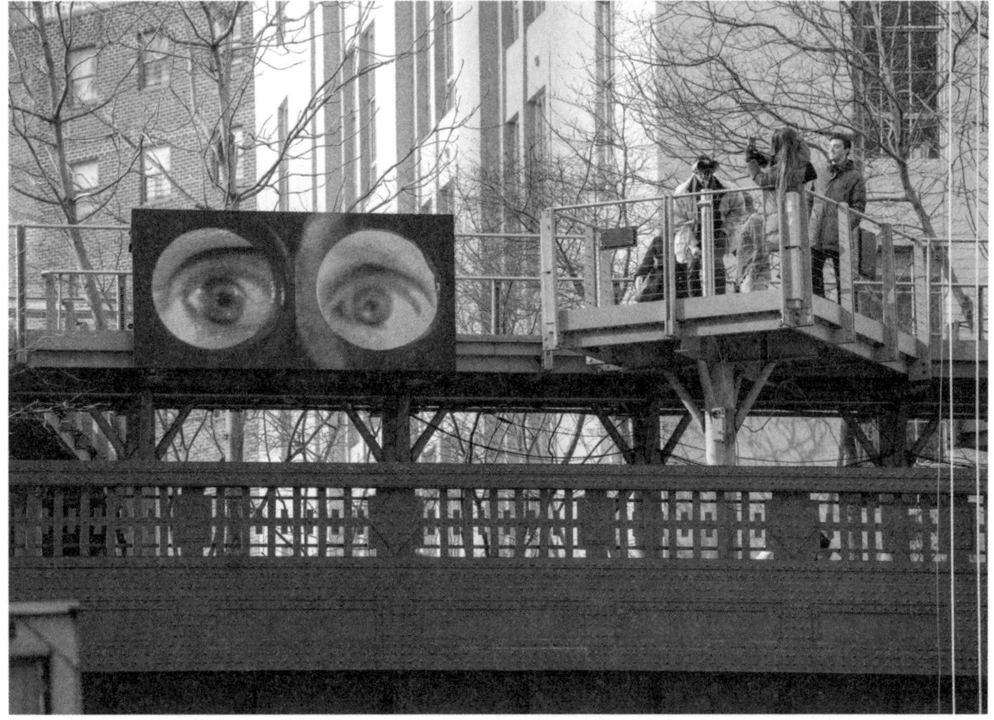

Observer, Observed, 2022. Bronze, stainless steel, binoculars, beamsplitter mirror, USB camera, LED video wall, Sculpture 138-178 × 54 × 70 cm; 54¼-70¼ × 21 × 27½, LED wall 305 × 153 × 11 cm; 120 × 60 × 4 inches © Julia Phillips, courtesy of High Line Art. Commissioned and produced by High Line Art, presented by Friends of the High Line and the New York City Department of Parks and Recreation. Photo by Timothy Schenck

FIA BACKSTRÖM   I'm excited to have this energy exchange with you today. We have had exchanges since 2013, when you started grad school, where I first met you. Your studio was sparse, with printed-out websites on the walls. It was unclear where your practice would go. I had no inkling that it would become so material- and object-committed. I would have guessed it might be more of a social practice, using interactive sensorial qualities to dismantle power structures.

In the second year, more material- and body-related work appeared. There were casts of your own body and index prints as traces of the body, and you started to work with ceramics—techniques and materials you still cling to. The sculpture work began to exhibit an apparatus-like quality, in which power dynamics were investigated.

Here's a good, sort of strange way to start: I've been thinking about hinges in your work. The body, or rather fragments of its anatomical parts, are a frequent reference. One body part that seems central is the pelvis, which also is the main hinge of the body. How do you think about hinges in your work?

JULIA PHILLIPS   I could address the question of hinges in two ways: mechanically or anatomically. My work borrows the language of functional objects and apparatuses. Hinges, or rather joints, play a central role in how different elements come together. The hardware that I use is integral to my work. It determines the formal language. And at the same time, it functions as a conceptual metaphor for physical and bodily relations. And then there are joints that are part of the body's anatomy, appearing in fragments, as you say. Showing certain joints, like the pelvis or the neck, gives the viewer a clue as to where the imagined body continues.

The Body as a Machine and the Playful Side of Grips:

Julia Phillips in Conversation with Fia Backström

FIA   The pelvis is also the part where sex difference is most clearly articulated in the skeleton. It is interesting that the pelvic representation in your early work seems gender neutral or gender ambiguous, as if you've literally drained it of its skeletal specificity, although there are many indexical surface marks of your body being cast, like pubic hair. One of the works that exemplifies this is *Drainer I* (2018), (p. 80) in which there is a representation of a pelvic bone, a flexible part used for bending the entire body.

(p. 82) JULIA   In both that work and *Drainer II* (2021), the body is in a folded-over position and presented in an unusual orientation, suspended from the pelvic bone. It is meant to read as somewhat gender-neutral, though there is a female quality to the simplicity of the pelvic shape, as well as the soft, folded abdomen.

(p. 107)   *Bower* (2021–22) is another work where the pelvis plays a central role. It's an apparatus that illustrates the motion of bowing. Here, the pelvis is represented by a cast of the lower back and hips, so gender specificity is left out. This work addresses the question of hinges or joints more mechanically, since there is the potential for motion built in. In *Bower*, I used springs as a new element. The apparatus could be set in motion by two points, either the forehead going forward or the hip tilting. I was interested in these two impulses that could cause this motion of bowing—the forehead as a symbol of consciousness and the hip as a symbol of impulse.

FIA   Both *Drainer* (*I* and *II*) and *Bower* suggest bending. In *Bower* there is a possibility of the body in a forward-moving slant, and with *Drainer* the pelvis is suspended, as if motion has already happened. That forward body movement makes me think of forms of submission, perhaps even of a religious kind.

JULIA   Yes, there is a sense of surrender. But unlike in *Bower*, where the body has a choice of bending, there is something inherently violent in *Drainer*. The inspiration for *Drainer* came from an acrobatic practice called aerial silks that I tried while doing a residency in Brazil. I remember associating one of the poses with a body hanging and being drained of its last drop of blood. *Bower*, on the other hand, is an apparatus of much more agency. When I titled the work, I made a conscious decision to call it *Bower* as opposed to *Prostrator*. The Latin word clearly implies an Other: prostrating in front of or for someone, whereas bowing is much more a motion that can be practiced in solitude.

FIA   You mentioned the spring as a new addition to the apparatus, a new technical piece of hardware in *Bower*. What does the spring do? And are you still working with springs in newer works?

JULIA   I am. Springs are a mechanical metaphor for flexibility and also tension and resistance. They appear again in my recent *Attachment* series (2022). Some of the works have stainless steel springs that are connecting two sets of grips. The springs allow for a changing distance between the users and for pulling with different forces while being in physical relation to each other.

(p. 113-117)

FIA   This is interesting in how the joint or hinge operates. In the *Attachment* series, the mobility is multidirectional in a different way than in both *Bower* and *Drainer*, which are more stationary. There seems to be a freer imagined range of motion.

JULIA   Yes, the word "play" comes to mind. I conceptualized the *Attachment* series after having entered motherhood, and thinking about mother-infant or parent-infant relationships, also from the child's perspective. And gripping can be such a playful way of interacting.

FIA   In the *Attachment* series there are many grips, not as representations of the hand gripping, but the actual imprint of the grip. This kind of imprint also exists in earlier works, for example in *Operator I* and *II* (2017/2018). Yet the grip seems to have different functions in your work.

(p. 75-79)

JULIA   You're right. Grips are a recurring element, but they play completely different roles from *Operator I* and *II* to *Fixator* (2017) to the *Attachment* series. Both *Operator* works look like medical trolleys that have different elements sitting on them. I refer to each of the *Operator* works as an analogy to a relationship, and the tools on the trolley as elements that appear in these relationships. The two sets of handles represent two bodies that are in collaboration. So, in this case, the handles are simply a symbol for two individuals.

(p. 67-69)

In a work like *Fixator*, the grips give much more of a clue as to which position the imagined body could be in. There are two interacting agents implied, one of them represented by grips. The grips are downward-facing and give a hint that one of the bodies is bent over. It's a way of positioning the imagined bodies in interaction. In the *Attachment* series, the grips are the primary element. The work is about gripping as a human gesture and an infant's instinct to grab and attach.

FIA   In *Operator I* and *II* you set up a relation of a two-bodied experience, whereas in *Fixator* the grip works like an instruction, as in the gym, gripping onto those apparatuses. and in the *Attachment* series, they are a way of thinking through early developmental psychology. It's interesting how young children use the tongue and the nose to explore the entire world, but also the hands by gripping—this instinct to take hold of things as a way of making sure that there is a world outside of the body. In *Operator I* and *II* the interaction happens between two bodies, while *Bower* implies only one body. Has there been a shift from a form of relationality into a solipsistic gaze that views the body as solitary? And then in the *Attachment* series you are focusing on an inner experience of an Other that is almost yourself, or barely separated from you, the child.

JULIA   Very interesting! This question of "barely separated from you" is exactly what led me to think about attachment theory. I wanted to articulate the ability or inability, the necessity and challenge, to separate from infant, or from mother. The psychoanalyst Jennifer Stuart writes: "As analysts, we know that attachment and autonomy *both* are critically important—to babies and to the adults who care for them."[1] The grips represent the gesture of attaching, while medical tubes hold some of the pieces together as a literal element of the physical connection, the shared nutrients, "barely separated," as you say. The springs, as I mentioned, stand for flexibility, tension, and resistance. And one of the works has metal quick releases, representing a potential for letting go, separation, and autonomy.

FIA   An interest in mechanics is also a recurring feature of your work, as in the body as a machine, which is often articulated through apparatuses or display technologies. *Mediator* (2020), for instance, a larger work of yours, appears as an apparatus, a metal structure holding up fragments of two torsi, whereas *Impregnator and Aborter* (2022) is more intimately sized and relies more heavily on display technology. The pedestals simultaneously work as a display armature while also being part of the sculpture.

(p. 90-93)

(p. 118-123)

JULIA   Yes, we're getting at a question of scale. I have an interest in all kinds of functional objects, from dentist tools to large gym devices. I use different display structures to give the works spatial context. The metal pedestals for *Impregnator and Aborter*, these medical dishes, give the ceramic works a clinical appearance. I'm fascinated by medical environments and their clinical surfaces but also by the weird, ambiguous shapes of instruments that are somehow meant to control or measure the body.

FIA   Can you say more about how you became interested in the world of functional objects?

JULIA   Yes, it started with a visit to the amazing armor section of the Metropolitan Museum of Art in New York. Even with the little knowledge I had, there was still so much to glean about the pieces of armor, because armor directly relates to the human form. We can see ourselves in it, similar to clothing. Realizing that, I also started looking at other designed objects, such as instruments and hardware. I wanted the intuition about how to use objects that relate to the body to become part of my work so that more people could access it by envisioning a potential use. That was pretty much how I developed my formal language.

FIA   Depending on the scale of your works, they are approached quite differently by the viewer. There's a stage-set quality with the smaller works we've mentioned, *Operator I* and *II*, *Impregnator and Aborter*. Whereas in larger installations like *Drainer* or *Nourisher* (2022), the fragmentation of the body works differently and is more tied to the architecture of the space.

(p. 110)

JULIA   Yes, there is a scene-like quality to how I think of these larger works, with a narrative implied. In *Drainer*, the relationship between the suspended cast and the drain base creates a time aspect: the dripping liquid. *Nourisher* is combined with medical tubes (a new material I started working with) that pool underneath the sculpture and represent a narrative of exchange: extracting out of but also fueling into a body, again drop by drop.

FIA The tubes are a new material in your work, whereas ceramics and metal have been part of it since the very beginning. It almost comes off as a binary, but the way that you work with it is not so binary, obviously. Ceramics are breakable, hard but fragile, while metal is cold and unbendable. Medical tubing is flexible but not so fragile, with the added function of suction.

JULIA Yes, these are interesting observations! Using less fragile and soft materials is somehow connected to the idea of adding flexibility to my work. I'm developing an interest in soft sculpture, particularly elements that sit differently every time a piece is installed. So, in one way I am opening up to less controllable elements, such as the plastic tubes or even (p. 104) textiles in a work called *Veiled Purifier* (2021–22), which has a mauve silk veil.

FIA Speaking of colors, in *Drainer I* the surface is a matte black, as opposed to the glossy, representational, pinkish flesh tones inside the pelvis. You have mentioned your interest in Kerry James Marshall's use of what he calls "rhetorical black." In your earlier work, color seems to be put to more realistic or representational use than in newer works, such as the *Attachment* series. Here your palette seems freer, almost whimsical or circus-like, with predominantly pastels of yellows, purples, even greens. It seems like a more abstract use of color. How has color changed for you through the years?

JULIA For a while, I was using matte black but also dark blue to resemble the coldness of instruments. But then, as the body casts became larger, for instance with the masks (p. 57) (p. 64) for *Positioner* (2016) or *Extruder* (2017) or the abdominal cast of *Drainer I*, I saw the black surfaces as a rhetorical way to represent skin. Kerry James Marshall's ivory black, Mars black, and carbon black rhetorically speak to a Black experience that could be any shade of brown, beige, or black. But I wanted to show skin tones in their specificity, and (p. 87–89) turned toward different complexions in works like *Fake Truth (Witness I–III)* (2019) or *Mediator*. In the latter, two chest casts are mounted to a metal structure, opposing each other. One is of a darker complexion, the other one a lighter. The attempt was to avoid a construction of race, to not be ethnicity specific. And still, these skin-colored casts are specific to a colorist experience in our sociopolitical climate.

FIA It's interesting that you bring up *Mediator* in that sense, since that work shows two torsos in a binary relationship. It's similar to how race is often discussed in our society.

JULIA Yes! On one hand the work denies a specific read of ethnicity, and on the other hand it might expose the binary representations of Black and White culture that we live in at the moment.[2] It's a very narrowing way to discuss ethnicity or racism.

FIA Where have you since gone with your thinking about how to work with skin complexion?

JULIA I decided for now to turn away from representing complexion in a realistic way in sculpture. Colorism is such a complex discourse and seems under-discussed. Colorist experiences are tied not just to privilege but also to questions of belonging and diaspora. I'm in the position of what, in the US context, is called "light-skinned" and "biracial" (meaning, in my case, Black and White). It's worth mentioning that the majority of Black Germans (*Afrodeutsche*), which I am, share that identity. I would like to find more articulations of this complexity around colorism, but right now, I'm not sure if sculpture as a medium is serving me in the right way for that.

My recent work *Nourisher,* with relatively large casts of my chest and face, gave me an opportunity to think about skin again. The outside surface is glazed in a matte orange, which is almost a cartoonish way to represent skin. It resembles emojis. And the insides of the casts are glazed in a glossy deep pink, a symbol for flesh, life, and subjectivity.

Throughout my Western art education, I gained little to no understanding of the symbolic use of color, especially in contemporary visual culture. It was not until I traveled East for the first time, and went to Hong Kong in early 2019, that I had a very satisfying conversation with a vase shop owner who was able to answer all my questions about color. I asked him what red stands for (luck); yellow (imperialism); green (forever young); blue (bright sky/good future). So it was through my studies of Asian culture that I found symbolic meaning in color. Orange in the Vedantic tradition represents devotion to spiritual life and renunciation. So the color system is also a value system.

But to go back to the *Attachment* series, earlier we spoke about the playfulness of these devices. I intended to somehow reference the world of toys, but also to use color almost in a celebratory way. I conceptualized the show *Me, Ourself & You,* which the *Attachment* series is part of, in a joyful mood, having entered motherhood and wanting to embrace that experience by using color in a similar way as to how colorful flowers can symbolize celebration. Sentimental, in a sense.

FIA I have to admit, when I first saw them, I thought to myself, "This is kind of corny." We have moved from your earlier works, such as *Drainer,* which are quite dark with suggested expressions of violence, into the more recent works like the *Attachment* series, with its playful relationship to color and joint mobility. What do you think about the latter potentially being perceived as corny?

JULIA I think my work has been changing a lot in the past few years. I moved away from investigations of oppressive relationships and want to explore and articulate something else, new experiences. During these moments of figuring out where to go next, I think it's sometimes necessary to go through really weird stages.

Some jazz musicians have been a major source of inspiration for me in thinking about weird transformative phases. Certain musicians come to mind where encounters with spiritual practices drastically changed their work. For instance, Alice Coltrane's music transformed in a remarkable way after her exposure to Vedanta studies. Her musical aesthetics—an album like *Universal Consciousness* from 1971, for example—were quite unfamiliar to the jazz audience. Or the pianist Horace Silver, who even included vocals in his later works. Or Mary Lou Williams and her 1975 album *Mary Lou's Mass.* Now there's a historical genre for it, "spiritual jazz," that includes many more musicians: John Coltrane, Pharoah Sanders, Sun Ra, Don Cherry. But at that time, the music was new to people's ears. So this corniness that you mention is, I think, the clash between established, accepted aesthetics in a field (like jazz or contemporary art) and an artist's new embracing of unfamiliar elements such as beauty or new value systems.

FIA There's perhaps also a feeling of embarrassment in that corniness.

JULIA Maybe in the sentimentality of self-revelation and the hope of having found a truth that needs to be shared. I think there's a good potential for embarrassment about that because truth is so transformative in and of itself.

Something we discover today as the truth that needs to be shared might look very different in a year. So this revealing part, I think, is embarrassing but also very generative.

1   Jennifer Stuart, "Work and Motherhood: Preliminary Report of a Psychoanalytic Study," *Psychoanalytic Quarterly* 76, no. 2 (2007): 443.

2   The artist has chosen to capitalize "Black" and "White" in alignment with sociopolitical discourse that seeks to call attention to the construction of race. See for instance Ann Thúy Nguyễn and Maya Pendleton, "Recognizing Race in Language: Why We Capitalize 'Black' and 'White,'" Center for the Study of Social Policy, March 23, 2020, https://cssp.org/2020/03/recognizing-race-in-language-why-we-capitalize-black-and-white.

FIA BACKSTRÖM Ich freue mich, heute zu diesem Energieaustausch (*Energy Exchange*) mit Dir eingeladen zu sein. Wir haben uns seit 2013, als Du Dein Masterstudium aufnahmst und ich Dich zum ersten Mal traf, schon mehrfach ausgetauscht. Dein Atelier war damals ziemlich kahl, es gab nur ausgedruckte Webseiten an den Wänden. Noch war nicht klar, wohin sich Deine künstlerische Arbeit entwickelte. Ich hätte nicht gedacht, dass sie so material- und objektorientiert werden würde. Eher hätte ich mir vorstellen können, dass es in Richtung einer sozialen Praxis geht, die interagierende sensorische Eigenschaften nutzt, um Machtstrukturen aufzubrechen.

Im zweiten Jahr entstanden mehr material- und körperbezogene Arbeiten. Es gab Abformungen von Deinem eigenen Körper, Indexprints als Spuren des Körpers, und Du fingst an, mit Keramik zu arbeiten – Techniken und Materialien, die Du immer noch gerne verwendest. Die bildhauerischen Arbeiten erhielten zunehmend den Charakter von Apparaten zur Erforschung von Machtdynamiken.

Um mit einem schönen, etwas ungewöhnlichen Thema zu beginnen: Ich habe über Gelenke in Deiner Arbeit nachgedacht. Der Körper oder vielmehr Fragmente seiner Anatomie sind häufige Bezugspunkte in Deinen Werken. Eines der Körperteile, die eine zentrale Rolle zu spielen scheinen, ist das Becken, das zugleich das zentrale Gelenk des Körpers ist. Wie verstehst Du (die) Gelenke in Deiner Arbeit?

JULIA PHILLIPS Die Frage nach den Gelenken kann ich auf zweierlei Weise beantworten: zum einen technisch und zum anderen anatomisch. Mein Werk bedient sich der Sprache von Gebrauchsgegenständen und Apparaten. Gelenke oder, besser gesagt, Verbindungen sind entscheidend dafür, wie sich die Elemente zusammenfügen. Die verschiedenen verwendeten Schrauben und Armaturen sind ein wesentlicher Bestandteil meiner Arbeiten; sie bestimmen ihre Formensprache. Gleichzeitig fungieren sie als konzeptuelle Metaphern für physische und körperliche Beziehungen. Und dann gibt es noch die Gelenke, die zur Anatomie des Körpers gehören und als Fragmente vorhanden sind, wie Du sagst. Die Darstellung von Teilgelenken, etwa des Beckens oder des Halses, gibt den Betrachtenden einen Hinweis darauf, wie sich der imaginäre Körper fortsetzt.

Der Körper als Maschine und die spielerische Seite von Griffen.

Julia Phillips im Gespräch mit Fia Backström

FIA Das Becken ist auch derjenige Teil des Skeletts, an dem sich der Unterschied zwischen den Geschlechtern am deutlichsten zeigt. Es ist interessant, dass die Darstellung des Beckens in Deinen frühen Arbeiten geschlechtsneutral oder mehrdeutig zu sein scheint, als hättest Du ihm seine skelettale Spezifität genommen, obwohl es viele sichtbare Oberflächenspuren Deiner Körperabformung gibt wie etwa Schamhaare. Eines der Werke, die das veranschaulichen, ist *Drainer I* (2018), eine Abformung/ Repräsentations des Beckenknochens und somit einer beweglichen Stelle des Körpers, an der er sich insgesamt beugen lässt.

(p. 80)

(p. 82)

JULIA Sowohl bei *Drainer I* als auch bei *Drainer II* (2021) befindet sich der Körper in einer zusammengeklappten Haltung und wird in ungewöhnlicher Lage präsentiert: als ein am Beckenknochen hängender Körper. Die Darstellung soll weitgehend geschlechtsneutral sein, obwohl die minimale Form des Beckens/des Schoßes und der weich eingeknickte Unterleib eine weibliche Anmutung haben.

(p. 107) *Bower* (2021/22) ist eine weitere Arbeit, bei der das Becken eine zentrale Rolle spielt; es handelt sich um einen Apparat, der die Bewegung des Verbeugens veranschaulicht. Hier ist das Becken durch eine Abformung des unteren Rückens und der Hüften dargestellt, sodass die Geschlechtsspezifik ausgespart bleibt. Diese Arbeit behandelt die Frage der Gelenke oder Verbindungen eher technisch, da die Möglichkeit der Bewegung bereits eingebaut ist. In *Bower* habe ich als neues Element Metallfedern verwendet. Der Apparat kann von zwei Punkten aus in Bewegung gesetzt werden: entweder durch die Vorwärtsbewegung der Stirn oder durch das Kippen der Hüfte. Mich interessierten die beiden Impulse, die diese Beugebewegung auslösen können – die Stirn als Symbol des Bewusstseins und die Hüfte als Symbol für Triebkraft.

FIA   Sowohl *Drainer* als auch *Bower* weisen auf eine Beugung hin. Bei *Bower* besteht die Möglichkeit einer Vorbeugung des Körpers, und bei *Drainer* befindet sich das Becken in der Schwebe, als hätte eine solche Bewegung bereits stattgefunden. Diese Vorbeugebewegung des Körpers erinnert mich an Gesten der Unterwerfung, vielleicht sogar religiöser Art.

JULIA   Es hat tatsächlich etwas von Unterwerfung. Aber anders als bei *Bower*, wo der Körper die Wahl hat, ob er sich beugt oder nicht, wohnt *Drainer* etwas Gewaltsames inne. Zu *Drainer* hat mich die Vertikaltuchakrobatik inspiriert, die ich während eines Aufenthalts in Brasilien ausprobieren konnte. Ich weiß noch, dass ich eine der Posen mit einem Körper assoziierte, der so aufgehängt ist, als sollte Blut von ihm abtropfen. *Bower* hingegen ist ein Apparat mit weitaus mehr Handlungsmöglichkeiten. Beim Titel des Werks habe ich mich bewusst für *Bower* und nicht für *Prostrator* entschieden. Das lateinische Wort impliziert eindeutig ein Gegenüber: sich vor jemandem niederwerfen. Bei der Verbeugung hingegen geht es eher um eine Bewegung, die man auch alleine ausführen kann.

FIA   Du hast die Feder als Erweiterung des Geräts erwähnt, als neues technisches Bauteil von *Bower*. Welche Funktion hat die Feder – arbeitest Du in neueren Werken weiterhin damit?

JULIA   Ja. Federn sind eine technische Metapher für Flexibilität, aber auch für Spannung und Widerstand. Sie tauchen auch (p. 113-117) in meinen letzten Skulpturen, der *Attachment* Serie (2022), wieder auf. In einigen der Arbeiten gibt es Federn aus Edelstahl, die zwei Griffpaare miteinander verbinden. Durch die Federn lässt sich die Distanz zwischen den Beteiligten verändern, und man kann unterschiedlich stark an ihnen ziehen, während die physische Verbundenheit bestehen bleibt.

FIA   Das ist interessant hinsichtlich der Funktionsweise der Verbindung/des Gelenks. Bei der *Attachment* Serie ist die Beweglichkeit auf andere Weise multidirektional als bei *Bower* und *Drainer*, die eher stationär sind. Die Bewegungsfreiheit scheint bei diesen Skulpturen größer zu sein.

JULIA   Ja, dazu fällt mir das Wort „spielen" ein. Ich habe mir diese neue Serie von Skulpturen, die *Attachment* Serie, überlegt, nachdem ich Mutter geworden war und über die Mutter-Kind- oder Eltern-Kind-Beziehung nachgedacht habe, auch aus der Perspektive des Kindes. Greifen kann eine spielerische Art der Interaktion sein.

FIA   In der *Attachment* Serie gibt es eine Reihe von Griffen, nicht als Darstellungen der greifenden Hand, sondern als tatsächlicher Abdruck eines Griffs. Diese Art von Abdruck kommt auch in früheren Arbeiten vor, zum Beispiel *Operator I* und *II* (2017/18). Aber trotzdem scheint der Griff in Deinem Werk verschiedene Funktionen zu haben.

(p. 75-79)

JULIA   Du hast Recht. Griffe sind in meinen Arbeiten ein wiederkehrendes Element, aber sie spielen vollkommen unterschiedliche Rollen, von *Operator I* und *II* über *Fixator* (2017) bis hin (p. 67-69) zur *Attachment* Serie. Die beiden *Operator*-Arbeiten sehen aus wie medizinische Instrumentenwagen, auf denen verschiedene

Gegenstände liegen. Ich betrachte jede der *Operator*-Arbeiten als Analogie zu einer Beziehung und die Werkzeuge auf den Wagen als in diesen Beziehungen vorkommende Elemente. Die beiden Griffpaare stehen für zwei Körper, die zusammenwirken. In diesem Fall sind die Griffe also einfach Symbole für zwei Personen.

In *Fixator* dagegen dienen die Griffe eher dazu zu verdeutlichen, in welcher Position sich der vorgestellte Körper befinden könnte. Von den beiden implizierten Interaktionspartner_innen wird eine_r durch die Griffe dargestellt. Sie zeigen nach unten und geben so einen Hinweis darauf, dass einer der Körper vorgebeugt ist. Das ist eine Möglichkeit, die imaginären Körper bei ihrer Interaktion zu positionieren. In der *Attachment* Serie sind die Griffe das zentrale Element. In dieser Arbeit geht es um das Greifen als menschliche Geste und um den Instinkt des Säuglings, zu greifen und sich festzuhalten.

FIA   In *Operator I* und *II* schaffst Du eine Beziehung zwischen zwei Körpern, während die Griffe bei *Fixator* als Anweisung zum Greifen funktionieren, wie im Sportstudio. In der *Attachment* Serie schließlich sind die Griffe ein Anlass, über die frühe Entwicklungspsychologie nachzudenken. Es ist interessant, wie kleine Kinder die Zunge und die Nase zur Erkundung der ganzen Welt und die Hände zum Greifen nutzen – dieser Instinkt, Dinge zu greifen, um sich zu vergewissern, dass es eine Welt außerhalb des eigenen Körpers gibt.

Bei *Operator I* und *II* geschieht die Interaktion zwischen *zwei* Körpern, während *Bower* nur *einen* Körper voraussetzt. Gab es eine Verschiebung von einer Art Relationalität hin zu einem solipsistischen Blick, der den Körper als solitär betrachtet? Und in der *Attachment* Serie konzentrierst Du Dich auf die innere Erfahrung einer anderen Person, die fast Du selbst oder kaum von Dir getrennt ist, die Erfahrung des Kindes.

JULIA   Sehr interessant! Die Frage des „kaum von Dir getrennt"-Seins ist genau das, was mich dazu veranlasst hat, über die Bindungstheorie nachzudenken. Ich wollte die Fähigkeit oder Unfähigkeit, die Notwendigkeit und die Schwierigkeit, sich vom Säugling beziehungsweise von der Mutter zu trennen, zum Ausdruck bringen. Die Psychoanalytikerin Dr. Jennifer Stuart schreibt: „Als Analytiker_innen wissen wir, dass Bindung und Autonomie *beide* von entscheidender Bedeutung sind – für Babys und für die Erwachsenen, die für sie sorgen."[1] Die Griffe stehen für die Geste des Verbindens, während medizinische Schläuche als buchstäbliches Element der physischen Verbindung die einzelnen Teile der Skulptur zusammenhalten. Die Schläuche sind eine Metapher für die geteilten Nährstoffe, die Vereintheit/Einigkeit oder, wie Du sagst, das „kaum getrennt"-Sein. Die Federn repräsentieren, wie schon gesagt, Flexibilität, Spannung und Widerstand, und eine der Arbeiten enthält Schnellspannhaken aus Metall, die die Möglichkeit des Loslassens, der Trennung und der Autonomie darstellen.

FIA   Das Interesse an Mechanik zieht sich ebenfalls als roter Faden durch Dein Werk, zum Beispiel wenn der Körper in Form von Apparaten oder durch die Präsentationstechnik als Maschine dargestellt wird. *Mediator* (2020) zum Beispiel, eines Deiner größeren Werke, erscheint als Apparat, als Metallkonstruktion, die die Fragmente zweier Torsi hält, während *Impregnator and Aborter* (2022) kleinformatiger ist und stärker auf die Präsentationstechnik setzt. Die Unterbauten fungieren als Podest und sind gleichzeitig Teil der Skulptur.

(p. 90-93)

(p. 118-123)

JULIA   Ich glaube, das ist eine Frage des Maßstabs. Ich interessiere mich für alle möglichen Arten von Gebrauchsgegenständen, von zahnärztlichen Instrumenten bis hin zu großen Fitnessgeräten. Ich verwende unterschiedliche Präsentationsformen, um den Arbeiten einen räumlichen Kontext zu geben. Die Metallgestelle für *Impregnator and Aborter*, diese medizinischen Schalen, verleihen den keramischen Arbeiten eine klinische Anmutung. Mich faszinieren medizinische Umgebungen und ihre klinischen Oberflächen, aber auch die seltsamen mehrdeutigen Formen von Instrumenten zur Kontrolle oder Vermessung des Körpers.

FIA   Kannst Du etwas mehr darüber erzählen, wie Du auf die Welt der Gebrauchsgegenstände aufmerksam geworden bist?

JULIA   Es begann mit einem Besuch in der erstaunlichen Rüstungsabteilung des Metropolitan Museum of Art. Bei meinen geringen Vorkenntnissen konnte ich anhand der verschiedenen Teile von Rüstungen noch einiges lernen, denn sie haben einen direkten Bezug zur menschlichen Gestalt. Wir können uns selbst darin sehen, ähnlich wie bei der Kleidung. Als ich das verstanden hatte, fing ich an, mir auch andere Gebrauchsgegenstände anzuschauen, zum Beispiel Werkzeuge und Armaturen. Ich wollte das intuitive Verständnis vom Gebrauch von Gegenständen, die mit dem Körper zu tun haben, in meine Arbeit einbeziehen, damit mehr Menschen einen Zugang zu ihr finden, indem sie sich eine mögliche Verwendung vorstellen können. Auf diese Weise habe ich meine Formensprache entwickelt.

FIA   Je nachdem, wie groß Deine Werke sind, werden sie von den Betrachter_innen ganz unterschiedlich wahrgenommen. Die kleineren Werke, über die wir gesprochen haben (*Operator I* und *II*, *Impregnator and Aborter*), erinnern an Objekte in einem Bühnenbild. Bei größeren Installationen wie *Drainer* oder *Nourisher* (2022) hingegen funktioniert die Fragmentierung des Körpers anders und ist stärker an die Architektur des Raums gebunden.

(p. 110)

JULIA   Bei diesen größeren Werken denke ich an etwas Szenenhaftes, das ein Narrativ impliziert. Bei *Drainer I* sorgt das Verhältis zwischen dem hängenden Körperabdruck und der Abflussplattform für einen zeitlicher Faktor: die tropfende Flüssigkeit. In *Nourisher* kommen medizinische Schläuche zum Einsatz (ein neues Material in meiner Arbeit), die sich unter der Skulptur aufstauen und ein Narrativ des Austauschs darstellen: der Entnahme von Flüssigkeit aus dem Körper, aber auch der Zufuhr in den Körper, wiederum Tropfen für Tropfen.

FIA   Die Schläuche sind innerhalb Deines Werks ein neues Material, während Keramik und Metall von Anfang an dazugehörten. Das wirkt fast schon binär, aber die Art und Weise, wie Du mit den Materialien arbeitest, ist offensichtlich nicht binär. Keramik ist zerbrechlich und hart, während Metall kalt und unflexibel ist – zwei unterschiedliche Qualitäten im Verhältnis zum Körper. Medizinische Schläuche sind flexibel, nicht zerbrechlich und können außerdem zum Absaugen verwendet werden.

JULIA   Ja, das sind wirklich interessante Beobachtungen! Die Verwendung weniger empfindlicher und weicher Materialien hat etwas mit dem Wunsch zu tun, meine Arbeiten flexibler zu machen. Ich beschäftige mich zunehmend mit *soft sculpture*, insbesondere indem ich Elemente verwende, die bei jeder neuen Installation der Werke leicht abweichend platziert sind. So erschließe ich mir gewissermaßen weniger beherrschbare Elemente wie die PVC-Schläuche oder sogar Stoffe in einem Werk wie *Veiled Purifier* (2021–22), das mit einem malvenfarbenen Seidenschleier versehen ist.

(p. 104)

FIA   Da wir gerade von Farben sprechen: Bei *Drainer* ist die Oberfläche mattschwarz und steht damit im Gegensatz zu den glänzenden rosafarbenen Fleischtönen im Inneren des Beckenabdrucks. Du hast einmal gesagt, dass Du Dich für Kerry James Marshalls Verwendung von „rhetorischem Schwarz", wie er es nennt, interessierst. In Deinen früheren Arbeiten scheint mir die Farbe realistischer oder repräsentativer zu sein als in neueren Werken wie der *Attachment* Serie. Hier wirkt Deine Farbpalette mit überwiegend pastelligen Gelb,

Violett- und sogar Grüntönen und einer abstrakteren Verwendung von Farbe freier, fast schon verspielt oder zirkushaft. Wie hat sich der Einsatz von Farbe für Dich im Laufe der Jahre verändert?

JULIA Eine ganze Zeit lang habe ich ein mattes Schwarz und auch Dunkelblau verwendet, um die Kälte von Instrumenten zu vermitteln. Als dann aber die Körperabformungen größer wurden, zum Beispiel die Masken für *Positioner* (2016) oder *Extruder* (2017) oder die Beckenabformung bei *Drainer I*, wurden die schwarzen Oberflächen für mich zu einem rhetorischen Mittel für die Darstellung von Haut. Kerry James Marshalls Elfenbeinschwarz, Marsschwarz und Kohlenschwarz sind rhetorische Mittel, die auf eine Schwarze Erfahrung hinweisen, die allen Schattierungen von Braun, Beige und Schwarz zugrunde liegen kann. Aber ich wollte Hauttöne auch in ihrer spezifischen Beschaffenheit zeigen und wandte mich in Werken wie *Fake Truth (Witness I–III)* (2019) und *Mediator* verschiedenen Schattierungen zu. Bei Letzterem sind zwei Brustabformungen einander gegenüberstehend an einer Metallkonstruktion befestigt. Die eine ist von einer dunkleren, die andere von einer helleren Hautfarbe. Damit sollte eine Konstruktion von *race* vermieden und keine spezifische Ethnie dargestellt werden. Und dennoch sind diese hautfarbenen Abformungen in unserem gesellschaftspolitischen Klima typisch für eine koloristische Wahrnehmung und Erfahrung.

(p. 57)
(p. 64)
(p. 87-89)

FIA Es ist interessant, dass Du in diesem Zusammenhang *Mediator* erwähnst – das Werk, das zwei Torsi in dieser binären Beziehung darstellt. Ähnlich wird in unserer Gesellschaft häufig über *race* diskutiert, indem man über Schwarz und Weiß redet.

JULIA Genau! Einerseits leugnet die Arbeit eine bestimmte Lesart von Ethnizität, und andererseits könnte sie die binären Darstellungen von Schwarzer und Weißer[2] Kultur aufzeigen, in denen wir zurzeit leben. Es ist eine sehr verengte Sichtweise auf Ethnizität und auch auf Rassismus.

FIA In welche Richtung haben sich Deine Überlegungen zur Arbeit mit Hautfarben und Hauttönen seitdem entwickelt?

JULIA Ich habe beschlossen, die realistische Darstellung von Hautfarben in der Bildhauerei vorerst einzustellen. Kolorismus ist ein äußerst komplexer Diskurs, über den viel zu wenig gesprochen wird. Koloristische Erfahrungen haben nicht nur mit Privilegien zu tun, sondern auch mit Fragen der Zugehörigkeit und der Diaspora. Ich gehöre zu den Menschen, die in den USA als „hellhäutig" und „*biracial*" bezeichnet werden (was in meinem Fall Schwarz und Weiß bedeutet). Dazu sollte man wissen, dass das auf die meisten Schwarzen Deutschen (Afrodeutschen) wie mich zutrifft. Ich würde gerne mehr Ausdrucksformen für die vielschichtige Thematik des Kolorismus finden, aber zurzeit bin ich nicht sicher, ob das Medium der Bildhauerei dafür der richtige Weg ist.

Meine letzte Arbeit *Nourisher* mit relativ großen Abformungen meiner Brust und meines Gesichts war ein Anlass, noch einmal über Haut nachzudenken. Die Außenseiten sind in einem matten Orange glasiert, das fast schon eine karikaturistische Darstellung von Haut ist; es erinnert an Emojis. Die Glasur der Innenseiten ist in einem glänzenden, satten Rosa gehalten, ein Symbol für Fleisch, Leben und Subjektivität.

In meinem gesamten westlichen Kunststudium habe ich wenig bis nichts über die symbolische Verwendung von Farbe, insbesondere in der zeitgenössischen visuellen Kultur, gelernt. Erst als ich zum ersten Mal in Richtung Osten reiste, nämlich im Frühjahr 2019 nach Hongkong, hatte ich eine sehr aufschlussreiche Unterhaltung mit dem Besitzer eines Vasengeschäftes, der mir all meine Fragen zum Thema Farbe beantworten konnte. Ich fragte ihn, wofür Rot steht – für Glück; Gelb – für Imperialismus; Grün – für ewige Jugend; Blau – für einen klaren Himmel/eine gute Zukunft. So habe ich die symbolische Bedeutung von Farben erst durch die Auseinandersetzung mit asiatischer Kultur entdeckt. Orange symbolisiert in der vedantischen Tradition Hingabe an das spirituelle Leben und Entsagung. Das Farbsystem ist somit auch ein Wertesystem.

Aber um noch einmal auf die *Attachment* Serie zurückzukommen: Vorhin haben wir über die Verspieltheit dieser Geräte gesprochen. Ich wollte einen Bezug zur Welt der Spielzeuge herstellen, aber auch Farben auf fast festliche Art und Weise einsetzen. Die Ausstellung *Me, Ourself & You*, zu der die *Attachment* Serie gehört, habe ich in freudiger Stimmung konzipiert, nachdem ich gerade Mutter geworden war, und ich wollte diese Erfahrung auf fast sentimentale Weise würdigen: durch die Verwendung von Farben … ähnlich wie bunte Blumen Festlichkeit symbolisieren.

FIA   Als ich sie das erste Mal sah, dachte ich ehrlich gesagt: „Das ist schon ein bisschen schnulzig." Nach Deinen früheren Arbeiten, zum Beispiel *Drainer*, die ziemlich düster sind und die Andeutung von Gewalt enthalten, sind wir nun bei den neueren Werken aus der *Attachment* Serie angelangt, die einen spielerischen Zugang zu Farbe und zur Beweglichkeit von Verbindungen haben. Was denkst Du darüber, dass sie womöglich als schnulzig wahrgenommen werden könnten?

JULIA   Ich glaube, meine Arbeit hat sich in den letzten paar Jahren stark verändert. Ich habe die Untersuchung unterdrückender Beziehungen hinter mir gelassen und möchte etwas anderes erforschen und ausdrücken, neue Erfahrungen. In diesen Zeiten, in denen ich versuche herauszufinden, wie es weitergehen soll, ist es meiner Meinung nach manchmal notwendig, wirklich seltsame Phasen zu durchlaufen.

Was diese abgedrehten, seltsamen Transformationsphasen betrifft, waren vor allem einige Jazzmusiker_innen wichtige Inspirationsquellen für mich. Ich meine Musiker_innen, die spirituelle Praktiken in ihr Leben einbezogen haben und deren Schaffen sich seitdem drastisch verändert hat. Alice Coltranes Musik zum Beispiel verwandelte sich durch ihre Auseinandersetzung mit Vedanta auf bemerkenswerte Weise. Die musikalische Ästhetik ihres Albums *Universal Consciousness* von 1971 war für das Jazzpublikum ziemlich ungewohnt. Oder nehmen wir den Pianisten Horace Silver, der in seinen späteren Werken sogar Gesang verwendete. Oder Mary Lou Williams und ihr Album *Mary Lou's Mass* von 1975. Inzwischen ist der „Spiritual Jazz" bereits als historisches Genre anerkannt, an dem noch viele weitere Musiker_innen teilhatten: John Coltrane, Pharoah Sanders, Sun Ra, Don Cherry. Aber damals war das neu für die Ohren des Publikums. Ich denke, dass die von Dir erwähnte Schnulzigkeit aus dem Zusammenprall der etablierten, akzeptierten Ästhetik des jeweiligen Bereichs (wie Jazz oder zeitgenössische Kunst) mit ungewohnten Elementen wie Schönheit oder neuen Wertesystemen, die von den Künstler_innen eingeführt werden, resultiert.

FIA   Vielleicht führt diese Schnulzigkeit auch zu einem Gefühl von Peinlichkeit.

JULIA   Das liegt womöglich an der Emotionalität der Selbstoffenbarung und an der Hoffnung, eine Wahrheit gefunden zu haben, die man allen mitteilen muss. Ich glaube, das kann potenziell sehr peinlich sein, weil die Wahrheit an und für sich so wandelbar ist. Was wir heute als Wahrheit entdecken, die wir glauben mitteilen zu müssen, kann in einem Jahr ganz anders aussehen. Es ist also diese Offenherzigkeit, die meiner Meinung nach peinlich ist, aber auch sehr fruchtbar.

Übersetzt von Sylvia Zirden

1 Jennifer Stuart, „Work and Motherhood. Preliminary Report of a Psychoanalytic Study", in: *The Psychoanalytic Quarterly* 76, Nr. 2 (2007), S. 443, https://doi.org/10.1002/j.2167-4086.2007.tb00264.x.

2 Die Künstlerin hat sich für die Großschreibung von Schwarz und Weiß entschieden, um auf den gesellschaftspolitischen Diskurs über die Konstruktion von *race* aufmerksam zu machen. Ann Thúy Nguyễn und Maya Pendleton, „Recognizing Race in Language. Why We Capitalize ‚Black' and ‚White'", Center for the Study of Social Policy, 23. März 2020, https://cssp.org/2020/03/recognizing-race-in-language-why-we-capitalize-black-and-white.

I remember the feeling of walking into the side gallery at Kunstverein Braunschweig when Julia Phillips' exhibition *Fake Truth* was opening. I had arrived early, and the space was empty. I paused at the edge of the gravel-covered floor and considered whether I was meant to step on it; upon recalling the importance of the body to the artist's work, I walked in. My shoes crunched along, each step different, uneven, and requiring attention. I started to hear ambient sound radiating, arrhythmically, from an unidentifiable source. I approached the first of three hanging sculptures, a ceramic set of lungs framed by an upper back (from below the top of the shoulders to halfway up the skull). As I turned to face it, a microphone grille greeted me, and I said hello. Some moments later, the sound in the space changed, and I heard a distorted version of my voice emerge from the sculpture in waves that overlapped with the ambient sound already present. The work was speaking back to me. I repeated this act with the other two sculptures, with each of the three works resulting in a different sound experience: one was slightly delayed, one steady and monotonous, and the last a mix of high and low feedback.

The Atmosphere of a Body   Magdalyn Asimakis

Technologically, the microphones were picking up my voice and sending it to a computer, from whence it came back in an altered state through speakers hidden in the lungs. Under my shoes, my steps were picked up by contact microphones and projected through a subwoofer under the ceiling. As a result, my body was in conversation with the sculptures and the space that held them; each of us presented a different affect to the same phrase, "hello," and we were, as a result, in social relation. Phillips' practice tends to exceed strictly cognitive or symbolic interactions, in which the viewer receives information through an established vocabulary of representation and display. Rooted in interaction between the physical and the psychological self, the artist's work often consists of sculptures that, through their titles and bodily cues, instruct viewers to imagine themselves enacting physical gestures that speak to societal power dynamics. I noted that *Fake Truth (Witness I–III)* (2019) took on more ambiguous titular instructions than, say, *Observer* (2016/20), *Mediator* (2020), *Destabilizer* (2018/21), or *Drainer* (2018/21). The role of *Fake Truth (Witness I–III)* is indeed to witness—that is, to confirm the truth of an event or idea through experiential knowledge. In this context, it was me who created the event to which the other bodies were witnesses.

(p. 87-89) (p. 90-93) (p. 141-143) (p. 80-83)

    It was around this time, 2019 to be precise, that the idea of fake truth—or "fake news" as it was called—became political rhetoric, specifically in the United States, where Phillips lives. Public accessibility to whatever truth one desires has now neutralized into reality, but the transparency of this was somewhat new at the time. The varied repetitions and interpretations of my voice in the exhibition space were comparatively opaque, but legible, and drew attention to the fact that we all exist in relation and that the instability of truth has material effects. The scenario that Phillips set up did not interpret or represent this cultural phenomenon; it restaged it, including the element of liveness and presence. In a departure from museological rhetoric that requires fixing, narrativization, and contextual distancing, Phillips did not use sound technology simply for the sake of contemporaneity, but rather to introduce an element of precarity, movement, and bodily implication to her repertoire, placing viewers in the position of a subject being interpreted—that is, in the traditional position of a political subject or museological object. Established curatorial strategies emerging from colonial practices of collecting, ordering, and displaying position objects and art as containers of information that can be cognitively read, sidestepping the fact that art and objects emerge from the material conditions of their context and cannot be severed from this through display. Phillips, importantly, subverts this colonial assumption in requiring the viewer to connect "inside" and "outside" of the gallery and the body.

The sculptures themselves also speak to the importance of embodiment in *Fake Truth* and in Phillips' practice at large. The meticulous sculpting and glazing of the "witnesses" suggests their different identities through unique heights, complexions, and scars that inevitably contribute to their varied interpretations by visitors. Up close, ruptures and tears visible on the "flesh" indicate psychological scarring and traumas obtained through living, or the categorization of being a "marked" body, which further contributes to the shaping of individual perspectives. These sculptural marks speak volumes about the correlation between body and psyche in Phillips' work, and how both manifest in the material world.

It is not the first time Phillips has suggested this. Material ruptures also appear in her earlier series of colographs titled (p. 135-139) *Expanded X, In Treatment* (2018), in which she ran pantyhose—to her, symbolic of the body and the psyche—through a printing press, making visible the tears, mending, and threading of the material. Similar to *Fake Truth (Witness I–III)*, Phillips forfeits a level of control in *Expanded X*, allowing space for bodies—both actual and metaphorical—to explore, interact, warp, and be altered by surrounding conditions. This attention to embodiment and lived experience shifts her practice from representational to atmospheric, allowing it to flow around and through the viewer's space and body in a microcosm of widespread patterns. The works experience us as we experience them.

An interest in stability underpins Phillips' language around the body's experience in the material world. As an exhibition, *Fake Truth* considered the instability of truth as reliable when sensorial perceptions hold the same weight as objective facts. Though a timely topic at the time of the exhibition, the ability to create truth through mere articulation also preceded that historical moment in multiple instances, the museum as a space of colonial display being one. Much of the way we encounter art has been learned through generations of conditioning that objects hold absolute truths that are static, completely knowable, and only related to their contexts representationally. From this perspective, knowledge is acquired through the mediator (the museum), or, in the case of *Fake Truth*, the witnesses. But these truths are at least once removed from the original context or event, which creates at least a minor destabilization. The phenomenology of walking through *Fake Truth*, then, with its disorientation, opacity, and unpredictability, quite intentionally mimicked the incompatibility between subjects and biased infrastructures of analysis. The stable value in *Fake Truth* was the body of the visitor.

Three years later, Phillips followed the conceptual thread of stability to a suite of sculptures for the 59th Venice Biennale, *The Milk of Dreams*, curated by Cecilia Alemani. The three included works—*Bower, Veiled Purifier*, and *Stabilizer* (p. 107) (p. 104) (p. 109) (all 2021–22)—turn to the internal self and the body's ability to stabilize through gestures of support, spiritual practices, and architecture. A ceramic cane with a fleshy handle, ideal for gripping with a human hand, *Stabilizer* is in many ways the bridge into this series from *Fake Truth*, due in part to its title and interest in truth. The base of the cane branches into three feet, creating a triangle—the geometric embodiment of stability—and from the handle hangs a plumb, an indicator of the perfect vertical. To use this cane would be to encounter deep grounding: the handle provides comfort, the three-legged base provides stability, and the plumb would ensure sound posture and orientation based on a relationship with gravity. Typical of Phillips' practice, the cane is ultimately unusable due to its material fragility, yet it has a phenomenological effect that invites us to imagine that level of physical stability. The work includes its own structure for display: a triangular wall-mounted shelf and a custom display case resembling a crystal (an extremely stable geological structure). Installed, the work at once mimics a seismograph on a museum wall—a measure of ground stability—and a shrine in a space of worship—a guide of spiritual stability. These affinities are emphasized by *Stabilizer*'s installation at eye level and further Phillips' redefining of display as a non-neutral element of exhibition. An attention to the ground is maintained in all three works from the Venice suite. While *Stabilizer* points to grounding through literal gravity, *Bower* and *Veiled Purifier* possess strong physical foundations made of heavy stone tiles. The former is a brass apparatus with ceramic supports for the forehead and lower back, creating negative space for a body being guided to bow to the ground. There are springs near the back support that would create resistance when the body bows, resulting in repetition and a general physical tension related to this act. In this gesture representing a spiritual lowering of the ego, Phillips suggests the difficulty in humbling oneself, or shrinking in the context of a capital- and growth-driven society. So much so, that acts of grounding are commonly relegated exclusively to spheres of the spiritual. Yet through this work Phillips points to how the psychic experience of spirituality is extended to, and can traverse, the boundary of the physical body.

If one manages to reach the ground of *Bower*—which, like *Stabilizer*, is not meant to be physically used—they would come face to face with dark gray tiles in a pattern inspired by the sixteenth-century church of San Giorgio Maggiore in Venice. According to Phillips, this artistic choice is a conscious reference to places of worship as spaces for introspection as a form of stabilization, while also acknowledging the specificity of when and for what site the work itself was made. Inserting herself into the dialogue by referencing the site of exposition is an unexpected and significant move that grounds the work in our lived reality. In a sense, Phillips once again breaks a fourth wall that divides representation and context. Reflecting this, in *Bower* the artist once again notes the importance of the body as a living, stabilizing entity that is malleable according to context, and while the granite tiles seem immovable, the body is enacting the struggle to stabilize.

Seemingly in relation, the hypothetical bowing individual was positioned facing *Veiled Purifier* in the Venice installation. *Veiled Purifier* also has a tiled base, this one referencing one of the most tourist-visited sites in Venice: Saint Mark's Basilica. In contrast to *Bower*, the tiles on this work are white marble and triangular, referencing the Moorish patterning of the basilica's floor. Draped over the tiles is a purple silk veil hanging from a ceramic cast of a forehead with a mouthpiece and handlebars, inviting a divine or physical other to step up onto the tiles and blow into another person's third eye—the energy center of the body, through which one can be spiritually cleansed or toxified. The veil here creates a space of introspection for the person being "purified" in which they can exclusively address the soul and spirit, away from the gaze of the viewer. Notably, the long silk fabric is very light and only fixed at the top of the sculpture, making this boundary precarious and unstable, particularly with the movement of people in the gallery.

The veil joins the plumb and springs as a sculptural component that builds precarity into the conceptual functionality of Phillips' Venice suite and, recalling *Fake Truth*, acknowledges the destabilizing reality of existing in relation to others within an individual-focused neoliberal capitalist framework. The artist's search for stability as a reliable value has a limit, which she acknowledges and folds into her sculptures and installations. While she may locate stability in the body, it is relations between bodies that contain dynamics of power that can quickly throw off this security, which Phillips centrally addresses through the fragility of her main material: ceramic. Indeed, Phillips' use of ceramic is transformative in its ability to at once invite you to touch, grip, and maneuver, and yet repel you with the fear of shattering the objects themselves. This indicates that Phillips does not believe that stability equates fixity, but that bodies remain in constant negotiation of the social power dynamics they are embedded in.

It is thus important to bring ourselves to Phillips' work while also considering the objects in relation to their display in colonial infrastructures like museums and biennials. The artist's eschewing of so-called traditional display structures in both *Fake Truth* and the Venice suite; her emphasis on malleability (the gravel), site specificity (the Venice tiles), and display affinities (the gem-shaped case); and her embracing of ambiguity and precarity in the sculptures themselves cut into the way we have been conditioned to understand the power of the museum as a mediator or translator of facts. In these projects, as in her larger search for internal stability through specific forms, media, and presentations, Julia Phillips scrupulously conveys varied dynamics of power at play both in the museum and outside of it.

Ich erinnere mich noch gut an die Eröffnung von Julia Phillips' Ausstellung *Fake Truth* 2019 im Kunstverein Braunschweig. Ebenso deutlich sind mir die Gefühle in Erinnerung, die mich beim Betreten der Seitengalerie beschlichen, in der sie stattfand. Ich war etwas zu früh gekommen und der Ausstellungsraum war noch leer. Daher blieb ich kurz zögernd am Rande der Galerie stehen, unsicher, ob ich den mit Kies gefüllten Raum überhaupt betreten sollte. Aber dann fiel mir ein, dass der Körper im Werk dieser Künstlerin eine ganz besondere Rolle spielt, und ich wagte den Schritt über die Türschwelle. Meine Schuhe knirschten auf dem Boden, jeder Schritt war prekär und erforderte eine gewisse Aufmerksamkeit. Von irgendwoher drangen arhythmische Geräusche zu mir. Ich ging auf die ersten von drei im Raum hängenden Skulpturen zu: ein menschliches Lungenpaar aus Keramik, eingerahmt vom oberen Teil des Rückens von der Schulter bis hoch zur Hälfte des Schädels. Als ich mich ihm zuwendete, begrüßte mich ein Mikrofongitter, und ich sprach „Hallo" hinein. Kurz darauf änderte sich der Klang im Raum, meine eigene Stimme drang verzerrt in Wellen aus der Skulptur heraus und überlagerte sich mit den anderen Geräuschen im Raum. Die Skulptur sprach nun mit mir. Ich wiederholte den Vorgang bei den anderen beiden Skulpturen, jedes Mal mit anderem Ergebnis: Das soeben beschriebene Klangerlebnis trat mit leichter Verzögerung ein, das zweite bestand aus einem anhaltenden, monotonen Ton und das dritte war eine Mischung aus hohen und tiefen Rückkopplungen.

Die Atmosphäre eines Körpers

Magdalyn Asimakis

Die Mikrofone nahmen meine Stimme auf, übermittelten sie an einen Computer und gaben sie schließlich durch Lautsprecher, die verborgen im Lungenpaar angebracht waren, verfremdet wieder zurück. Meine Schritte wiederum wurden von Kontaktmikrofonen aufgezeichnet und über einen an der Decke montierten Subwoofer zurück in den Raum projiziert. Das Ergebnis war ein Dialog zwischen meinem Körper und den drei Skulpturen; unsere affektiv unterschiedlich gefärbten „Hallos" ergaben ein soziales Beziehungsgefüge.

Wie oft in Phillips' Arbeit ging auch hier die im Raum erschaffene Beziehung über die rein intellektuelle oder symbolische Interaktion hinaus, mit der wir aus der konventionellen Ausstellungspraxis her vertraut sind. Ihre Arbeiten setzen vielmehr eine Interaktion zwischen unserer physischen und psychischen Identität in Gang. Durch ihre Titel, aber auch durch ihre körperliche Signalgebung fordern sie die Betrachtenden zum imaginativen Nachvollzug von Bewegungsgesten auf, die gesellschaftliche Machtdynamiken kommentieren. Dabei sind die Werktitel *Witness I–III* in *Fake Truth* (2019) (p. 87-89) im Unterschied zu Phillips' sonstigen so indikativen, Funktionen oder Aktionen bezeichnenden Werktiteln wie *Observer* (2016/20), (p. 141-143) *Mediator* (2020), *Destabilizer* (2018/21), oder *Drainer* (2018/21) un- (p. 80-83) (p. 90-93) gewöhnlich unkonkret. Die Rolle der *Fake Truth*-Werke besteht in der Zeug_innenschaft, also darin, die Wahrheit eines Ereignisses oder einer Hypothese durch Erfahrungswissen zu bezeugen und zu bestätigen. In diesem Fall war das Ereignis von mir selbst in Gang gesetzt und wurde von den skulpturalen Körpern bezeugt und jeweils unterschiedlich interpretiert.

Ungefähr zur Zeit von Phillips' Ausstellung (2019) wurde das Konzept der Falschwahrheit – der sogenannten Fake News – in den Vereinigten Staaten, wo die Künstlerin lebt, zur politischen Rhetorik. Wenn auch die öffentliche Aneignung einer gerade erwünschten, opportunen Wahrheit inzwischen Teil der politischen Realität geworden ist, handelte es sich zur Zeit der Ausstellung noch um eine recht neue Entwicklung. Die vielfältigen Wiederholungen und Modulationen meiner Stimme im Raum waren zwar relativ undurchsichtig, aber doch als individuell erkennbar. Das Klangerlebnis machte darauf aufmerksam, dass die menschliche Existenz eine relationale ist und die Instabilität von Wahrheit tatsächliche, materielle Auswirkungen hat. Bei Phillips' Skulpturen-Installation handelt es sich insofern nicht um eine Interpretation oder Darstellung dieses kulturellen Phänomens, sondern um dessen Neuinszenierung, live und in Präsenz. In Abkehr von der museologischen Rhetorik, die Fixierung, Narrativierung und kontextuelle Distanzierung verlangt, setzte Phillips die Tontechnik hier nicht allein wegen der zeitgenössischen Relevanz des Mediums ein. Vielmehr erweitert sie damit ihr Repertoire um ein Element der Prekarität, der Bewegung und der körperlichen Implikation, indem sie die Betrachtenden in die Rolle des interpretierten Subjekts versetzt – in die Rolle also, die klassischerweise dem politischen Subjekt oder musealen Ausstellungsobjekt zukommt. Etablierte kuratorische Strategien – das Ergebnis kolonialer Praktiken des Sammelns, Ordnens und Ausstellens – positionieren Objekte und Kunst als kognitiv zu entschlüsselnde Informationsträger. Dabei wird die Tatsache missachtet, dass Kunstwerke und Objekte aus den materiellen Bedingungen ihres Kontextes hervorgegangen sind und durch ihr Ausgestelltwerden nicht einfach aus diesen Kontexten gelöst werden können. Die koloniale Grundposition unterläuft Phillips, indem sie den Betrachtenden abverlangt, sich sowohl „innerhalb" als auch „außerhalb" der Galerie und des Körpers mit den Arbeiten in Beziehung zu setzen.

Auch die Beschaffenheit der Skulpturen selbst in *Fake Truth* wie in Phillips' künstlerischer Praxis überhaupt sagt etwas über die Bedeutung von Körperlichkeit aus. In der akribischen Modellierung und Glasur dieser „Zeug_innen" mit unterschiedlicher Körpergröße, Hautfarbe und Narben drückt sich ihre je eigene Identität aus, die selbstverständlich auch je unterschiedlich von den Betrachtenden interpretiert wird. Von Nahem betrachtet werden Brüche und Risse auf der „Haut" sichtbar, Hinweise auf seelische Narben und erlittene Traumata oder auf die Zuschreibung eines „markierten" Körpers, was wiederum weitere individuelle Interpretationen zuließe. Diese skulpturalen Gesten sprechen Bände über die Wechselbeziehung zwischen Körper und Psyche in Phillips' Werk und ihren Ausdruck in der materiellen Welt.

Nicht zum ersten Mal kommen diese skulpturalen Spuren zum Vorschein. Auch in Phillips' früherer Collagrafie-Druck-Serie *Expanded X, In Treatment* (2018) tauchen Risse im Material auf. Hier (p. 135-139) ließ Phillips mit Rissen, Flicken und Fäden versehene Strumpfhosen – bei ihr Symbole für Körper und Psyche – durch eine Druckpresse laufen und bildete ihre Struktur auf Papier ab. Ähnlich wie in der *Witness*-Serie gibt Phillips in *Expanded X* ein gewisses Maß an Kontrolle ab: Sie lässt den Körpern – sowohl realen als auch symbolischen – Raum, in die Umgebung einzudringen, mit ihr zu interagieren, sie zu verzerren und von ihr verändert zu werden. Durch diese Sensibilität für Körperlichkeit und erlebte Erfahrung verschiebt sich der Schwerpunkt in Phillips' Werk vom rein Darstellerischen hin zum Atmosphärischen. Die Arbeiten schwingen buchstäblich um und durch die Betrachtenden hindurch und werden durch den Mikrokosmos eines raumgreifenden Musters zusammengehalten. Die Werke erleben uns und wir erleben sie.

Das Vokabular, das Phillips für die körperliche Erfahrung der materiellen Umwelt aufgebaut hat, wird von einem Interesse an Stabilität durchzogen. Die Ausstellung *Fake Truth* untersucht die Instabilität von verlässlicher Wahrheit, indem Sinneseindrücken das gleiche Gewicht gegeben wird wie objektiven Fakten.

Auch wenn das Thema *Fake Truth* zum Zeitpunkt der Ausstellung gerade aktuell war, den Mechanismus, Wahrheit durch bloße Behauptungen zu schaffen, gab es bereits lange zuvor – eines von vielen Beispielen dafür wäre etwa das Museum als Ort der kolonialen Ausstellung. Kunst nehmen wir meist so wahr, wie wir es über Generationen erlernt haben: als seien die Werke Träger einer absoluten, unveränderlichen und vollständig erfassbaren Wahrheit; als stünden sie mit ihrem Kontext in einem reinen Abbildungsverhältnis. Aus dieser Perspektive wird Wissen durch eine Vermittlungsinstanz, das Museum oder, im Falle von *Fake Truth*, durch Zeug_innen erworben. Diese Wahrheiten sind jedoch aus ihrem ursprünglichen Kontext entfernt (und meist mehrfach herumgereicht) worden, was bereits eine geringfügige Destabilisierung erzeugt. Die Phänomenologie des Durchwanderns von *Fake Truth* ahmt also mit ihrer Orientierungslosigkeit, Undurchsichtigkeit und Unvorhersehbarkeit ganz bewusst die Inkompatibilität zwischen Subjekten und voreingenommenen Analysestrukturen nach. Der einzig stabile Wert in *Fake Truth* ist der Körper der Besucher_innen.

Mein Besuch von *Fake Truth* liegt inzwischen drei Jahre zurück. Aber das Motiv der Stabilität durchzieht als konzeptueller Faden auch einige in der Folgezeit entstandene Arbeiten von Julia Phillips, so etwa die drei Skulpturen, die die Künstlerin auf der 59. Biennale in Venedig gezeigt hat, *The Milk of Dreams* (kuratiert von Cecilia Alemani). Die drei Werke – *Bower, Veiled Purifier und* (p. 107) (p. 104) (p. 109) *Stabilizer* (alle 2021–22) – wenden sich dem inneren Selbst und der Fähigkeit des Körpers zu, sich durch unterstützende Handlungen, spirituelle Praktiken und Architektur zu stabilisieren. *Stabilizer* bildet in gleich mehrfacher Hinsicht die Brücke von *Fake Truth* zu dieser neuen Serie, dies aufgrund des Titels, aber auch aufgrund des Interesses an (wissenschaftlicher) Wahrheit. Die Skulptur stellt einen keramischen Gehstock mit fleischigem Griff dar. Das untere Stockende verzweigt sich in drei Füße, die ein Dreieck bilden – ein geometrisches Symbol der Stabilität. Vom Griff am oberen Ende hängt ein Lot – Indikator für die perfekte, der Schwerkraft zu verdankenden Vertikale. Mit diesem Stock in der Hand könnte man sich erden: Der Griff sorgt für Komfort, der dreiteilige Fuß für Stabilität und das Lot für eine aufrechte Körperhaltung basierend auf einer Beziehung zur Schwerkraft. Aber es ist kennzeichnend für Phillips' Kunst, dass der Gehstock aufgrund seiner materiellen Zerbrechlichkeit letztlich unbrauchbar ist. Dennoch hat er eine phänomenologische Wirkung, die die Betrachtenden dazu einlädt, sich dieses Maß an physischer Stabilität vorzustellen.

Dazu trägt auch die Präsentationsform des Objekts bei: Es steht auf einem dreieckigen Wandsockel in einer maßgefertigten Vitrine von kristalliner Form – repräsentativ für eine extrem stabile geologische Materie. Beim Betrachten der Arbeit fühlt man sich an einen Seismografen an einer Museumswand erinnert – ein Maß für Bodenstabilität – oder einen Schrein in einem Gebets- oder Andachtsraum – Zufluchtsort auf der Suche nach spiritueller Stabilität. Diese Assoziationen werden einerseits durch die Installation auf Augenhöhe betont und andererseits durch Phillips' Neudefinition der Präsentationsform als nicht neutrales Ausstellungselement.

In allen drei Werken der Venedig-Werkreihe spielt die Ausrichtung auf den Boden eine große Rolle. Während *Stabilizer* durch buchstäbliche Schwerkraft auf Erdung hinweist, stehen *Bower* und *Veiled Purifier* auf mächtigen steinernen Fliesen-Plattformen. *Bower* ist ein Messingapparat mit keramischen Passformen für die Stirn und den unteren Rücken, die einen Negativraum für den Körper schaffen. Die Skulptur suggeriert die Ausführung einer Beugung zum Boden. Rückenstütze und Querachse sind mit Federn verbunden, die Widerstand bei einer Beugung erzeugen und damit zu Wiederholungen und körperlicher Anspannung bei der Ausführung führen würden. Mit der Verneigung als Geste der spirituellen Überwindung des Egos deutet Phillips auf die Schwierigkeit hin, sich im Kontext der kapital- und wachstumsorientierten Gesellschaft in Demut und Verneigung zu üben. Die Schwierigkeit ist gesellschaftlich so erheblich, dass Praktiken der bewussten Besinnung und Erdung oft in die Sphäre des Spirituellen verdrängt werden. Mit dieser Skulptur weist Phillips jedoch darauf hin, dass Spiritualität nicht nur eine psychische Erfahrung ist, sondern auch die Grenze zum Körperlichen überschreiten und sich auf den Körper erstrecken kann.

Wenn man *Bower* betätigt und es schafft, sich dem Boden zuzuneigen, obwohl der Apparat ebenso wenig wie *Stabilizer* zur tatsächlichen Nutzung bestimmt ist, stößt man auf dunkelgraue Fliesen. Das Muster ist von der venezianischen Kirche San Giorgio Maggiore aus dem 16. Jahrhundert inspiriert. Nach Aussage der Künstlerin ist die Wahl der kirchlichen Referenz ein bewusster Hinweis auf Orte der Kontemplation, der Selbstbeobachtung und der Stabilisierung. Gleichzeitig wird durch diese örtliche Bezugnahme auch auf den besonderen Anlass für die Entstehung der Arbeit verwiesen. Durch den Venedig-Verweis entsteht ein Dialog mit dem Ausstellungsort; ein unerwarteter und bedeutender Schritt, der die Arbeit in unserer momentanen Gegenwart und Realität verankert. In gewisser Weise durchbricht Phillips erneut eine vierte Wand zwischen Darstellung und Kontext: Auch in *Bower* betont die Künstlerin die Bedeutung des Körpers als lebendige, stabilisierende Instanz, die abhängig vom Kontext formbar ist. Der Körper ringt auf den unbeweglich erscheinenden Granitfliesen um Stabilisierung.

Das sich hypothetisch verbeugende Individuum von *Bower* stand in der Ausstellung in Venedig direkt ausgerichtet auf die Skulptur *Veiled Purifier* und insofern dazu in Beziehung. Auch dieses Werk hat einen Fliesen-Sockel, der an eine der meistbesuchten Sehenswürdigkeiten Venedigs erinnert, den Markusdom. Im Gegensatz zu *Bower* sind die Fliesen in dieser Arbeit aber dreieckig, aus weißem Marmor und zitieren die maurischen Muster des Dombodens. Über die Fliesen gebreitet liegt ein violetter Seidenschleier, der an einem Keramikabdruck einer Stirn mit einem Mundstück und Griffstangen hängt. Das Mundstück auf der Stirn scheint eine göttliche oder physische Präsenz einzuladen, auf die Fliesen zu steigen und Atem in das dritte Auge der anderen Person zu hauchen – das Energiezentrum des Körpers, durch das man geistig gereinigt oder vergiftet werden kann. Der Schleier schafft hier einen Raum der Introspektion für die zu „läuternde" Person: Den Blicken anderer entzogen, kann sie sich seelisch und geistig versenken. Bemerkenswert ist, dass der lange Seidenstoff sehr leicht und nur an der Oberseite der Skulptur befestigt ist. Insbesondere bei der Bewegung von Menschen im Ausstellungsraum macht dies diese Grenze prekär und instabil.

Ähnlich wie das Lot und die Federn trägt auch der Schleier als skulpturale Komponente zu einer Prekarität der konzeptionellen Funktionalität von Phillips' Venedig-Werkreihe bei. Wie auch bei *Fake Truth* steht die Frage nach einer destabilisierenden Realität im Raum, deren Wesen es ist, in Beziehung zu anderen zu existieren, und zwar im Rahmen eines neoliberalen, auf das Individuum ausgerichteten kapitalistischen Systems. Die Suche der Künstlerin nach Stabilität und Verlässlichkeit hat eine Grenze, die sie in ihre Skulpturen und Installationen einarbeitet. Während Phillips Stabilität innerhalb des Körpers verorten mag, enthalten Beziehungen zwischen Körpern Machtdynamiken, welche diese Sicherheit schnell aus dem Weg räumen können. Dies thematisiert Phillips durch die Zerbrechlichkeit ihres Hauptmaterials: Keramik. Das Material lädt einerseits zum Berühren, Greifen und Manövrieren ein, lässt andererseits aber aufgrund seiner Zerbrechlichkeit davor zurückschrecken – ein Hinweis darauf, dass Phillips Stabilität nicht mit Beständigkeit gleichsetzt, sondern dass Körper in ständiger Verhandlung mit der sozialen Machtdynamik verharren, in die sie eingebettet sind.

Daher ist es bei der Begegnung mit Phillips' Arbeit wichtig, die Objekte auch in Bezug auf ihre Präsentation in kolonialen Infrastrukturen wie Museen und Biennalen zu betrachten. Der Verzicht auf die traditionellen musealen Präsentationsformen zeigt sich sowohl bei *Fake Truth* als auch in der Venedig-Werkreihe. Die Betonung von Formbarkeit (Kies), Ortsspezifität (Venedig-Fliesen) und eine Affinität für Displays (die kristallförmige Vitrine) sowie die Inkaufnahme von Mehrdeutigkeit und Prekarität ihrer Skulpturen, dies alles untergräbt unsere Konditionierung darauf, Museen als Vermittlungs- oder Übersetzungsinstanzen von Fakten anzuerkennen. In diesen Arbeiten wie auch auf ihrer allgemeineren Suche nach innerer Stabilität vermittelt die Künstlerin durch ihre Formen, Medien und Präsentationsformen akribisch unterschiedliche Dynamiken von Macht, die sowohl im Museum als auch außerhalb des Museums im Spiel sind.

Übersetzt von Magnus Elias Rosengarten und Julia Phillips

WRITERS

DANIELLA ROSE KING

Daniella Rose King is a writer and curator concerned with artistic practices of the Caribbean and its diaspora, with a particular focus on feminist readings of transatlantic geographies and their histories of extraction. She is currently an adjunct curator of Caribbean diasporic art at Hyundai Tate Research Centre: Transnational. Her writing has appeared in *Life between Islands: Caribbean-British Art 1950s–Now* (Tate Publishing, 2021), *Deborah Anzinger: An Unlikely Birth* (ICA Philadelphia, 2019), *The Last Place They Thought Of* (ICA Philadelphia, 2018), *Women and Performance: A Journal of Feminist Theory*, and *Other Cinemas: Politics, Culture and Experimental Film in the 1970s* (IB Tauris, 2017).

FIA BACKSTRÖM

Fia Backström is an artist based in New York. Backström represented Sweden in the 2011 Venice Biennale (for which a monograph of her work was produced) and was included in the 2008 Whitney Biennial and *Greater New York* at MoMA PS1 in 2015. Backström's work was the focus of the fall 2015 season at the Artist's Institute, and has been shown at the Museum of Modern Art, New York; The Kitchen, New York; Serpentine Galleries, London; De Appel, Amsterdam; Centre Pompidou, Paris; and the Moderna Museet, Stockholm. Her writings have been published in *COOP A-script* (2016). In 2018 she received the Prix Littéraire Bernard Heidsieck – Centre Pompidou. Backström is an associate professor at the Cooper Union.

JAMIESON WEBSTER

Jamieson Webster, PhD, is a psychoanalyst based in New York. She teaches at the New School for Social Research and is on the board and faculty of Pulsion Institute. She is the author of *The Life and Death of Psychoanalysis* (Routledge, 2011), *Stay, Illusion!* with Simon Critchley (Vintage, 2013), *Conversion Disorder* (Columbia University Press, 2018), and *Disorganisation and Sex* (Divided, 2022). She writes regularly for *Artforum*, the *New York Review of Books*, the *New York Times*, and *Spike Art Quarterly*.

JANET DEES

Janet Dees is the Steven and Lisa Munster Tananbaum Curator of Modern and Contemporary Art at the Block Museum of Art, Northwestern University, where she is an affiliate of the Department of Art History and the Center for Native American and Indigenous Research. Trained as a historian of American art, she focuses her curatorial work on contemporary artists' engagements with history, archives, and transformational practices and inclusive museum methodologies. Dees was the recipient of a 2018 curatorial fellowship from the Andy Warhol Foundation for the Visual Arts for the development of *A Site of Struggle: American Art against Anti-Black Violence* (2022) and is a 2023 fellow of the Center for Curatorial Leadership.

MAGDALYN ASIMAKIS

Magdalyn Asimakis is a curator and writer living in Toronto. Her practice centers on inherited knowledge and lived experience in relation to Western display practices and methods of knowing. She has organized exhibitions and programs in Toronto and New York, and cofounded the roving project space and collective ma ma in 2018. She is currently a PhD candidate at Queen's University.

AUTORINNEN

DANIELLA ROSE KING

Daniella Rose King ist Autorin und Kuratorin und beschäftigt sich mit künstlerischen Praktiken in der Karibik und ihrer Diaspora. Ihr besonderer Schwerpunkt liegt auf feministischen Lesarten der transatlantischen Geografie und deren Ausbeutungsgeschichte. Zurzeit arbeitet sie als Assistenzkuratorin für karibische Diasporakunst am Hyundai Tate Research Centre: Transnational. Sie veröffentlichte Beiträge in *Life Between Islands. Caribbean-British Art 1950s to Now* (Tate Publishing 2021), *The Last Place They Thought Of* (ICA University of Pennsylvania 2018), Deborah Anzinger: *An Unlikely Birth* (ICA UPenn 2019), *Women and Performance. A Journal of Feminist Theory* (Juli–Nov. 2018) und *Other Cinemas. Politics, Culture and Experimental Film in the 1970s* (IB Tauris 2017).

FIA BACKSTRÖM

Fia Backström ist Künstlerin und lebt in New York. Sie vertrat Schweden im Jahr 2011 auf der Biennale von Venedig und war 2008 auf der Whitney Biennale vertreten sowie 2015 bei *Greater New York*, MoMA PS1. Im Herbst 2015 bildeten ihre Arbeiten den Schwerpunkt des Artist's Institute. Backströms Werke wurden in New York im MoMA und in The Kitchen, in der Londoner Serpentine Gallery, im Amsterdamer De Appel, im Centre Pompidou in Paris und im Moderna Museet in Stockholm ausgestellt. Anlässlich der Biennale von Venedig erschien eine Monografie über ihre Arbeit. Ihre Schriften wurden 2016 in dem Band *COOP A-script* publiziert. 2018 erhielt sie den Bernhard-Heidsieck-Literaturpreis des Centre Pompidou. Fia Backström ist Professorin an der Cooper Union.

JAMIESON WEBSTER

Dr. Jamieson Webster ist Psychoanalytikerin in New York. Sie unterrichtet an der New School for Social Research und gehört zum Kuratorium und zum Kollegium des Pulsion Institutes. Zu ihren Publikationen gehören *The Life and Death of Psychoanalysis* (Routledge, 2011), *Stay, Illusion!* mit Simon Critchley (Vintage, 2013), *Conversion Disorder* (Columbia University Press, 2018) und *Disorganisation and Sex* (Divided, 2022). Sie schreibt regelmäßig für *Artforum*, *The New York Review of Books*, *The New York Times* und *Spike Art Quarterly*.

JANET DEES

Janet Dees ist Steven-und-Lisa-Munster-Tananbaum-Kuratorin für moderne und zeitgenössische Kunst am Block Museum of Art an der Northwestern University, wo sie Mitglied des Fachbereichs Kunstgeschichte und des Center for Native American and Indigenous Research ist. Als ausgebildete Kunsthistorikerin mit dem Schwerpunkt amerikanische Kunst widmet sie sich in ihrer kuratorischen Arbeit der Auseinandersetzung zeitgenössischer Künstlerinnen und Künstler mit Geschichte, Archiven und Transformationsverfahren sowie integrativen Museumsmethoden. Dees erhielt 2018 ein Kuratorenstipendium von der Andy Warhol Foundation for the Visual Arts für die Entwicklung von *A Site of Struggle. American Art against Anti-Black Violence* (2022) und ist 2023 Fellow am Center for Curatorial Leadership.

MAGDALYN ASIMAKIS

Magdalyn Asimakis ist Kuratorin und Autorin und lebt in Toronto. Schwerpunkt ihrer Arbeit sind ererbtes Wissen und gelebte Erfahrungen im Zusammenhang mit westlichen Ausstellungspraktiken und Erkenntnismethoden. Sie hat Ausstellungen und Projekte in Toronto und New York organisiert und war 2018 Mitbegründerin des mobilen Projektraums und Kollektivs *ma ma*. Zurzeit ist sie Doktorandin an der Queen's University.

TRANSLATORS

MELODY MAKEDA LEDWON

Melody Makeda Ledwon is a bilingual translator and interpreter (German/English) who calls both Berlin and New York home. Her work critically engages intersectional perspectives on African American and African diasporic history and literature, with a specific focus on Black feminisms. She has translated and authored a wide range of texts, including "Combahee River Collective: Ein Schwarzes feministisches Statement," published in *Schwarzer Feminismus: Grundlagentexte* (Unrast, 2019), and *Entangled (Hi)stories: A Conversation between Iman Attia and Michael Rothberg* (S. Fischer Verlag und Transit).

MAGNUS ELIAS ROSENGARTEN

Magnus Elias Rosengarten primarily works as a writer and curator in the fields of performance, discourse, and film/video, recently for the Gropius Bau in Berlin. He has written and produced for *C& Magazine, Artforum*, the Berlin Biennale, and ZDF/Arte, among others. He has presented work at the Kraine Theater, New York (2016), the California African American Museum, Los Angeles (2018), and Ballhaus Naunynstraße, Berlin (2023).

SYLVIA ZIRDEN

Sylvia Zirden, PhD, is a translator, editor, and artist who lives and works in Berlin. She studied philosophy and German language and literature in Munich and Berlin, specializing in aesthetics. Her 2003 doctorate was on Theodor W. Adorno's *Theorie des Neuen* (Theory of the New). She has produced manifold translations and editing work in the fields of aesthetics, art, and culture for museums, publishers, galleries, and artists. She is also trained in photography and has presented numerous exhibitions.

ÜBERSETZER_INNEN

MELODY MAKEDA LEDWON

Melody Makeda Ledwon ist bilinguale Übersetzerin und Dolmetscherin (DE/EN), die in Berlin und New York lebt. Der Fokus ihrer Arbeit liegt auf rassismuskritischen, intersektionalen Perspektiven und Ansätzen. Schwerpunktthemen sind afroamerikanische und afro-diasporische Geschichte und Literatur, speziell Schwarze Feminismen. Übersetzt hat sie eine große Bandbreite an Texten unter anderem *Combahee River Collective: Ein Schwarzes feministisches Statement* in Schwarzer Feminismus – Grundlagentexte (Unrast, 2019) und *Entangled (Hi)stories: A Conversation between Iman Attia and Michael Rothberg* (S. Fischer Verlag und TRANSIT).

MAGNUS ELIAS ROSENGARTEN

Magnus Elias Rosengarten arbeitet vor allem als Autor und Kurator in den Bereichen Performance, Diskurs und Film/Video, zuletzt für den Gropius Bau in Berlin. Er hat unter anderem für das Magazin Contemporary And (C&), Artforum, die Berlin Biennale und ARTE/ZDF geschrieben und produziert. Zudem präsentierte er auch Arbeiten im Kraine Theatre, New York City (2016), im California African American Museum, Los Angeles (2018) und im Ballhaus Naunynstraße, Berlin (2023).

SYLVIA ZIRDEN

Dr. Sylvia Zirden ist Übersetzerin, Lektorin und Künstlerin. Sie studierte Philosophie und Germanistik mit dem Schwerpunkt Ästhetik in München und Berlin. 2003 Promotion über Theodor W. Adornos *Theorie des Neuen*. Vielfältige Übersetzungen und Lektorate im Bereich Ästhetik, Kunst und Kultur für Museen, Verlage, Galerien, Künstlerinnen und Künstler. Ausbildung in künstlerischer Fotografie 2017–2019, seitdem zahlreiche Ausstellungen. Sylvia Zirden lebt und arbeitet in Berlin.

CV
JULIA PHILLIPS

Born 1985 in Hamburg, lives and works in Chicago and Berlin / geb. 1985 in Hamburg, lebt und arbeitet in Chicago und Berlin

SOLO EXHIBITIONS / EINZELAUSSTELLUNGEN

2022
Observer, Observed, High Line Art, New York (commission / Auftragsarbeit)
Me, Ourself & You, Matthew Marks Gallery, New York

2021
Between Love and Loss, Matthew Marks Gallery, Los Angeles

2020
New Album, Matthew Marks Gallery, New York

2019
Fake Truth, Kunstverein Braunschweig, Germany

2018
Failure Detection, MoMA PS1, Queens, New York

2016
Impenetrable Entry, Campoli Presti, London

GROUP EXHIBITIONS / GRUPPENAUSSTELLUNGEN

2023
Words Don't Go There, Kunstverein Braunschweig, Germany
Of Mythic Worlds: Works from the Distant Past through the Present, The Drawing Center, New York

2022
Future Bodies from a Recent Past, Museum Brandhorst, Munich*
The Milk of Dreams, Venice Biennale, 59th International Art Exhibition*

2021
Grief and Grievance: Art and Mourning in America, New Museum, New York*

2020
Nothing Is So Humble: Prints from Everyday Objects, The Whitney Museum of American Art, New York
1 Million Roses, Albertinum, Dresden, Germany*
Grace Before Jones: Camera, Disco, Studio, Nottingham Contemporary, United Kingdom
Studio Berlin, Berghain in collaboration with the Boros Foundation, Berlin*
Frank Walter — Eine Retrospektive, MMK Museum für Moderne Kunst, Frankfurt, Germany*
Duro Olowu: Seeing Chicago, Museum of Contemporary Art Chicago*
Haptic Feedback, Galerie Thomas Schulte, Berlin

2019
Contemporary Art: Five Propositions, Museum of Fine Arts, Boston
Feminist Histories: Artists After 2000, Museu de Arte de São Paulo, Brazil*
I campi magnetici (Magnetic Fields), Gió Marconi, Milan
Performing Society: The Violence of Gender, Tai Kwun, Hong Kong*

2018
Positioner, Matthew Marks Gallery, Los Angeles
In The Air, ma ma, Toronto
We don't need another hero, 10th Berlin Biennale for Contemporary Art*
Face of Another, Galleri Susanne Ottesen, Copenhagen
Songs for Sabotage, New Museum Triennial, New York*

2017
We Go As They, artist-in-residence exhibition, The Studio Museum in Harlem, New York*
Dreamers Awake, White Cube (Bermondsey), London*
That I am reading backwards and into for a purpose, to go on, The Kitchen, New York*

2016
The Whitney Museum of American Art Independent Study Program exhibition, The Elizabeth Foundation for the Arts, New York
In Place Of, Miguel Abreu Gallery, New York

2015
A Constellation, The Studio Museum in Harlem, New York*

*

(Exhibition catalog /Ausstellungskatalog)

MUSEUM AND PUBLIC COLLECTIONS / MUSEEN UND ÖFFENTLICHE SAMMLUNGEN

The Art Institute of Chicago
Fondazione Memmo, Rome
Hammer Museum, Los Angeles
Hessel Museum of Art, Bard College, Annandale-on-Hudson, New York
Marciano Art Foundation, Los Angeles
MUSEUM MMK für Moderne Kunst, Frankfurt am Main, Germany
Moderna Museet, Stockholm
The Museum of Contemporary Art, Los Angeles
Museum of Fine Arts, Boston
The Museum of Modern Art, New York
The Studio Museum in Harlem, New York
UCLA Grunwald Center for the Graphic Arts, Hammer Museum, Los Angeles
The Whitney Museum of American Art, New York

PUBLICATIONS / VERÖFFENTLICHUNGEN

In addition to numerous exhibition and collection catalogues including *Four Generations: The Joyner Giuffrida Collection of Abstract Art*, Phillips has been featured in prestigious publications such as *Artforum*, *The New York Times*, *Sculpture Magazine*, *Texte zur Kunst*, *Frieze*, *ArtReview*, *Hyperallergic*, *The New Yorker*, and *Mousse Magazine*.

Zahlreiche Ausstellungskataloge (s.o.), darunter *Four Generations: The Joyner Giuffrida Collection of Abstract Art* und Artikel in namhaften Publikationen, unter anderem in *Artforum*, *The New York Times*, *Sculpture Magazine*, *Texte zur Kunst*, *Frieze*, *ArtReview*, *Hyperallergic*, *The New Yorker* und *Mousse Magazine*.

RESIDENCIES / KÜNSTLER_INRESIDENZEN

Phillips has been awarded artist residencies at the Skowhegan School of Painting and Sculpture as well as The Studio Museum in Harlem, among others.

Artist-in-Residence unter anderem bei der Skowhegan School of Painting and Sculpture und The Studio Museum in Harlem.

ACADEMIC APPOINTMENTS / LEHRTÄTIGKEITEN

2020–ongoing
Assistant Professor, Department of Visual Arts, University of Chicago

2018–2020
Postgraduate Fellow, Department of Visual Arts, University of Chicago

EDUCATION / AKADEMISCHER WERDEGANG

2015–2016
Independent Study Program, The Whitney Museum of American Art, New York

2013–2015
Master of Fine Arts, Columbia University, School of the Arts, New York

2006–2012
Diploma, HFBK Hamburg

VISUAL INDEX

ABBILDUNGSVERZEICHNIS

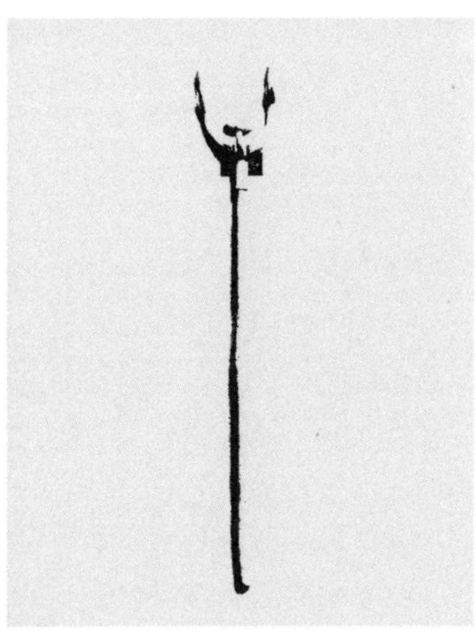

49
Objectifier I, 2014. Ceramic, steel,
84 × 16 × 7 cm; 33¼ × 6½ × 3 inches
© Julia Phillips, courtesy of Matthew Marks
Gallery

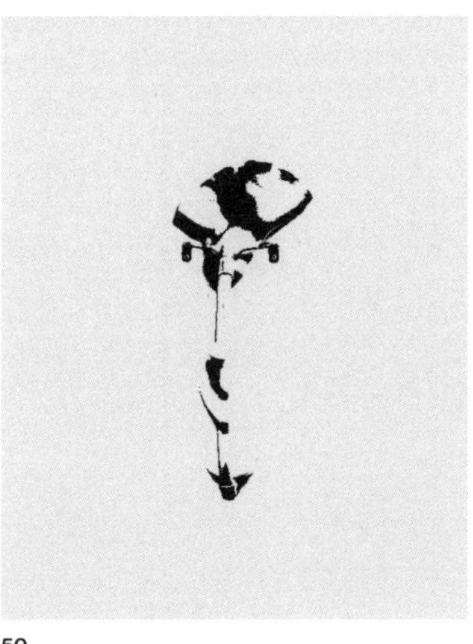

50
Objectifier II, 2014. Ceramic, steel,
46 × 22 × 18 cm; 18¼ × 8¾ × 7¼ inches
© Julia Phillips, courtesy of Matthew Marks
Gallery

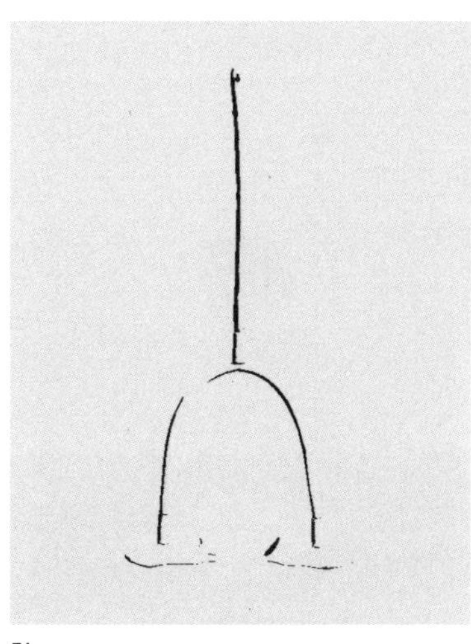

51
Objectifier III, 2014. Ceramic, steel,
128 × 29 × 15 cm; 50½ × 11½ × 6 inches
© Julia Phillips, courtesy of Matthew Marks
Gallery

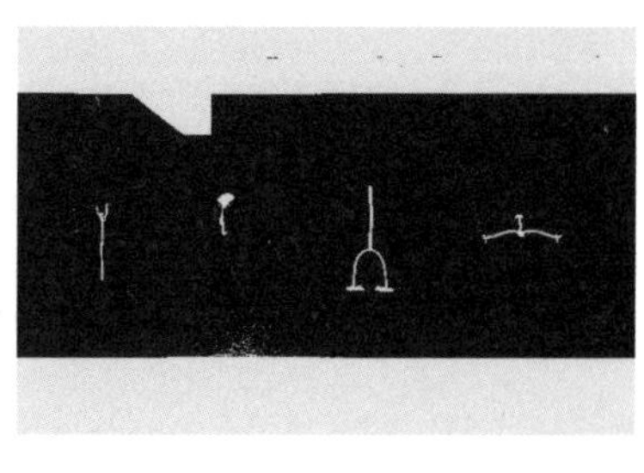

52
Impenetrable Entry, installation view, Campoli
Presti, London, 2016 © Julia Phillips, courtesy
of Matthew Marks Gallery

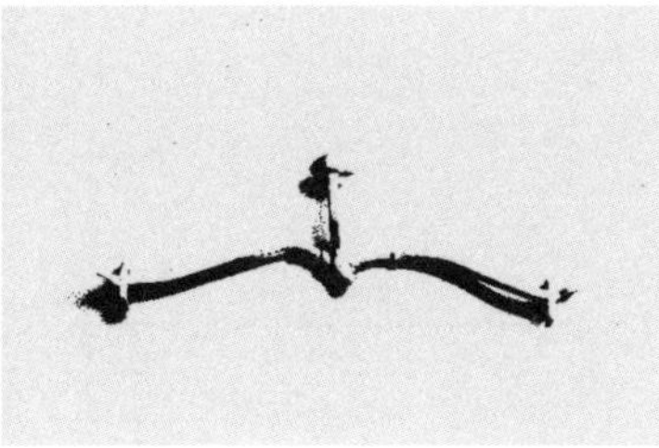

53
Objectifier IV, 2014. Ceramic, steel,
22 × 103 × 17 cm; 8¾ × 40¾ × 6¾ inches
© Julia Phillips, courtesy of Matthew Marks
Gallery

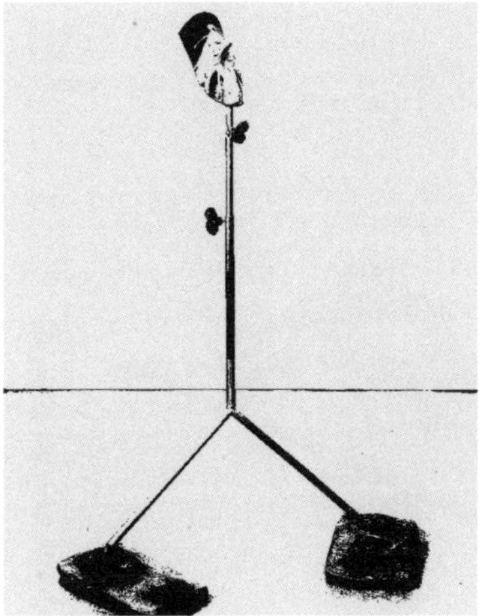

55
Regulator, 2014. Ceramic, steel,
65 × 112 × 50 cm; 25¾ × 44¼ × 19¾ inches
© Julia Phillips, courtesy of the artist

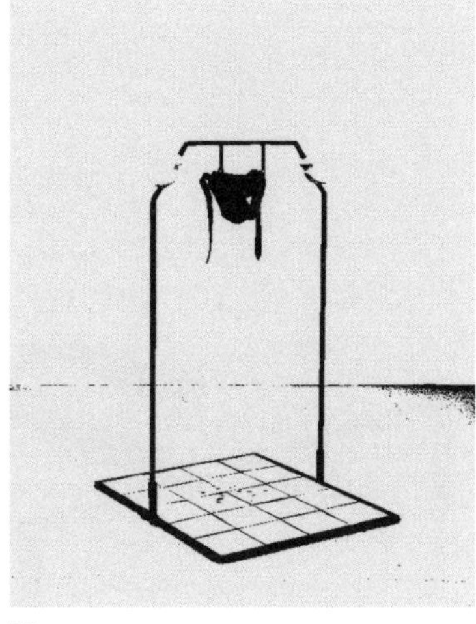

57
Positioner, 2016. Ceramic, steel,
112 × 62 × 78 cm; 44¼ × 24½ × 30¾ inches
© Julia Phillips, courtesy of Matthew Marks
Gallery

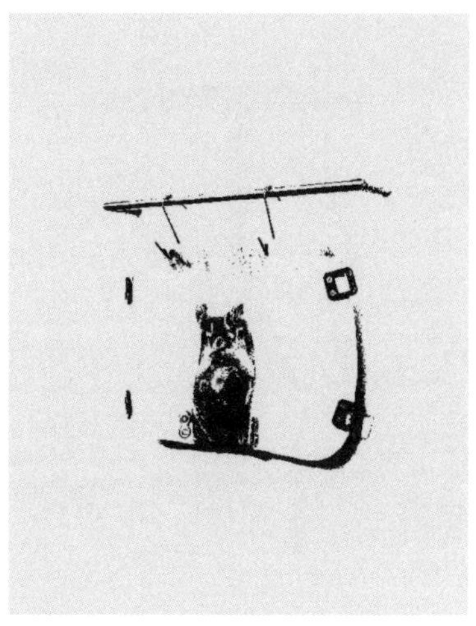

59
Protector I, 2016/18. Ceramic, metal
hardware, stainless steel, 30 × 38 × 6 cm;
12 × 15 × 2½ inches © Julia Phillips, courtesy
of Matthew Marks Gallery. Photo by Jeffrey
Sturges.

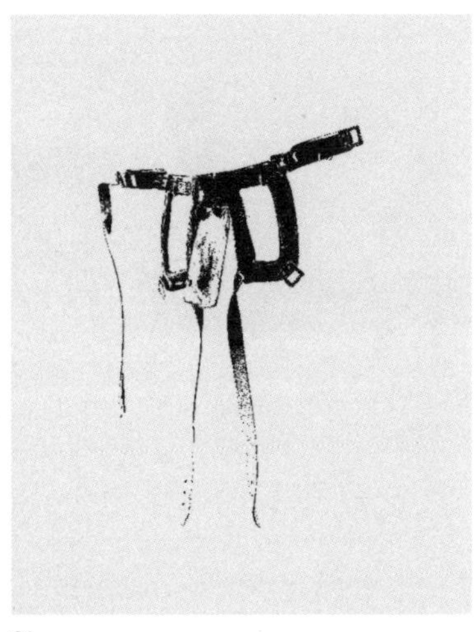

61
Protector II, 2016. Ceramic, metal hardware,
steel, 63 × 57 × 10 cm; 25 × 22½ × 4 inches
© Julia Phillips, courtesy of Matthew Marks
Gallery. Photo by Jeffrey Sturges. Collection
of The Studio Museum in Harlem

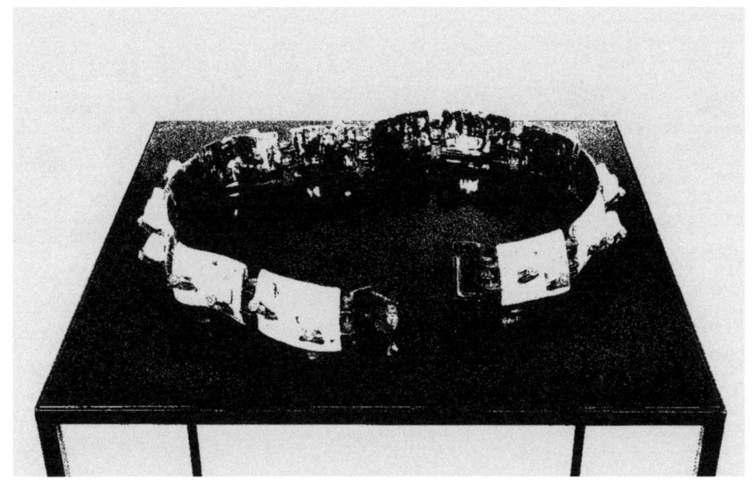

62
Exoticizer, Worn Out (Josephine Baker's Belt), 2017. Ceramic, brass hardware, steel,
Sculpture 7 × 33 × 38 cm; 2⅝ × 13 × 15 inches; Pedestal 94 × 41 × 41 cm; 37 × 16 × 16 inches
© Julia Phillips, courtesy of Matthew Marks Gallery. Photo by Jeffrey Sturges. Collection
of The Studio Museum in Harlem

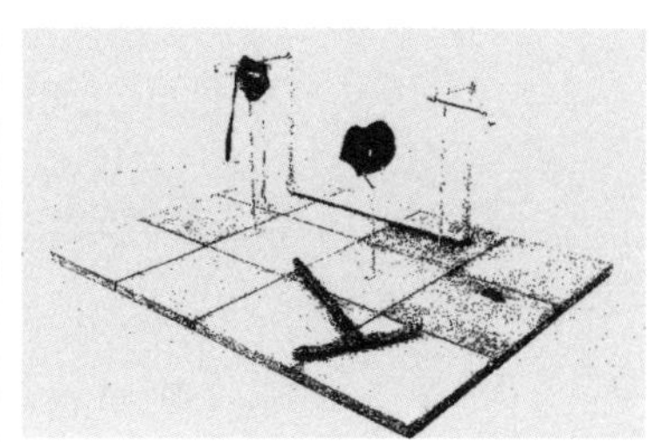

64
Extruder, 2017. Ceramic, nylon hardware,
steel, concrete, lacquer, 86 × 130 × 173 cm;
34 × 51¼ × 68¼ inches © Julia Phillips, courtesy
of Matthew Marks Gallery. Photo by Jeffrey
Sturges

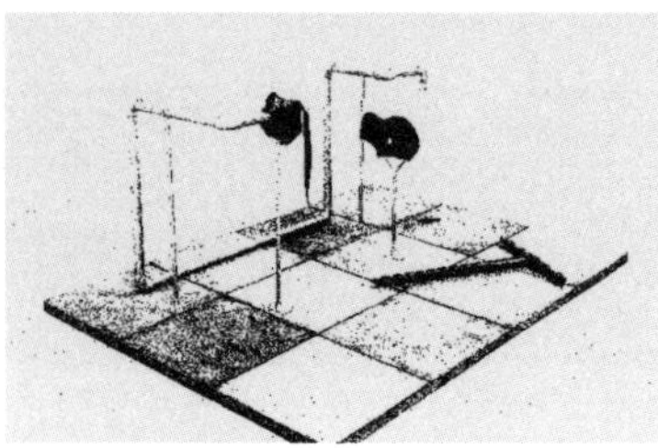
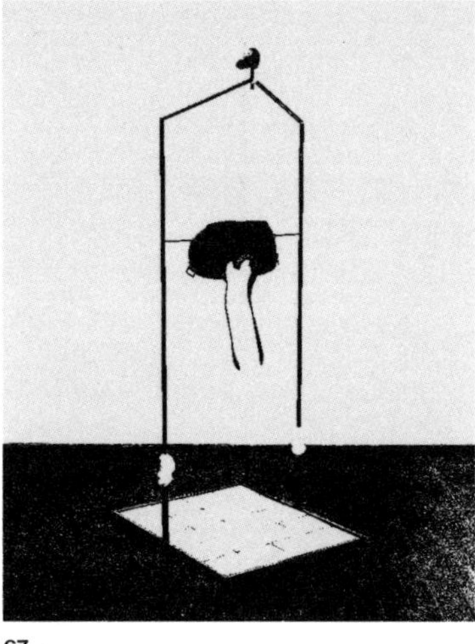
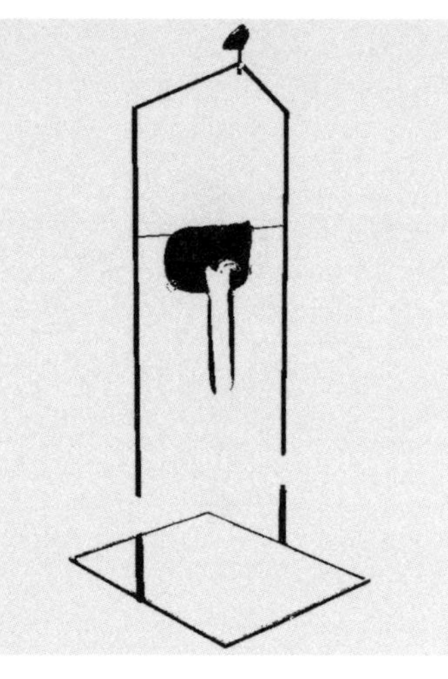
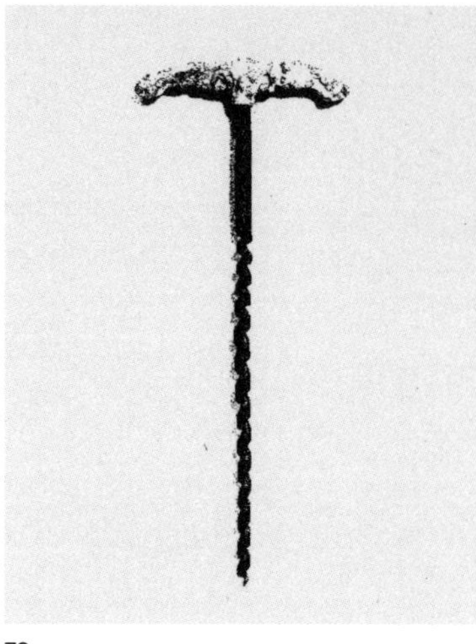

67
Fixator (#1), 2017. Ceramic, nylon hardware, steel, 177 × 64 × 79 cm; 69¾ × 25¼ × 31¼ inches © Julia Phillips, courtesy of Matthew Marks Gallery. Collection of The Whitney Museum of American Art

69
Fixator (#2), 2017. Ceramic, nylon hardware, steel, 177 × 64 × 79 cm; 69¾ × 25¼ × 31¼ inches © Julia Phillips, courtesy of Matthew Marks Gallery. Collection of The Museum of Contemporary Art, Los Angeles

70
Intruder Study VII, 2017. Ceramic, 62 × 24 × 4 cm; 24½ × 9½ × 1¾ inches © Julia Phillips, courtesy of Matthew Marks Gallery. Photo by Jeffrey Sturges

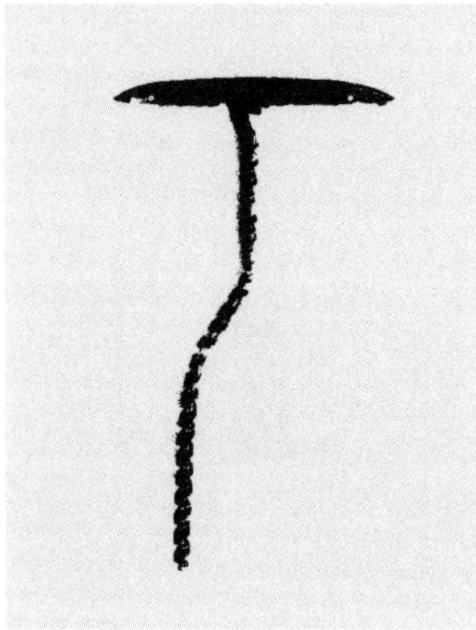
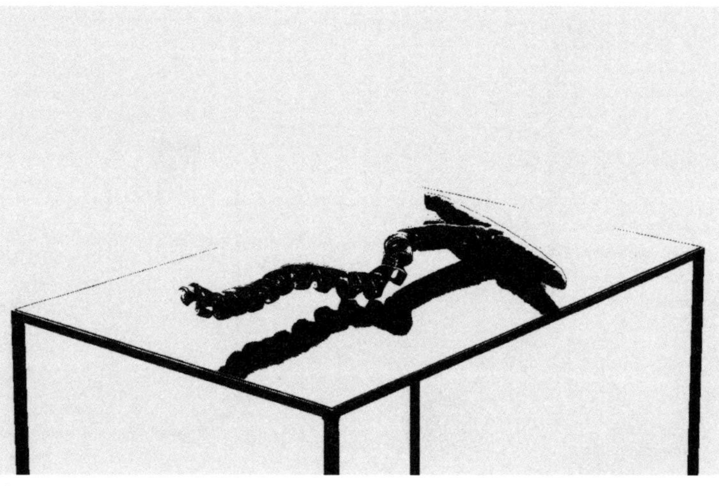
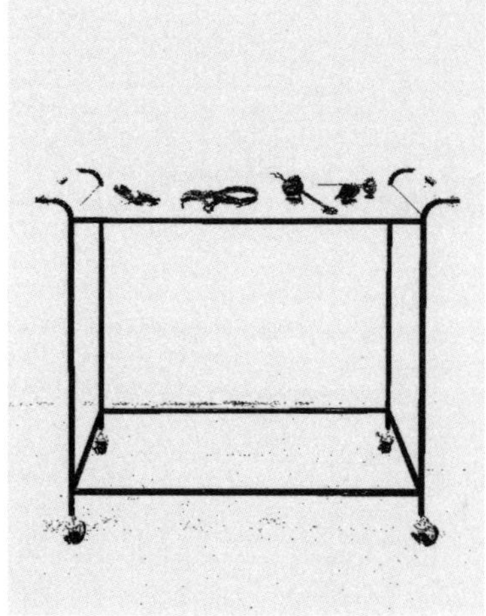

71
Intruder, Misused I, 2019. Ceramic, 64 × 36 × 3.5 cm; 25¼ × 14¼ × 1½ inches © Julia Phillips, courtesy of Matthew Marks Gallery. Photo by Jesse Meredith

72
Intruder, Misused II, 2019. Ceramic, steel, Sculpture 8 × 71 × 46 cm; 3¼ × 27¾ × 18¼ inches, Pedestal 94 × 81 × 51 cm; 37 × 32 × 20 inches © Julia Phillips, courtesy of Matthew Marks Gallery. Photo by Jesse Meredith

75
Operator I (with Blinder, Muter, Penetrator, Aborter), 2017. Ceramic, brass hardware, steel, wheels, 104 × 117 × 45.5 cm; 41 × 46¼ × 18 inches © Julia Phillips, courtesy of Matthew Marks Gallery. Photo by Jeffrey Sturges

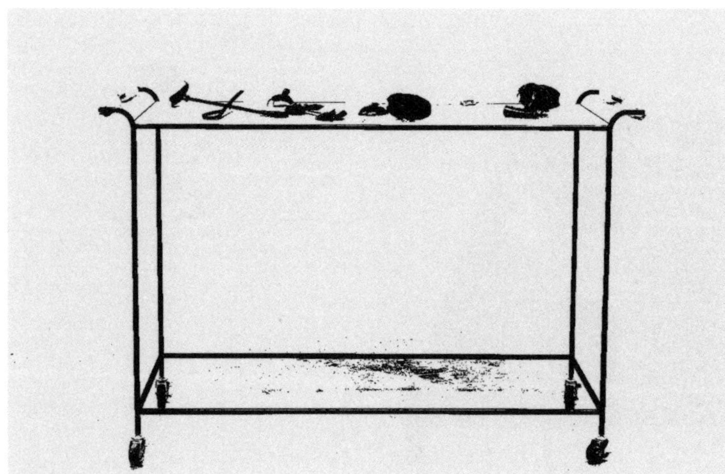
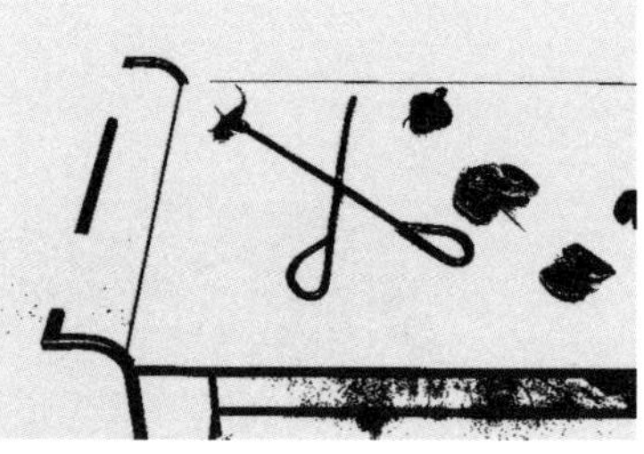
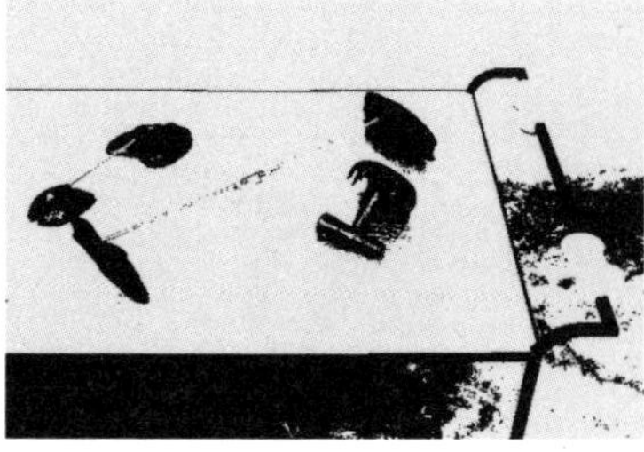

76-79
Operator II (with Opener, Destabilizer, Distancer, [R]Ejecter), Partially Dismantled, 2018. Ceramic, metal hardware, steel, wheels, 104 × 127 × 63.5 cm; 41 × 50 × 25 inches © Julia Phillips, courtesy of Matthew Marks Gallery

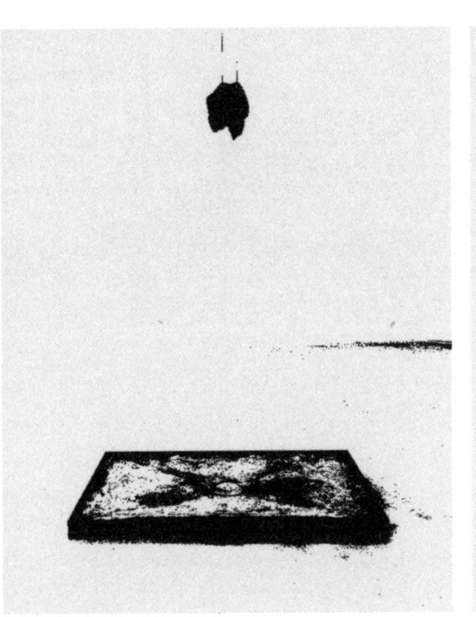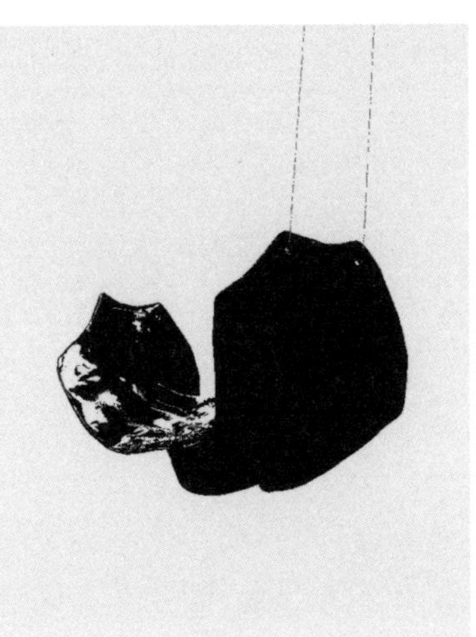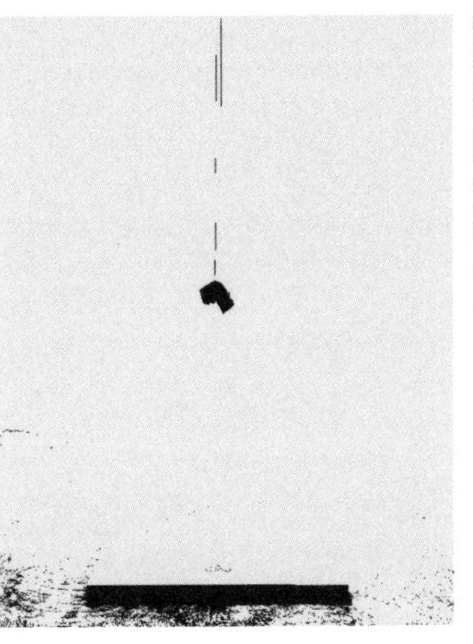

80
Drainer I, 2018. Ceramic, steel cable, limestone,
base: 9 × 152 × 89 cm; 3½ × 60 × 35 inches,
height to top edge of cast: 188 cm; 74 inches
© Julia Phillips, courtesy of Matthew
Marks Gallery. Collection of the Marciano
Art Foundation

82
Drainer II, 2021. Ceramic, steel cable, limestone,
base: 9 × 152 × 89 cm; 3½ × 60 × 35 inches,
height to top edge of cast: 188 cm; 74 inches
© Julia Phillips, courtesy of Matthew Marks
Gallery. Collection of the Hammer Museum

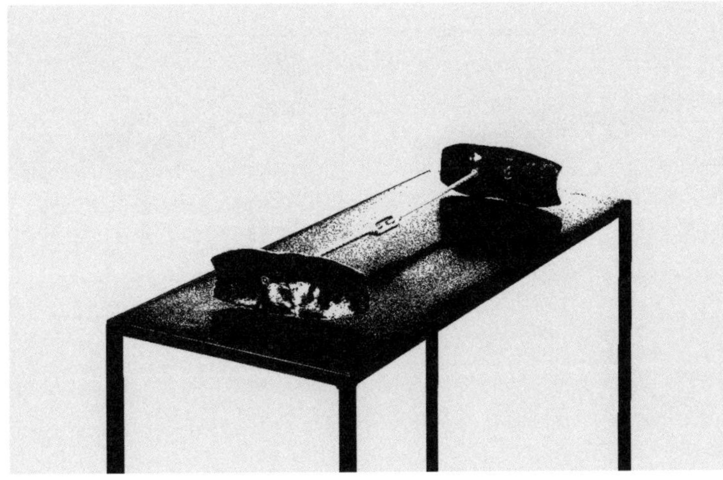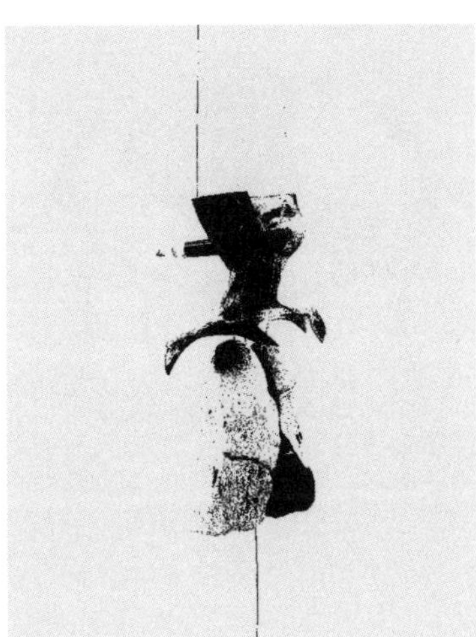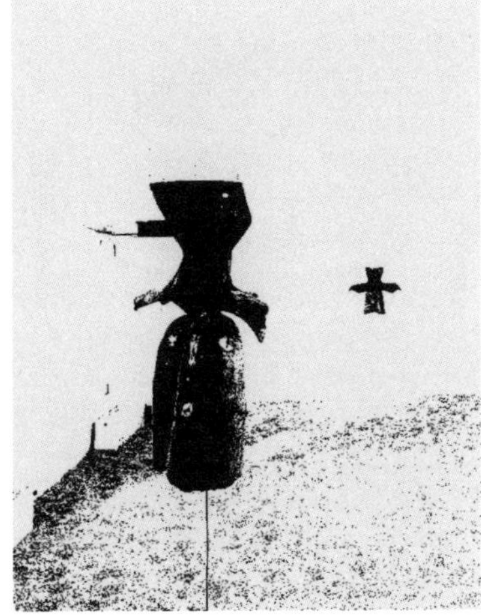

84
Distancer (#3), 2019. Ceramic, metal hardware, steel, Sculpture 7 × 47 × 17 cm;
2¾ × 18½ × 6¾ inches, Pedestal 95 × 64 × 28 cm; 37¼ × 25 × 11 inches © Julia Phillips,
courtesy of Matthew Marks Gallery. Photo by Jesse Meredith

87
Fake Truth (Witness I-III), Kunstverein
Braunschweig, 2019. Ceramic, cables, cardioid
microphones, contact microphones, speakers,
subwoofer, gravel, dimensions variable
© Julia Phillips, courtesy of the artist. Photo by
Stefan Stark

88-89
Fake Truth (Witness I-III), installation view,
Kunstverein Braunschweig, 2019. Ceramic,
cables, cardioid microphones, contact
microphones, speakers, subwoofer, gravel,
dimensions variable © Julia Phillips, courtesy
of the artist. Photo by Stefan Stark

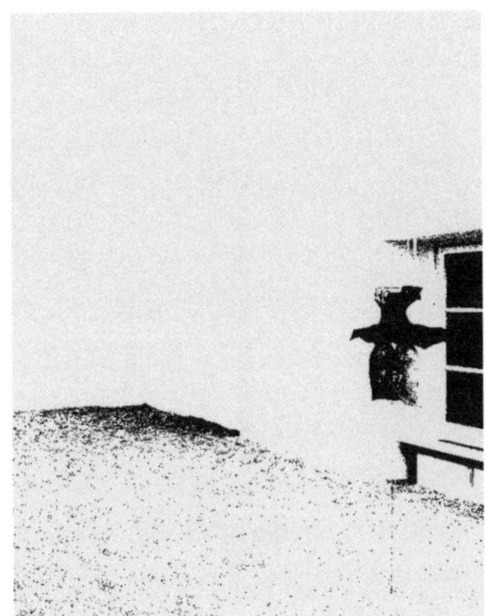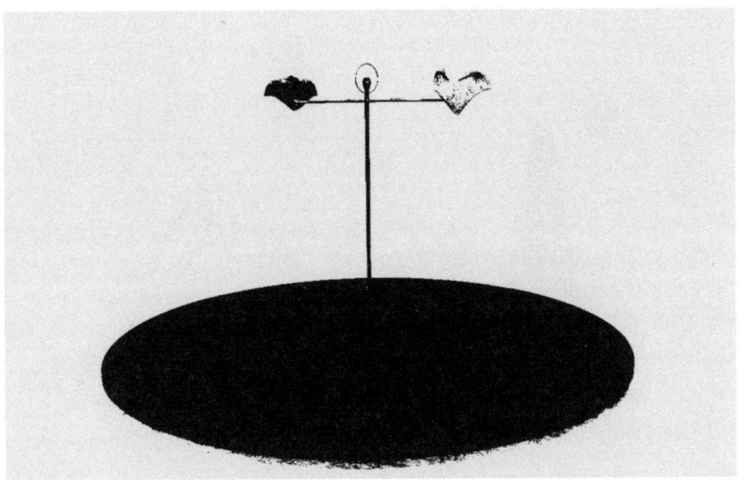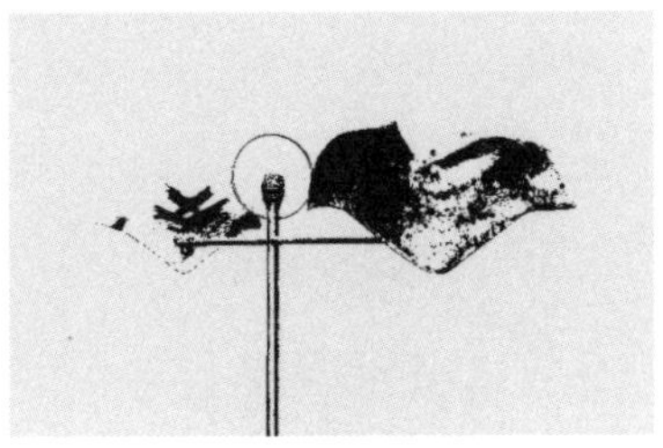

90-93
Mediator, 2020. Ceramic, stainless steel, granite, nylon hardware, 175 × 285 × 285 cm;
69 × 112¼ × 112¼ inches © Julia Phillips, courtesy of Matthew Marks Gallery. Collection
of The Art Institute of Chicago

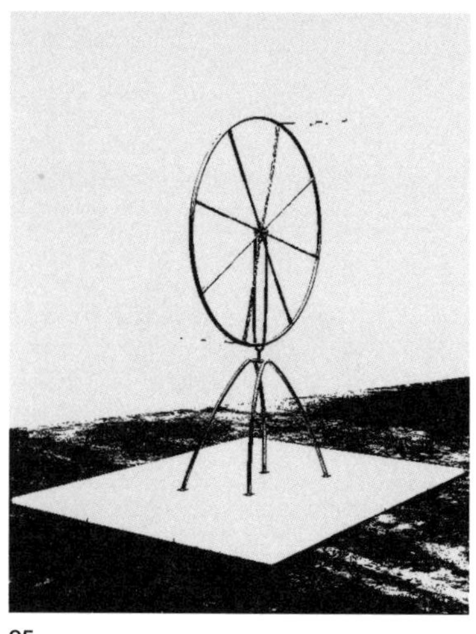

95
Negotiator (#1), 2020. Ceramic, stainless steel, marble, 196 × 150 × 201 cm; 77¼ × 59¼ × 79¼ inches © Julia Phillips, courtesy of Matthew Marks Gallery

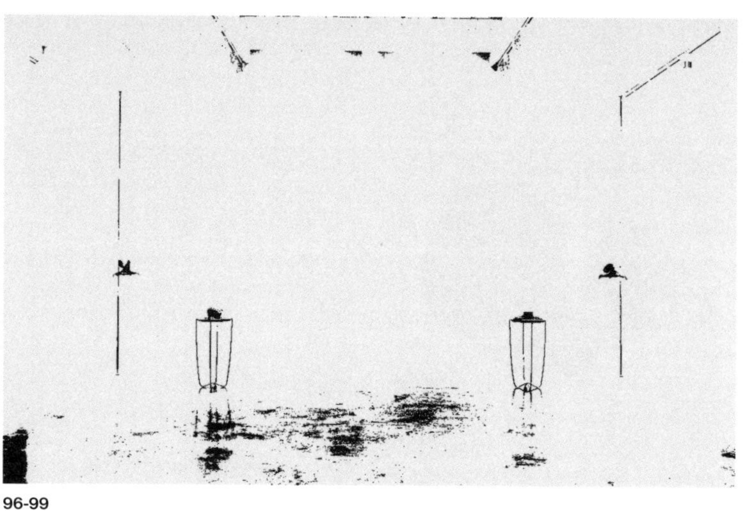

96-99
Oppressor with Soul, In Treatment & Suppressor with Spirit, In Treatment, 2020. Ceramic, stainless steel, nylon hardware, dimensions variable, Pedestal 97 × 50 × 50 cm; 38 × 19½ × 19½ inches each © Julia Phillips, courtesy of Matthew Marks Gallery

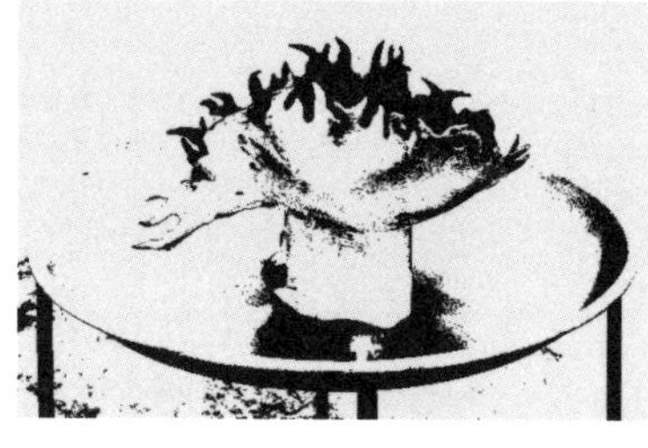

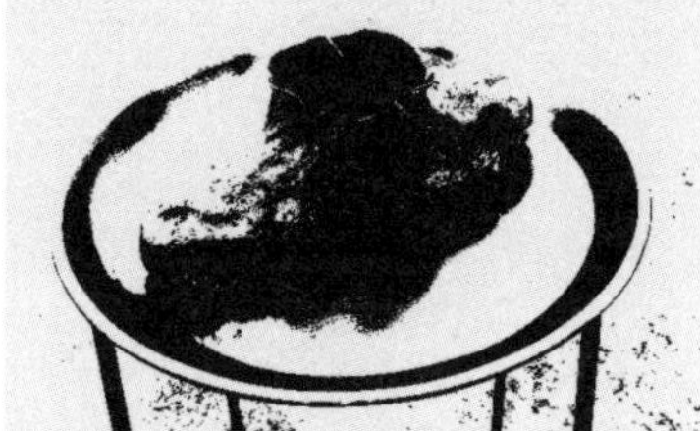

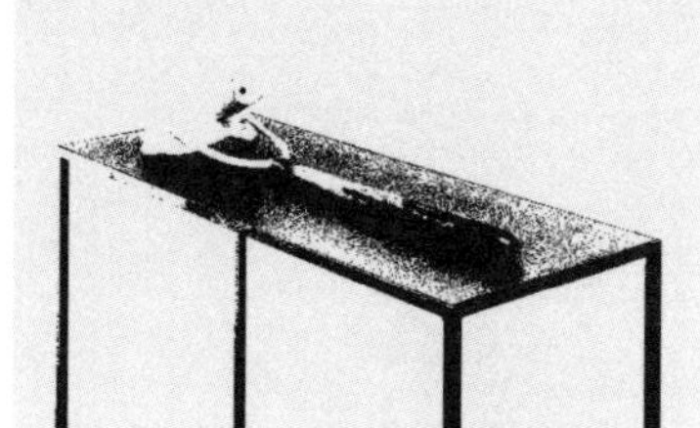

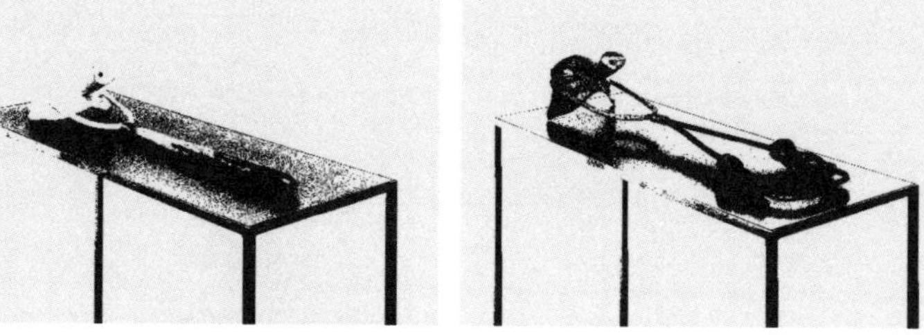

101
Purifier I, 2021. Ceramic, stainless steel, Sculpture 11 × 58 × 16 cm; 4⅛ × 22⅛ × 6¼ inches, Pedestal 94 × 71 × 28 cm; 37 × 28 × 11 inches © Julia Phillips, courtesy of Matthew Marks Gallery

103
Purifier II, 2021. Ceramic, stainless steel, Sculpture 13 × 63 × 17 cm; 5 × 24⅛ × 6⅛ inches, Pedestal 94 × 71 × 28 cm; 37 × 28 × 11 inches © Julia Phillips, courtesy of Matthew Marks Gallery

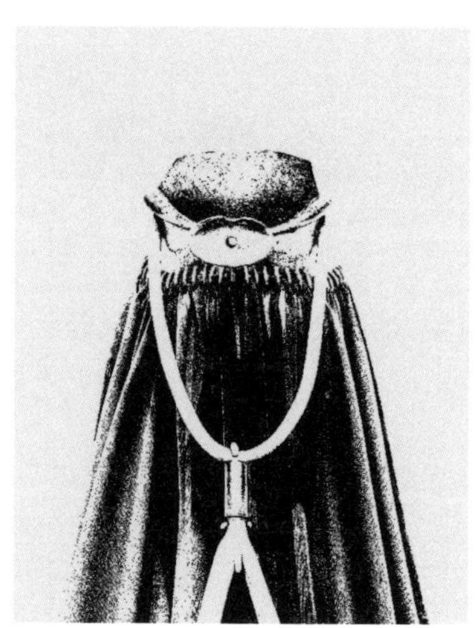

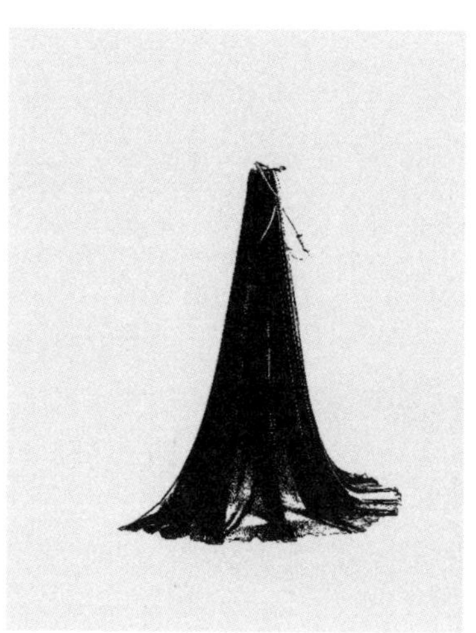

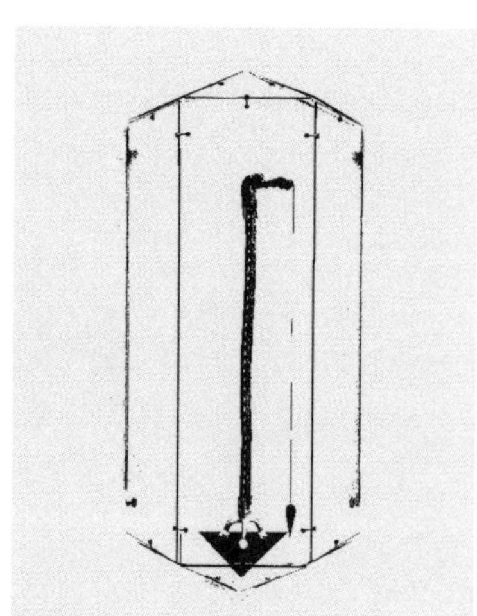

104
Veiled Purifier, 2021–22. Ceramic, silk, bronze, marble, 245 × 174 × 93 cm; 96½ × 68½ × 36¾ inches © Julia Phillips, courtesy of Matthew Marks Gallery

107
Bower, 2021–22. Ceramic, bronze, granite, nylon hardware, 175 × 81 × 138 cm; 69 × 32 × 54½ inches © Julia Phillips, courtesy of Matthew Marks Gallery

109
Stabilizer, 2021–22. Ceramic, bronze, brass cable, glass case, 136 × 61 × 27 cm; 53½ × 24 × 10½ inches © Julia Phillips, courtesy of Matthew Marks Gallery

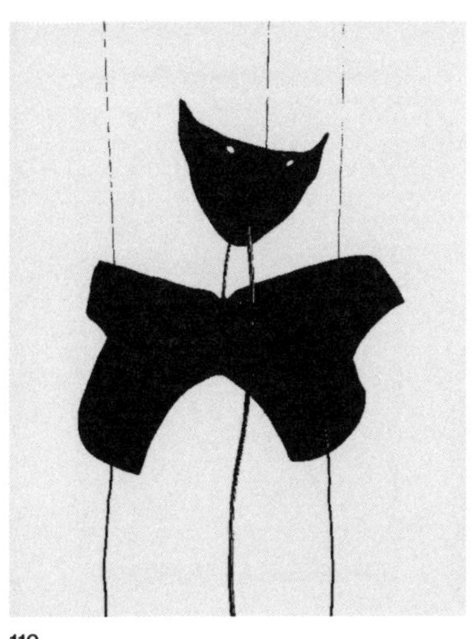

110
Nourisher, 2022. Ceramic, medical PVC tubes, stainless steel, steel cable, 177 × 81 × 61 cm; 69½ × 32 × 24 inches © Julia Phillips, courtesy of Matthew Marks Gallery. Collection of Hessel Museum of Art

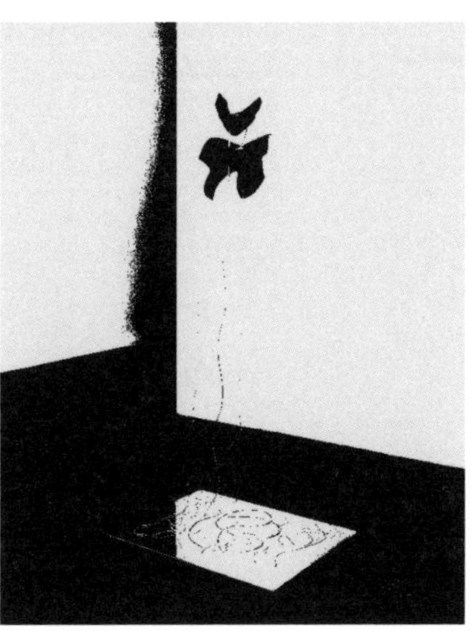

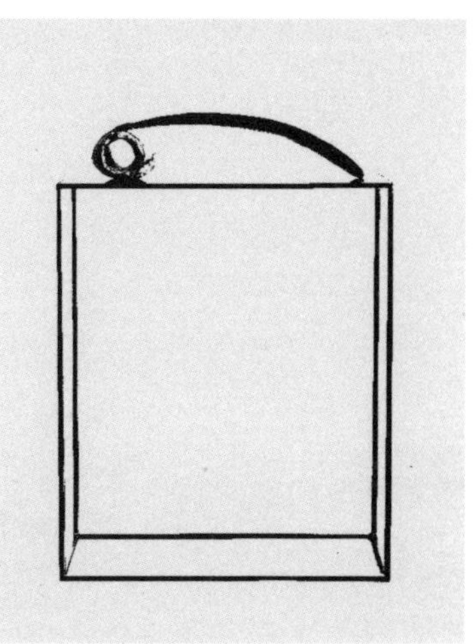

113
Attachment I, 2022. Ceramic, stainless steel, 118 × 27 × 13 cm; 46½ × 10½ × 5¼ inches © Julia Phillips, courtesy of Matthew Marks Gallery

114
Attachment II, 2022. Ceramic, stainless steel, Sculpture 16 × 64 × 23 cm; 6⅜ × 25 × 9 inches, Pedestal 94 × 76 × 31 cm; 37⅛ × 30 × 12 inches © Julia Phillips, courtesy of Matthew Marks Gallery

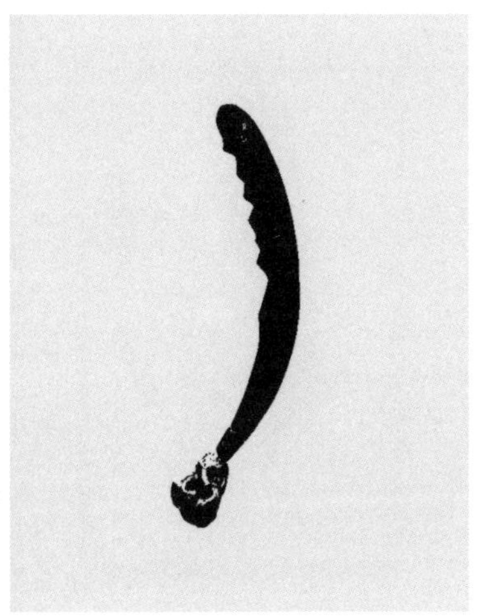

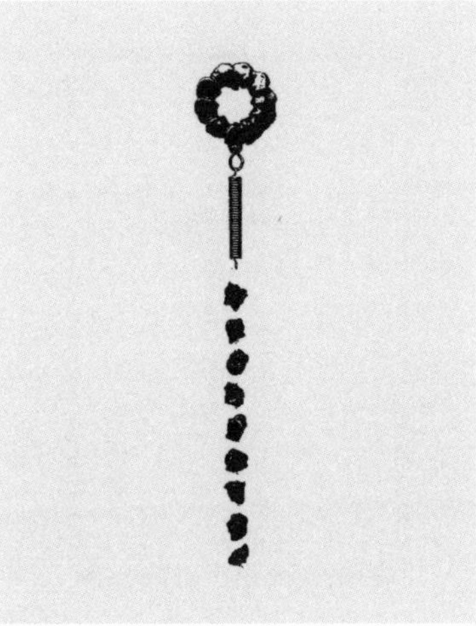

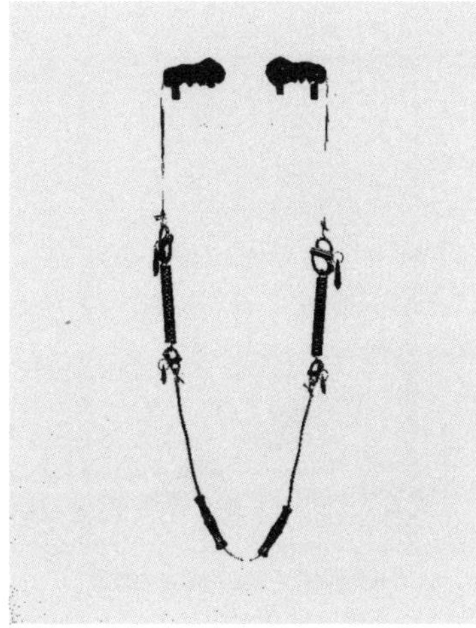

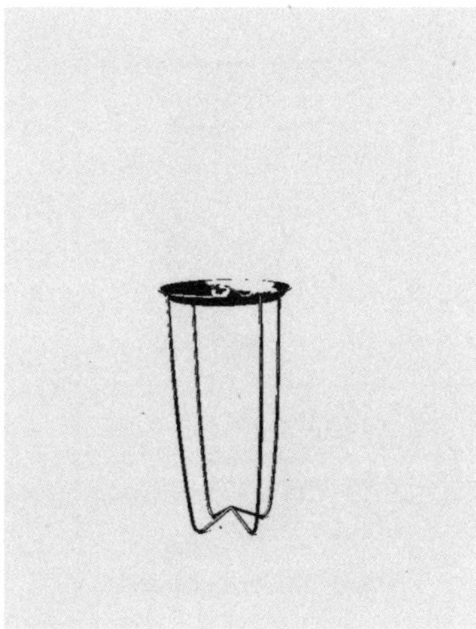

115
Attachment III, 2022. Ceramic, stainless steel, 65 × 20 × 13 cm; 25½ × 8 × 5 inches © Julia Phillips, courtesy of Matthew Marks Gallery

116
Attachment IV, Flexible, 2022. Ceramic, medical PVC tubes, stainless steel hardware, 78 × 13 × 9 cm; 30¾ × 5 × 3½ inches © Julia Phillips, courtesy of Matthew Marks Gallery

117
Attachment V, Flexible with Quick Release, 2022. Ceramic, medical PVC tubes, stainless steel hardware, wire rope, 86 × 34 × 13 cm; 33¾ × 13½ × 5 inches © Julia Phillips, courtesy of Matthew Marks Gallery

118-123
Impregnator and Aborter, 2022. Ceramic, stainless steel, medical PVC tubes, dimensions variable, Pedestal 97 × 50 × 50 cm; 38 × 19½ × 19½ inches each © Julia Phillips, courtesy of Matthew Marks Gallery. Collection of Moderna Museet Stockholm

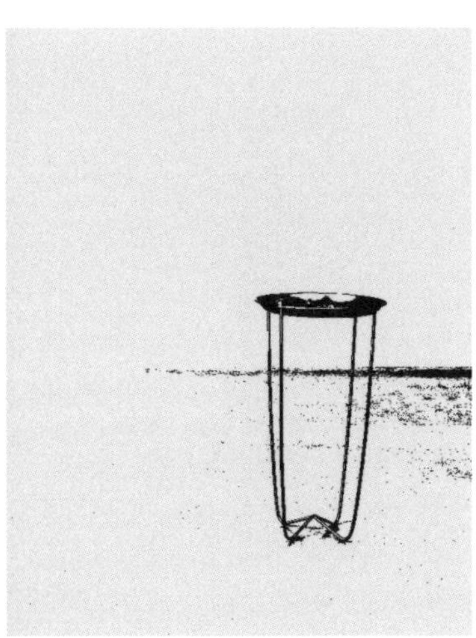

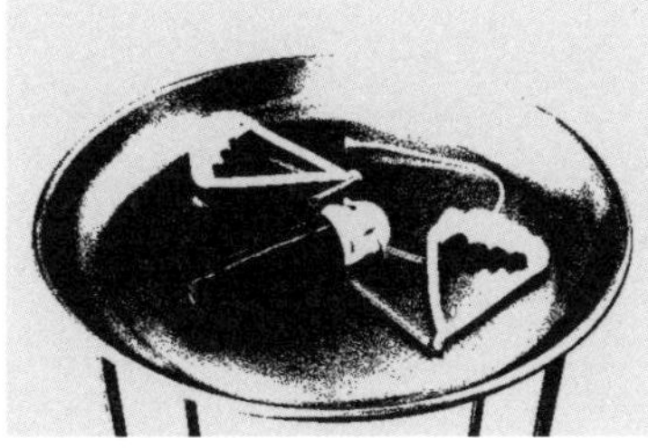

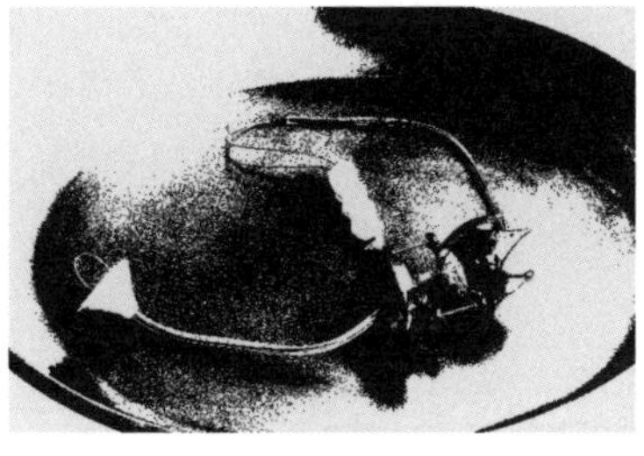

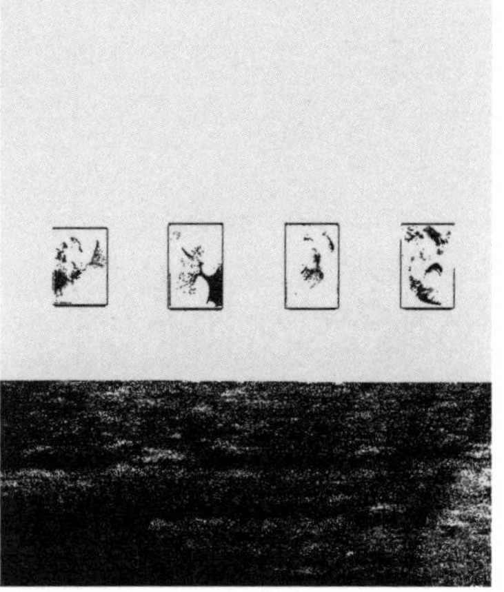

124
Me, Ourself & You, installation view, Matthew Marks Gallery, New York, 2022 © Julia Phillips, courtesy of Matthew Marks Gallery

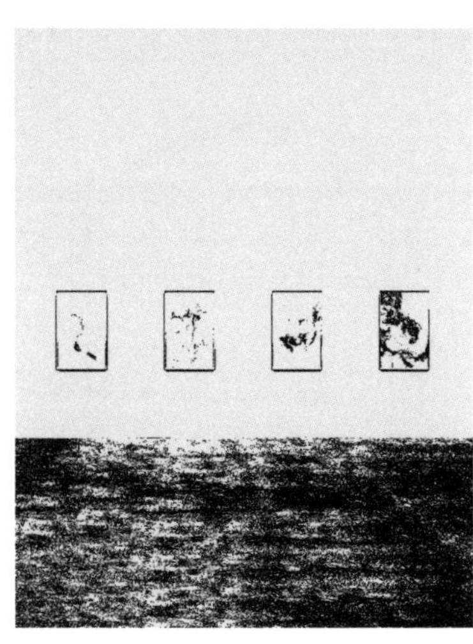
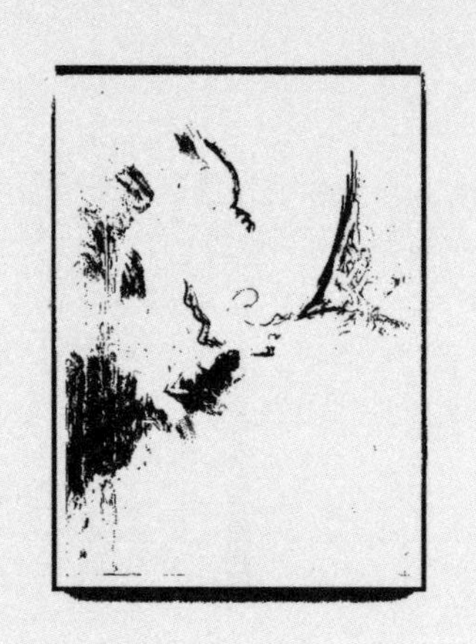

126
Conception Drawing I (Within Between?), 2020–21. Oil pastel and vegetable oil on Dura-Lar in artist's frame, 97 × 68 cm; 38 × 26⅞ inches © Julia Phillips, courtesy of Matthew Marks Gallery

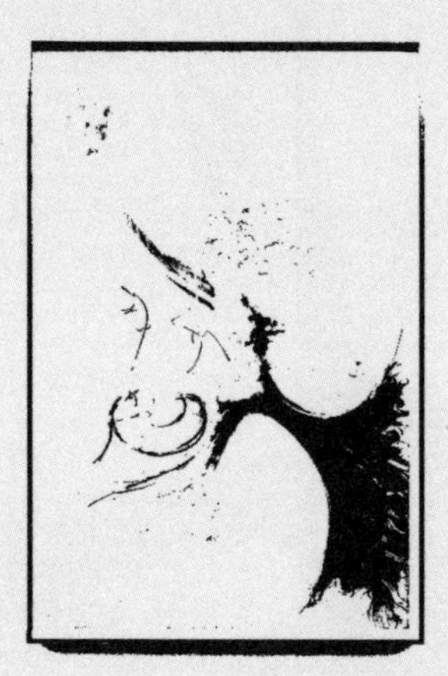

127
Conception Drawing II (Tissue?), 2020–21. Oil pastel and vegetable oil on Dura-Lar in artist's frame, 106 × 68 cm; 42 × 27 inches © Julia Phillips, courtesy of Matthew Marks Gallery

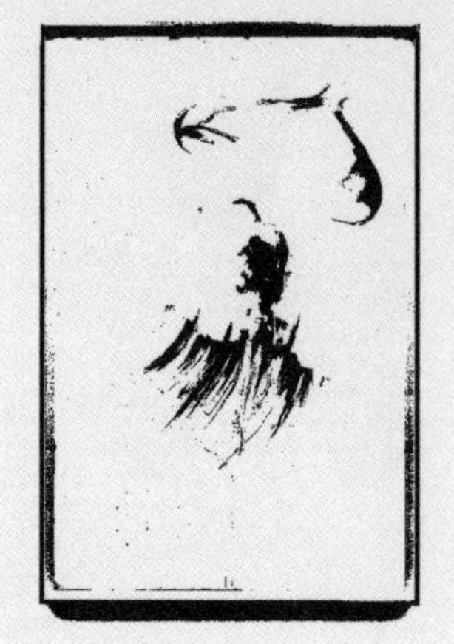

128
Conception Drawing III (Tube Suck / Float?), 2020–21. Oil pastel and vegetable oil on Dura-Lar in artist's frame, 106 × 68 cm; 42 × 27 inches © Julia Phillips, courtesy of Matthew Marks Gallery

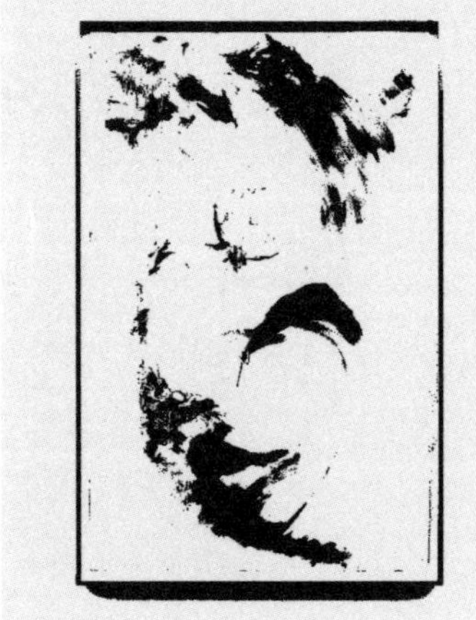

129
Conception Drawing IV (Ovulation / Eisprung?), 2020–21. Oil pastel and vegetable oil on Dura-Lar in artist's frame, 106 × 68 cm; 42 × 27 inches © Julia Phillips, courtesy of Matthew Marks Gallery

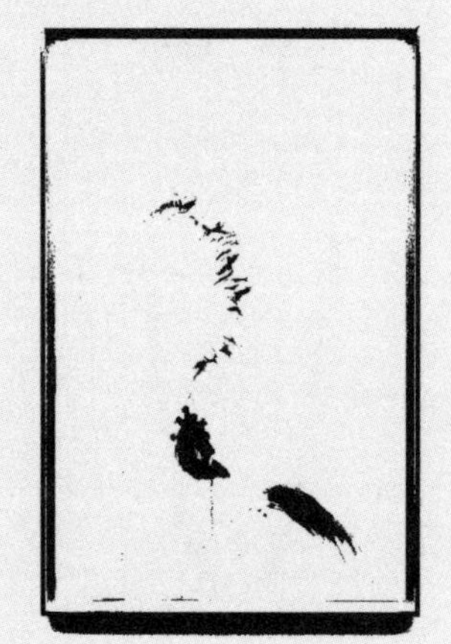

130
Conception Drawing V (Any Egg for a Big Flush?), 2020–21. Oil pastel and vegetable oil on Dura-Lar in artist's frame, 106 × 68 cm; 42 × 27 inches © Julia Phillips, courtesy of Matthew Marks Gallery

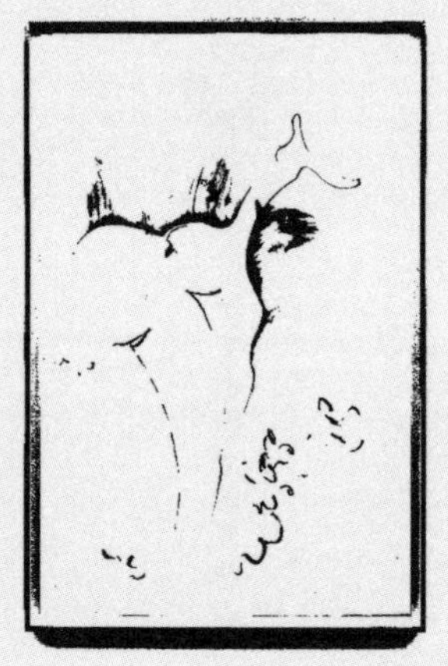

131
Conception Drawing VI (Soft Tubes?), 2020–21. Oil pastel and vegetable oil on Dura-Lar in artist's frame, 106 × 68 cm; 42 × 27 inches © Julia Phillips, courtesy of Matthew Marks Gallery

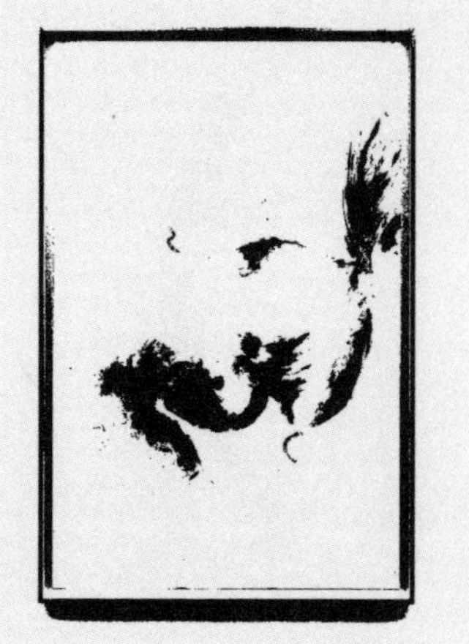

132
Conception Drawing VII (Implantation?), 2020–21. Oil pastel and vegetable oil on Dura-Lar in artist's frame, 106 × 68 cm; 42 × 27 inches © Julia Phillips, courtesy of Matthew Marks Gallery

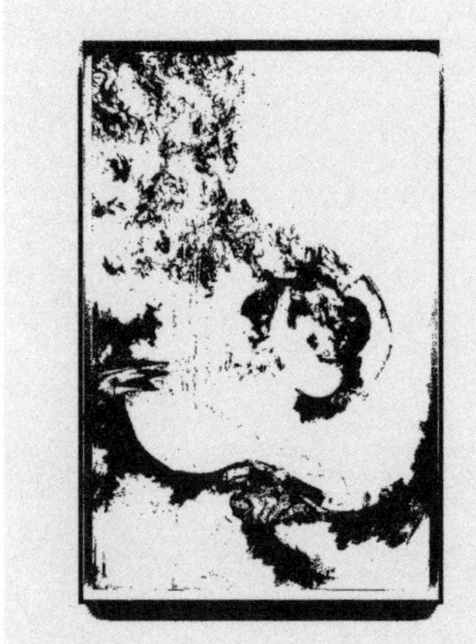

133
Conception Drawing VIII (Cell Accumulation / Embryo?), 2020–21. Oil pastel and vegetable oil on Dura-Lar in artist's frame, 106 × 68 cm; 42 × 27 inches © Julia Phillips, courtesy of Matthew Marks Gallery

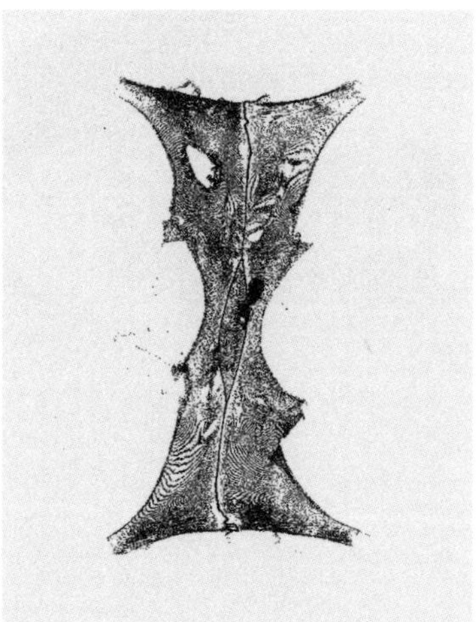
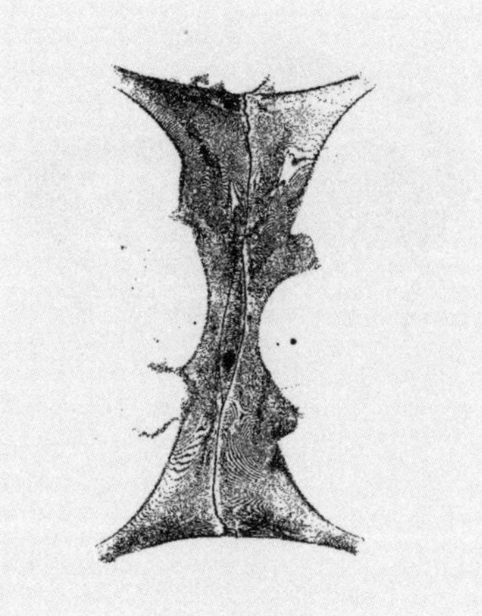
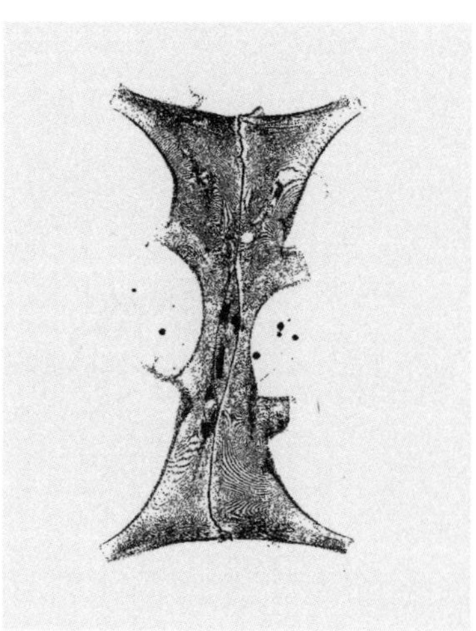

135-139
Expanded X, Treated Twice, 2018. Four collagraphs with blind embossing in artist's frames, 80 × 61 cm; 31¾ × 24⅛ inches each © Julia Phillips, courtesy of Matthew Marks Gallery. Photo by Jeffrey Sturges. Collection of The Museum of Modern Art

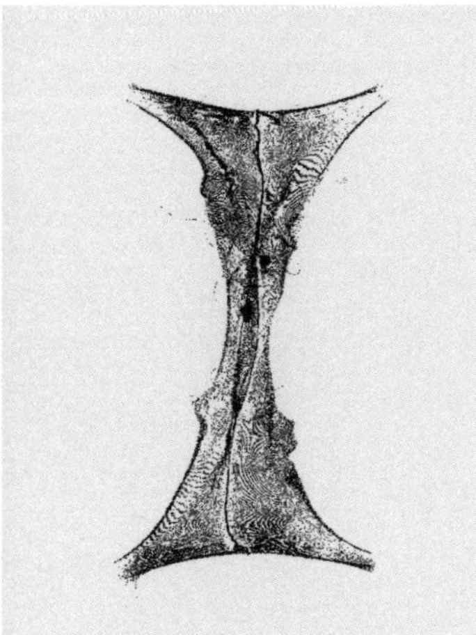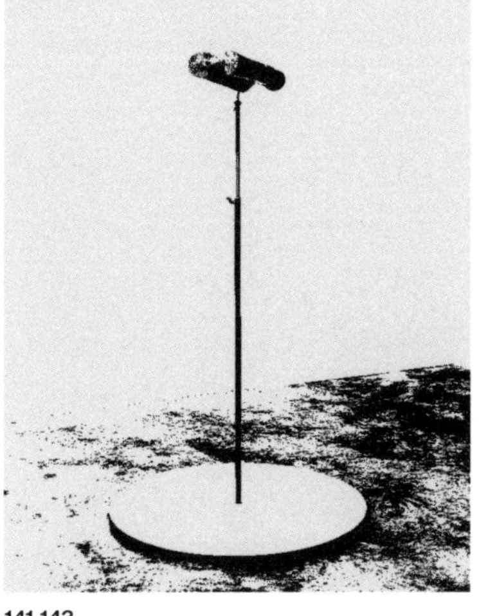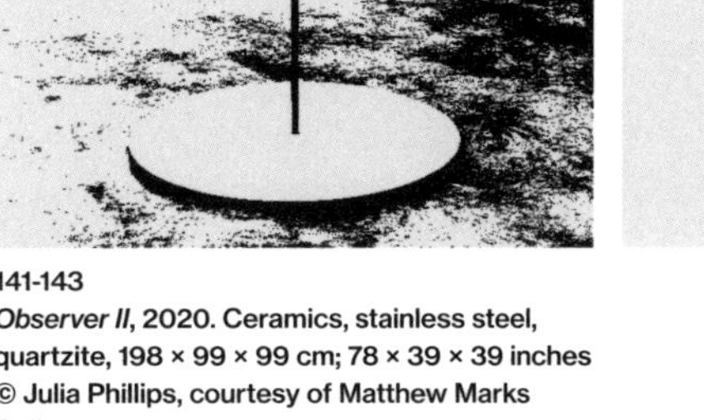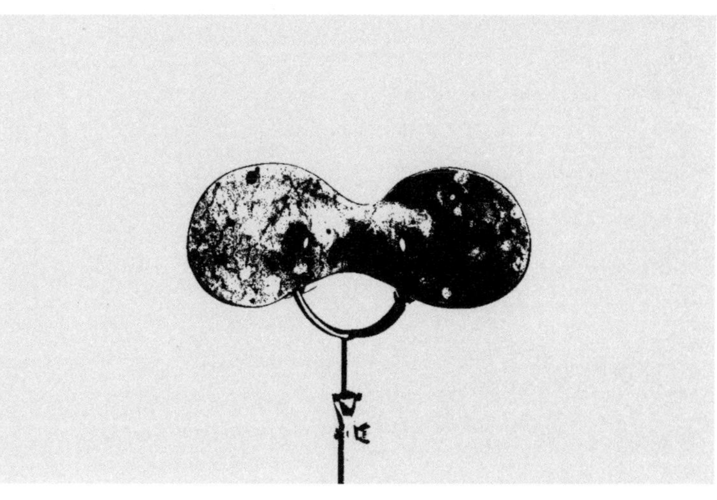

141-143
Observer II, 2020. Ceramics, stainless steel, quartzite, 198 × 99 × 99 cm; 78 × 39 × 39 inches
© Julia Phillips, courtesy of Matthew Marks Gallery

IMPRINT / IMPRESSUM

PUBLISHED AND DISTRIBUTED BY /
VERLAG UND VERTRIEB
Mousse Publishing / Contrappunto s.r.l.
via Pier Candido Decembrio 28,
20137, Milan–Italy

AVAILABLE THROUGH / ERHÄLTLICH DURCH
Mousse Publishing, Milan
moussemagazine.it
DAP | Distributed Art Publishers, New York
artbook.com
Les presses du réel, Dijon
lespressesdureel.com
Idea Books, Amsterdam
ideabooks.nl
Antenne Books, London
antennebooks.com
Motto Distribution, Berlin
mottodistribution.com

CONTRIBUTIONS / TEXTBEITRÄGE
Magdalyn Asimakis, Fia Backström,
Janet Dees, Daniella Rose King, Jamieson
Webster

TRANSLATIONS / ÜBERSETZUNGEN
Melody Makeda Ledwon, Julia Phillips,
Magnus Elias Rosengarten, Sylvia Zirden

PUBLISHING EDITOR / PUBLIKATIONSLEITUNG
Ilaria Bombelli (Mousse)

COPY EDITORS / LEKTORAT
Magdalyn Asimakis, Fiammetta
Duke (Mousse), Sarah Kramer, Marny
Garcia Mommertz, Julia Phillips,
Anne Vonderstein, Lindsey Westbrook

MANAGING EDITOR / REDAKTION
Caitlyn Au

GRAPHIC DESIGN / GRAFISCHE GESTALTUNG
Massimiliano Pace (Mousse)

PRINTED IN ITALY BY / DRUCK (ITALIEN)
Grafiche Zanini, Bologna

FIRST EDITION / ERSTAUSGABE
2023

ISBN 978-88-6749-588-7

€ 30 / $ 35

© 2023 Julia Phillips, Mousse Publishing,
the authors of the texts / © 2023 Julia
Phillips, Mousse Publishing, Autor_innen

WITH THE GENEROUS SUPPORT OF /
MIT GROSSZÜGIGER UNTERSTÜTZUNG VON
Center for the Study of Race, Politics,
and Culture at the University of Chicago
Matthew Marks Gallery
Stiftung Kunstfonds
The University of Chicago, Division of the
Humanities

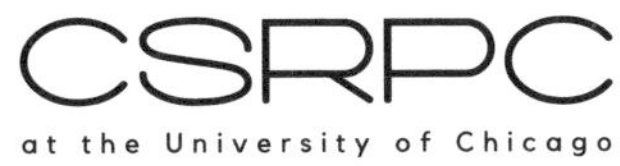

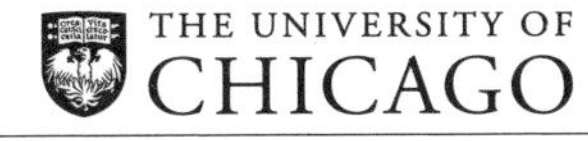

ACKNOWLEDGMENTS / DANKSAGUNGEN
I express special gratitude to the contributors, translators, and editors of this book. I extend this gratitude to those who make my physical works possible, my production team and collaborators: / Mein besonderer Dank gilt den Verfasserinnen der Beiträge, den Übersetzer_innen und Lektorinnen dieses Buches sowie all jenen, die es mir ermöglichen, meine Arbeiten physisch zu realisieren – meinem Produktionsteam, Werkstätten und Kollaborationspartner_innen:

PRODUCTION / PRODUKTION
Conservation / Restauration Kendra Roth, Christian Scheidemann
Design and Engineering Support / Konstruktion und Entwicklung Casey Lurie
Metal Fabricators / Schlosserei Stuart Sobczynski, Joel Fisher
Slipcasting / Gießerei Francisca Villagrana
Stone Fabrication / Steinmetzerei Quarra Stone Company

COLLABORATIONS / KOLLABORATIONEN
Headshot (2018)
with photographer Keisha Scarville
Fake Truth (Witness I–III) (2019)
with sound engineer Kenneth Klemaier
Stabilizer (2021–22)
with furniture designer Casey Lurie
Veiled Purifier (2021–22)
with fashion designer Rey Pador
Observer, Observed (2022)
with technical engineer Jordan Benke,
High Line Art; designer Casey Lurie;
bronze foundry Stratton Sculpture Studios

Over the past ten years I have been in inspiring and generative conversations with critical dialogue partners: / In den vergangenen zehn Jahren habe ich durch die kritische Auseinandersetzung mit meinem Werk zahlreiche Inspirationen und Anregungen erhalten von: Nana Adusei-Poku, Cecilia Alemani, Deborah Anzinger, Magdalyn Asimakis, James Gregory Atkinson, Fia Backström, Rina Banerjee, Naomi Beckwith, Matthew Buckingham, Jordan Carter, Elesa Commerce, Janet Dees, Michael Diers, Nadja Frank, Jenny Gheith, Lars Hinrichs, Swami Ishatmananda, Ruba Katrib, Daniella Rose King, Autumn Knight, Melody LaVerne Bettencourt, Simone Leigh, Casey Lurie, Matthew Marks, Nomaduma Masilela, Michelle Millar Fisher, Marny Garcia Mommertz, Alida Müschen, Natacha Nsabimana, Lorraine O'Grady, Sondra Perry, Leah Pires, Andy Robert, Magnus Elias Rosengarten, Beau Rutland, Jennifer Stuart, Monika Szewczyk, Johanna Tiedtke, Andreas Waldburg-Wolfegg, Patrice Washington, Alexander Weheliye

Gratitude is also expressed to the institutions that helped me mature as an artist: / Mein Dank gilt auch den Institutionen, die mir Gelegenheit zur künstlerischen Weiterentwicklung gegeben haben: HFBK Hamburg, Columbia University School of the Arts, the Independent Study Program of The Whitney Museum of American Art, Skowhegan School of Painting and Sculpture, The Studio Museum in Harlem

I thank my studio and research assistants of the past several years: / Ich danke meinen Assistentinnen, die mir bei der administrativen und handwerklichen Arbeit der letzten Jahre zur Seite gestanden haben: Caitlyn Au, Maia Johnson, Jasmin Liang, Anh Thuy Nguyen, and Elissa Osterland, as well as the staff at / sowie den Mitarbeiter_Innen von Matthew Marks Gallery, MoMA PS1, and / und Kunstverein Braunschweig. I would also like to acknowledge the work of our child caregivers / Ebenso möchte ich die Arbeit unserer Kinderbetreuung anerkennen: Coco Bookmyer and / und Sophie Senard.

And finally I thank my family—biological and chosen—for their love, support, and inspiration. / Und schließlich danke ich sowohl meiner Herkunfts- als auch meiner Wahlfamilie für ihre Liebe, Unterstützung und Inspiration.